Advance Praise for *The Power of the 2 × 2 Matrix*

"Although we see four quadrant matrices used frequently in business settings, there is altogether too much hit and miss in their application. The culprit, pure and simple, is a lack of appreciation of what is really at work in these models. Hood and Lowy have beautifully filled that gap with their straightforward examples and clearly written guidelines. In the hands of a master, this under-appreciated management tool becomes a powerful catalyst for innovation. Reading this book is a wonderful step towards attaining that mastery."

> —Verna Allee, author, *The Future of Knowledge*

"This is a significant work, not one that just has academic appeal to a few people and then is buried, but something with classic character and wide practical application."

> —Dr. Stephen R. Covey, author, *The 7 Habits of Highly Effective People*

"Lowy and Hood's new book on resolving management dilemmas is wonderfully thought provoking and fun to read. Not only do the authors treat us to a rich collection of insights, wisdom, and case examples, but they also provide a framework for how to construct and use 2 × 2 Thinking for decision making and problem solving. This book is destined to become a classic for management decision making."

> —Charles Fine, Chrysler LFM Professor of Management, MIT Sloan School of Management, and author, *Clockspeed*

"Multidimensionality is perhaps one of the most potent principles of systems thinking. But a fallacy to treat complementary tendencies as duality in zero sum game is responsible for the sad fact that we have kept on producing the same set of non-solutions all over again. *The Power of the 2 × 2 Matrix,* as the authors have chosen to name this exciting conception, is an excellent contribution towards initiating a long due cultural transformation. It goes a long way to operationalize a different way of seeing and thinking about our troubled world. A great job."

> —Jamshid Gharajedaghi, managing partner and CEO, INTERACT, and author, *Systems Thinking: Managing Chaos and Complexity*

"As apologists for the 2 × 2 matrix, we are delighted that Alex Lowy and Phil Hood wrote this book. We applaud them for taking the initiative to organize and prioritize representative models that illustrate the usefulness of 2 × 2 Thinking. Frankly, such a tome is long overdue, and readers will greatly benefit from the insightful selection of 2 × 2's made by Lowy and Hood."

> —James H. Gilmore and B. Joseph Pine II, coauthors, *The Experience Economy*

"Four decades of developing leaders has convinced me that the tools we rely on most often are simple, relevant, and have purpose. *The Power of the 2 × 2 Matrix* explains why this is the case, and delivers a unique and timeless collection of many of the best tools the behavioral sciences have to offer today's leader."

> —Dr. Paul Hersey, founder and chairman of the board, Center for Leadership Studies, the home of Situational Leadership®

"As a downstream result of our workshop with Lowy and Hood, we re-tuned our Vision, Value Proposition, Mission, Goals, and Business Strategy (and a whole lot more). We turned the business around using the output as the platform for our drive to the next level of business performance. These ideas are rock solid. I strongly recommend them based on real and positive business impact."

> —Austen Mulinder, president and CEO, Fujitsu Corporation's North American Retail Business

"In *The Power of the 2 × 2 Matrix*, Lowy and Hood present an innovative way to solve an array of complex problems. Based on an extensive review of management classics, the book advocates that qualitative 'both-and' thinking is more effective in the long run than the more fashionable and often easier-to-define quantitative 'either-or' approach. Applied properly, the 2 × 2 matrix is a most powerful and groundbreaking tool. The book will be extremely useful to consultants, managers, and academics committed to conceptualizing new solutions through the successful application of dialectical reasoning."

> —Ikujiro Nonaka, visiting dean and professor at the Center for Knowledge and Innovation Research, Helsinki School of Economics and Business Administration, and coauthor, *The Knowledge-Creating Company*

"This book is a brilliant addition to the arsenal of tools people can use to resolve dilemmas in their everyday business lives. It offers a novel and practical perspective that is relevant to anyone who exercises leadership."

> —Hubert Saint-Onge, CEO, Konvergeandknow, and author, *Leveraging Communities of Practice for Strategic Advantage*

"The 2 × 2 matrix is the simplest expression of contingency. In a complex and dynamic world filled with critical uncertainties the most common strategy is denial. Decision makers are trapped by seeing a linear future, and mislead their organizations by failing to rigorously think through the possibilities. The need to think contingently is what scenario planning is all about and is what *The Power of 2 × 2 Matrix* makes possible."

> —Peter Schwartz, chairman, Global Business Network, and author, *The Art of the Long View*

"When Alex Lowy first told me about his and Phil Hood's book, my immediate reaction was: Wow, that's a book I'd like to read! This is a book for those who, like me, apply dialectical models all the time but can never remember what is on the axes of the Johari Window and the BCG matrix. The inventory of 50-plus classic 2 × 2's is a very valuable time saver, and the tips on how to construct them are as relevant to the seasoned consultant as they are to busy corporate executives."

—Karl-Erik Sveiby, professor of knowledge management,
Swedish Business School, Hanken, in Helsinki, and author,
The New Organizational Wealth

"In a world of trite management tomes, recycling tired themes, it is indeed refreshing to find a book that discovers a completely original truth. Who would have thought that investigating the familiar 2 × 2 matrix as a generic construct could reveal profound insights into business strategy and possibly even human thought? I am thankful to Lowy and Hood for unlocking this treasure."

—Don Tapscott, chairman, New Paradigm Learning Corporation,
and coauthor, *The Naked Corporation*

"Managers are far too prone to leap to the 'answer,' often basing their conclusions on poor assumptions or inadequate problem diagnosis. Alex Lowy and Phil Hood have masterfully documented the art of asking the right question. This book should be required reading in any organization coping with the challenge of making critical decisions under conditions of risk or uncertainty."

—Paul Wiefels, managing director, The Chasm Group, LLC, and author,
The Chasm Companion

The Power of
the 2 × 2 Matrix

Using 2 × 2 Thinking to Solve Business Problems and Make Better Decisions

Alex Lowy
Phil Hood

Foreword by James H. Gilmore and B. Joseph Pine II

JOSSEY-BASS
A Wiley Imprint
www.josseybass.com

Published by Jossey-Bass
A Wiley Imprint
989 Market Street, San Francisco, CA 94103-1741   www.josseybass.com

Jossey-Bass books and products are available through most bookstores. To contact Jossey-Bass directly call our Customer Care Department within the U.S. at 800-956-7739, outside the U.S. at 317-572-3986, or fax 317-572-4002.

Jossey-Bass also publishes its books in a variety of electronic formats. Some content that appears in print may not be available in electronic books.

Credits are on page 321.

Library of Congress Cataloging-in-Publication Data
Lowy, Alex.
The power of the 2x2 matrix : using 2x2 thinking to solve business problems and make better decisions / Alex Lowy, Phil Hood ; foreword by James H. Gilmore and B. Joseph Pine II.
    p. cm.— (The Jossey-Bass business & management series)
Includes bibliographical references and index.
ISBN 0-7879-7292-4 (alk. paper)
1. Problem solving. 2. Decision making. 3. Industrial management.
I. Hood, Phil, 1951- II. Title. III. Series.
HD30.29.L69 2004
658.4'03—dc22
                                                                2003026851

Printed in the United States of America
FIRST EDITION
HB Printing   10 9 8 7 6 5 4 3 2

The Jossey-Bass
Business & Management Series

CONTENTS

FOREWORD

T he 2 × 2 matrix represents the most notable analytical tool ever to emerge in business management. Yet as a genre, this conceptual framework has been greatly misunderstood, misused, and mistrusted, even as it rose to prominence among management models. The 2 × 2 has been particularly maligned in recent years, perhaps in relation to the saturation of M.B.A. programs and the maturation of management consulting across the globe. All too often, eyes now roll whenever a work colleague or business consultant takes to a white board or flip chart to draw *x*- and *y*-axes.

Fast Company magazine's defunct "Consulting Debunking Unit" perhaps epitomized the tendency to throw the baby out with the bath water—to dismiss whole categories of business thinking, management practice, and professional services because of the lack of discipline or integrity on the part of a few poor professors and pitiful practitioners. But it's easy today to belittle bad apples (as we just did in our poor, pitiful selection of alliterative adjectives), for there's no lack of such inferior thinking to pick on. It's always safe to just get "back to basics." It's much harder to weed through the proliferation of management material churned out on endless fronts these days and find the true gems that can help businesses envision innovative possibilities and make better decisions. And many of these gems hold forth in the form of the venerable 2 × 2.

As apologists for the 2 × 2 matrix, we are delighted that Alex Lowy and Phil Hood wrote this book. We applaud them for taking the initiative to organize and prioritize representative models that illustrate the usefulness of 2 × 2 Thinking.

Frankly, such a tome is long overdue, and readers will greatly benefit from the insightful selection of 2 × 2s that Lowy and Hood made. We've pored over their work and find much relevant knowledge to be had from careful scrutiny of their study.

Too much management thinking today exists as what we like to call a "giant list of stuff" that lacks perspective on the underlying factors that contribute to items making the list, or misses linkages that connect various principles or other phenomena. Therein resides the beauty of the 2 × 2 matrix. The better ones (those well executed along the lines pointed out by Lowy and Hood) force new comparisons, foster fuller exploration of the subject at hand, and fashion creative tension between alternative points of view.

Consider for a moment an alternative topic—baseball—and this insightful quotation from George Will's wonderful book, *Men at Work:*

> Baseball is a game you cannot play with your teeth clenched. But neither can you play it with your mind idling in neutral. Baseball is a game where you have to do more than one thing very well, but one thing at a time. The best baseball people are (although you do not hear this description bandied about in dugouts) Cartesians. That is, they apply Descartes's methods to their craft, breaking it down into bite-sized components, mastering them and then building the craft up, bit by bit. Descartes, whose vocation was to think about thinking, said (I am paraphrasing somewhat): The problem is that we make mistakes. The solution is to strip our thought processes down to basics and begin with a rock-solid foundation, some certainty from which we can reason carefully to other certainties.[1]

We have René Descartes, of course, to thank for the 2 × 2 matrix! This model is nothing more than the first step in breaking a business down into manageable components and thereby stripping thinking down to some basics as a firm foundation. The best businesspeople too are Cartesians. Their use of any pertinent 2 × 2 matrix aims not at simplifying the world into four finite categories, but at moving to fuller, more reasoned certainties in an uncertain world—managing the complete Cartesian coordinate system that is business![2] Indeed, this book contains many fine examples of exemplary construction of 2 × 2 matrices and points out how lack of mastery on the part of matrix users can distort 2 × 2 applications.

We once heard a wrong-headed manager say to a peer, "I cannot relate to you because I'm ISTJ," referring to one of the sixteen types within the Myers-Briggs classification system. This gentleman was blatantly misusing Myers-Briggs to put himself in a sheltered box rather than using the tool to relate to others better or as a means to develop alternative thinking styles. Too many people similarly limit themselves when they encounter a useful 2 × 2 matrix, thinking the four quadrants represent the end-all and be-all of thinking on some subject (or outright dismissing the model as too simplistic). Shame, shame, shame. The power of any well-constructed 2 × 2 matrix rests in what one *does* with it once formulated.

For example, let's examine one of our own 2×2 models examined in this book (Figure 7.21, page 230). We once worked with a professor at Iowa State, an expert in pedagogical methods, who was interested in defending (much-maligned) "Edutainment" in teaching. We knew Edutainment to be a useful concept, but also knew it to be only one of a number of possibilities for enhancing the normally dry discourse of classroom discipline. So we brought to bear this particular model, which depicts four experiential realms—Entertainment, Educational, Escapist, Esthetic—that together make for a compelling experience. Edutainment was but one combination of the four realms, specifically:

Edutainment = Education + Entertainment (holding attention)

Realizing this, we together proceeded to identify five other dimensions worthy of further exploration as means to enhance learning:

Eduscapist = Education + Escapist (changing context)

Edusthetic = Education + Esthetic (fostering appreciation)

Escasthetic = Escapist + Esthetic (altering state)

Entersthetic = Entertainment + Esthetic (having presence)

Escatainment = Escapist + Entertainment (creating catharsis)

The results vary in how trippingly they fall from the tongue (although Edutainment flows smoothly primarily through familiarity and repetition), but the 2×2 matrix helped map out a richer territory of understanding. Indeed, debating the selection of prefixes and suffixes (and number of occurrences of each) helped us all to better understand not only each dimension, but the subject of pedagogy itself.

Lowy and Hood have done a great service in assembling this book. We particularly enjoyed seeing Pascal's Wager crafted as a 2×2 matrix, as Blaise Pascal was the intellectual and theological archrival to René Descartes in the early seventeenth century. (How edutaining!) Even with our great fondness for the 2×2 as a tool, we side with Pascal when he says, "The heart has reasons that Reason cannot understand." Recognize that no matter how brilliant a particular 2×2 matrix, its usefulness resides primarily in clarifying various managerial options. Ultimately, all decision making relies on gut feeling and intuition. At the end of the day, you must examine the Cartesian possibilities, and then go with your heart.

JAMES H. GILMORE
B. JOSEPH PINE II

ACKNOWLEDGMENTS

We owe a great deal to colleagues, clients, friends, and family who helped along the way. Without their inspiration and feedback, this book would not be. Contributions have taken many forms, each essential in its own way. Early in the life of the project, we needed to collect a large number of outstanding 2 × 2 business frameworks. We solicited suggestions from pretty much everyone we encountered, yielding a robust listing of over three hundred unique titles. Two people stand out in this effort. Andy De of i2 generously shared his collection of thirty-plus frameworks, and Derek Lennox added another dozen. Derek played a significant early role in gathering and organizing suggestions. Without their assistance, the project would probably never have gotten off the ground.

Many of the world's sharpest business consulting minds helped us to unravel the mysteries of 2 × 2 Thinking and to construct the meta-models that appear in Chapters One through Five. We conducted interviews between January and July 2003, asking three basic questions: Why do you use a 2 × 2 approach? What's key in designing them? What makes the application of a framework successful? Valuable discussions were held with the following people: Verna Allee, Nicole Boyer, Stephen Covey, Jamshid Gharajedaghi, Jim Gilmore, Paul Hersey, Barry Naelbuff, William Ralston, Hubert Saint-Onge, Joseph Pine, Karl-Erik Sveiby, Simon Trussler, Paul Weifels, and Watts Wacker. We owe a great deal to these individuals for their insights, personal stories, and willingness to engage in challenging dialogue. Encouragement and suggestions from Stephen Covey, Joseph Pine, and Jim Gilmore were particularly helpful in shaping the book.

A number of colleagues gave generously by reading and commenting on chapters. Tim Warner played an important ongoing role in this capacity, often acting as our conscience by asking the tough questions that needed to be addressed. Nancy Brown, Tom Emodi, Mike Dover, Dan Swedberg, and David Ticoll all read and reread material, offering helpful feedback and suggestions.

Iris Glaser provided critical design guidance and support. We were most fortunate to have the attention of this talented young artist early in her career.

The development of a structured 2 × 2 method was made possible by the brave and adventurous participation of two client organizations willing to experiment with us. The first was a New Jersey software firm, LegatoVideo. Many thanks to CEO Dave Reifsnyder and the rest of the LegatoVideo senior team. The second was the Fujitsu Corporation's North American Retail business unit led by CEO Austin Mulinder. The story of Fujitsu's strategic renewal experience is told in Chapter Five. Many thanks to this group for allowing us to learn with them and to recount their story to illustrate the steps of the Dialectical Solutions Method.

Sincere thanks are given to the team at Jossey-Bass—Susan Williams, Jeff Wyneken, and Rob Brandt—who guided our efforts and helped us through each of the critical book development phases. A special thank you goes to Beverly Miller for working out final kinks in the manuscript and getting it ready for publication. Noteworthy contributions of a more general and ongoing sort were offered by the following people: Paul Bates, Dan Brousseau, Dave Button, Ron Brunt, Bob Horenstein, Alan Hutton, Del Langdon, Rich Lauf, Mark Novak, Joe Sauer, Don Tapscott, and Steve Zlotolow.

The largest debt is owed to all the framework inventors and big thinkers whose ideas fill up the pages of this book. From the early dialecticians like Heraclitus and Hegel to the authors of the fifty-five 2 × 2 frameworks summarized in the book, we thank you. The opportunity to speak with close to a third of the author group enriched and strengthened our learning experience.

A very special thank you is owed to our close colleague and friend Eli Singer. Eli joined the project as research associate earlier on. His talents, resourcefulness, perseverance, and knowledge have made him a valued and essential member of the team. Eli's insights can be felt on each page of the book.

Finally, we thank our wives, Julia Mustard and Connie Hood, for their patience, encouragement, and support, and our children, André, Benjamin, Jack, and Pam, and Phil's grandchildren, Juliana, Isabella, Nicolas, and Alexie, for their interest, inspiration, and questions. This book is for them and all other future problem solvers.

February 2004

ALEX LOWY
Toronto, Canada
PHIL HOOD
San Jose, California

THE AUTHORS

A LEX LOWY specializes in the creation of innovative work, learning, and information systems. He is cofounder and past president of Digital 4Sight, a global technology think tank and strategy consulting firm with headquarters in Toronto, Canada. He has coauthored two best-selling business books, *Digital Capital: Harnessing the Power of Business Webs* (2000) and *Blueprint to the Digital Economy* (1998), with Don Tapscott and David Ticoll. He is a sought-after consultant and educator and has contributed award-winning articles to journals including *Business 2.0, Training and Development,* and the *Journal for Group and Organizational Studies.* In 2003, he formed the Transcend Strategy Group.

PHIL HOOD has been one of Silicon Valley's most thoughtful voices on the development and use of multimedia and pervasive computing technologies for the past twenty years. He is the former executive editor of *NewMedia* magazine and a contributing columnist to *Wired* and other publications. As the former chief executive officer of Digital 4Sight, he directed a series of multiyear research studies that explored the links between emerging technologies and business ethics and strategy. He is a senior consulting associate to Stanford Research International (SRI), an engaging speaker, and a partner with Alex Lowy in the Transcend Strategy Group.

The Power of the 2 × 2 Matrix

INTRODUCTION

If you are a business executive, reflective professional, or consultant, the book you hold in your hands is an embarrassment of riches. Fifty-five remarkable frameworks are presented here—exceptional frameworks with an unusual power to organize and marshal problem-solving efforts. As diverse as these frameworks are on the surface, they share a common structure, which is responsible for their strength. The book is about learning to recognize, appreciate, and exploit this commonality that is contained in the 2 × 2 design that sets tension between opposing forces as the prime source of problem-solving energy and direction.

We reviewed more than three hundred discrete models to arrive at our final set of frameworks and consulted widely with colleagues and acknowledged business experts from industry and academia. We selected frameworks based on two simple criteria: each must succinctly and uniquely help to solve a class of problem worth solving, and each must use the 2 × 2 matrix form. In every case, we asked our respected sources to recommend their three favorite frameworks, emphasizing usability and practical payoff. We told them that we were interested in approaches they had personally applied and benefited from—theory that had been tested in the real world.

The frameworks ranged from brilliant to sublime to highly idiosyncratic. To understand the frameworks better, we tested them on ourselves, our clients, and in some cases, our families and friends. At times, we felt like those old sci-fi depictions of research scientists drinking concoctions late at night in their lab in the search for a powerful elixir. A project that had started as a casual and professional interest, quickly became a more intense journey of personal meaning and transformation.

In the end, we settled on the fifty-five frameworks set out in Part Three of the book. Many of them are established classics developed by well-known business authors—frameworks such as the BCG Grid, Ansoff's Product-Market Portfolio, and Michael Porter's Generic Strategy. Others are lesser-known gems we encountered along the way—ones we believed brought something necessary to round out the collection. We are absolutely certain that we have overlooked some superb examples of 2 × 2 modeling, and this is unfortunate. But there is only so much room in one book, and arguably, there is a limit to the number of truly unique expressions of the form. In the spirit of opening a dialogue rather than delivering a finished, closed set of ideas, we encourage readers to share their own examples of best practices at our Web site, www.TranscendStrategy.com.

Frameworks range from the highly intuitive to the ingeniously complex. In many cases, they are the most accessible and important part of a larger body of work. For each of these, we offer essential information—enough to get you started and to whet your appetite. In some instances, we provide case-based examples to illustrate a complex or particularly important set of ideas. As a general rule, we present the frameworks in the simplest way possible, while still delivering full meaning and accessibility. To do the material justice, we urge readers to go to the source and read books, articles, and manuals written by the creators. They are worth the time.

The unifying theme to the frameworks is the use of a 2 × 2 matrix to represent the formulation and treatment of an important topic. The power of 2 × 2, however, goes far beyond the matrix itself. It is the underlying dynamic structure of 2 × 2 modeling that brings richness, depth, and a uniquely transformational power to the form. There is a right and wrong way to construct a 2 × 2 matrix, and the key lies in how the primary factors are selected and applied. Although the essence of the approach is contained within the matrix, successful application depends on a particular cognitive and emotional bias in approach. We refer to this style of problem solving as 2 × 2 Thinking, an open and integrative orientation that operates independent of any particular framework. By studying hundreds of unique and diverse frameworks and interviewing experts like Paul Hersey and Steven Covey, we have been able to construct a practical set of rules and structures that anyone can learn and apply.

WHAT IS 2 × 2 THINKING?

The very best instances of problem solving share a number of characteristics that comprise the core of 2 × 2 Thinking. 2 × 2 Thinking is open (as opposed to closed), proactive, and drawn toward inherent conflicts in search of resolution. The following seven points illustrate this more fully:

- 2 × 2 Thinking leads to an open exploration of issues to unearth inherent tensions. These tensions exist within an evolving context, where focus shifts as old points are resolved and new tensions emerge.

- 2 × 2 thinkers recognize the importance of learning as both a condition for change and a key enabler. Learning involves embracing the new and letting go of unhelpful and invalid views.

- 2 × 2 Thinking is often but not necessarily interpersonal. When others are involved, dialogue is rich, informative, and honest.

- 2 × 2 thinkers move toward, not away from, complexity. The act of focusing on a core set of variables does not reduce or simplify analysis. Rather, it enriches it.

- 2 × 2 Thinking requires openness, which leads to rapid modeling and reframing. Problems are reconsidered, and underlying assumptions are vigorously challenged.

- 2 × 2 thinkers are drawn to seeing both sides of an issue. This often leads to paradoxical situations, which are explored rather than denied or ignored.

- 2 × 2 thinkers simplify to intensify focus. Rather than being confused by the core dilemma, they use the framework to gain deeper meaning and arrive at more informed choices.

FROM 2 × 2 THINKING TO MANAGING DILEMMAS

The simplest 2 × 2 problem-solving behavior involves looking at the other side of an issue before reaching a conclusion. A simple "what-if" exercise will accomplish this. Dilemmas are a more interesting case. Dilemmas pull us simultaneously in competing directions, each compelling in its own right. Although dilemmas rarely feel good, they often contain the seeds of deeper understanding and a superior solution than we are otherwise capable of finding. The trouble with our experience of dilemmas is that they generally happen to us, and we feel out of control.

2 × 2 Thinking recognizes the power in exploring competing forces. By intentionally constructing dilemmas, we challenge ourselves to think at a higher logical level. Often it is not really about choosing one or another option. Something is missing in the decision process. It could be perspective, excitement, confidence, agreement among parties, or additional alternatives—for example, should

we invest in developing our business or take profit now? This simple dilemma (see Figure I.1) has caused thousands of business owners sleepless nights over the years. Viewed as a simple and straightforward choice, it is not very interesting or enlightening. However, a poorly thought-through decision based in fear, greed, or misplaced confidence can prove hazardous to the business over time. In contrast, we can construct a 2 × 2 decision matrix to intensify and deepen the way we think through the issue. Looked at in this way, there are really two sets of choices to make rather than one. And it may not have to be a forced choice between this and that. In the best of cases, it is possible to realize both ideals by reframing the question.

ISN'T THIS OBVIOUS AND SIMPLE?

It is tempting to dismiss 2 × 2 Thinking as stunningly simple and hardly worth the time and study. After all, the structure is self-evident, and the practice seems clear and to a degree, instinctive. Nevertheless, the apparent simplicity of the 2 × 2 matrix is deceptive. Einstein commented that models should be "as simple as possible and no simpler." Finding the perfect point of balance can be elusive; excursions of over- and underdevelopment are the norm, not exceptions.

The matrix is a clear and helpful starting point to achieving balance and clarity. We regard the matrix as one leg of a three-legged stool. The *form* of the matrix needs to be applied in a systematic manner (*method*) and with sensitivity and expertise (*mastery*). The combination of form, method, and mastery

Figure I.1. Profit Now or Later Matrix

imbues 2 × 2 Thinking with the power to realize more fully what is possible and to generate solutions characterized by what Bill Buxton, former chief scientist at Alias Research, calls "surprising obviousness."

HOW THE BOOK IS ORGANIZED

We suggest that readers treat this book as a rich resource and problem-solving aid. Reading it from end to end will not be meaningful in most cases. The jewel in the crown is the inventory of remarkable 2 × 2 frameworks in Part Three. These are organized to enable easy identification and application to different situations. Two other types of content complement and extend the value of the frameworks. The book opens with three chapters that explain the conceptual underpinnings and logic of 2 × 2 Thinking. These chapters set the context for the selection and use of all of the frameworks contained in the book. The third and final topic is methodology. Chapters Four and Five walk readers through two levels of application, making the design and use of 2 × 2 Thinking clear and explicit.

Part One looks at how 2 × 2 Thinking is constructed, when it is applicable, and why it is effective. The power of 2 x 2 Thinking derives from the creative tension established between carefully selected, primary forces. Drawing on archetypal and Hegelian lessons, the book establishes the rationale and conditions for effective application of this basic problem-solving and consulting method.

Chapter One, "The DNA of Great Problem Solving," provides an overview of the topic, setting it firmly in the context of business problem solving. It presents a number of classic 2 × 2 frameworks, along with stories of 2 × 2 Thinking on the fly.

Chapter Two, "Form, Method, and Mastery," explores the underlying structure of effective 2 × 2 modeling. Form (the matrix), method (systems and steps), and mastery (lessons of experience) are all necessary. The emphasis of the chapter is on mastery, highlighting many of the less obvious elements of design and application.

Chapter Three, "The Eight Archetypal Dilemmas," presents a powerful set of recurring dilemmas that are useful for diagnosis and idea generation. The chapter ends with a self-diagnostic survey suitable for organizational assessment.

Part Two offers the reader guidance in applying 2 × 2 Thinking in a structured and practical way. Drawing on the insights of dozens of 2 × 2 authors and expert implementers, the chapters in this part offer a clear and dependable methodology for home-grown modeling. The step-by-step process is accompanied by situational advice drawn from the field experiences of leading consultants and business leaders.

Chapter Four, "Designing 2 × 2 Matrices," walks readers through the basic mechanics of constructing a powerful 2 × 2 matrix. Simple, easy-to-relate-to examples illustrate design steps and decisions.

Chapter Five, "2 × 2 Thinking in Action," tells the real-world story of how the North American Retail Division of Fujitsu Corporation turned chronic loss to profit by addressing its clients' biggest dilemma with courageous and creative application of 2 × 2 Thinking.

Part Three contains an inventory of best-of-breed 2 × 2 frameworks. Fifty-five of the most powerful 2 × 2 models used in business are presented in three categories: strategic, organizational, and individual.

Chapter Six, "Strategic Frameworks," tackles the challenge of business competitiveness. Twenty-three frameworks address five strategic topics: customer needs, strategic context, strategic options, marketing and communications, and risk.

Chapter Seven, "Organizational Frameworks," focuses on effectiveness and adaptation. Twenty frameworks address four organizational topics: structure, leadership and culture, learning and change, and process.

Chapter Eight, "Individual Frameworks," helps us to increase personal effectiveness. Twelve frameworks address three individual topics: personal awareness and style, personal effectiveness, and decision making.

A STEP IN THE RIGHT DIRECTION

If this book could teach only one lesson, it would be to encourage people to learn and solve problems through the intentional creation and resolution of dilemmas. By challenging ourselves and those around us to think at higher logical levels, we raise the quality of deliberation and the decisions and agreements we reach.

2 × 2 Thinking is not a panacea. We believe it is definitely a step in the right direction, improving the clarity, honesty, and quality of problem solving. This is not a new idea; dialectical reasoning, which is explained in Chapter Two, is a tradition that is twenty-five hundred years old. By bringing many of the most impressive 2 × 2 frameworks together and by adding analysis and methodology, we hope more people and more organizations will open themselves to the practice. We will continue to collect and publish new and interesting frameworks and thoughts on our Web site, www.TranscendStrategy.com, and encourage readers to join us there.

PART ONE

2 × 2 THINKING

CHAPTER ONE

THE DNA OF
GREAT PROBLEM SOLVING

Everything craves its contrary, and not for its like.
—Socrates

I t was a snowy, winter night in 1994 at the Leadership Centre of the Canadian Imperial Bank of Commerce (CIBC) north of Toronto. A small group of executives had been working for many hours trying to solve an organizational crisis that was becoming more worrisome each day. The commercial part of the bank, serving roughly seventy-five thousand small to medium-sized businesses, was in need of serious redesign if the bank were to remain competitive and viable in this important sector. Several years of complacency had led to products falling out of touch with changing client needs. Add to this the growing ineffectiveness of the group's middle management to set meaningful performance standards and motivate staff, and prospects for a simple fix seemed dim. The bank's competitors were charging forward with newly found creativity and energy, and had started to make inroads into some of the CIBC's oldest and most secure client accounts.

At a critical juncture in the discussion, the vice president of leadership and learning, Hubert Saint-Onge, jumped to the white board and drew a simple diagram like the one in Figure 1.1. "Our problem," he began, "is striking a balance between Alignment on the one hand and Autonomy on the other. Some of our best staff are out of control . . . behaving like cowboys. They need to be reined in. Others have become too comfortable and passive. They act as if they expect the bank to tell them what to do at every moment; they're afraid to make decisions or take even the smallest risk. Well, that won't work. We need an approach that moves staff into the upper right quadrant [pointing to the 2 × 2 model]."

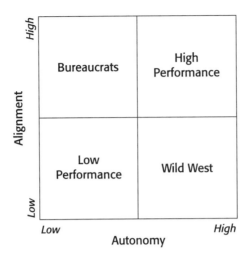

Figure 1.1. Alignment versus Autonomy Matrix

When he finished talking, there was a noticeable sense of relief among those in the room. Something important and profound had changed. The debate for the last while had raged over how to motivate loan officers to take more initiative without the bank losing control of assessing quality and riskiness of applicants. The Gordian knot was cut. A simple 2 × 2 framework intervention at the pivotal moment had reframed the crisis, allowing the group to move beyond the place where only moments before they had felt paralyzed.

2 × 2 THINKING:
A COMMON PATH TO EXTRAORDINARY ENDS

Although the facts of the case described above are specific to the financial industry, the method that Saint-Onge applied had little to do with banking. Rather, it is both universal and highly transferable. We call this approach 2 × 2 Thinking. A complex situation is modeled as a set of dueling interests. The hunt for a single correct solution is supplanted by the search for understanding, perspective, and insight. The game is in effect redefined:

- Tension becomes a good thing. Instead of trying to eliminate tension, we let it lead us to important topics and questions.

- Conflicting goals are seized upon, becoming useful markers that set the parameters for our search (in the example, these are Alignment and Autonomy).

- In place of a single right answer, a set of plausible options is created by considering high and low cases of the two conflicting needs.

- The four options may be illuminating or not. Generally, if the two axes are well defined, the options will be rich in explanatory or provocative power. If this not the case, it is usually worth redefining one or both of the axes and trying again.

In the bank example, introduction of the 2×2 matrix did several things. By naming the two issues, the group acknowledged a core dilemma that had been getting in the way of progress. The matrix provided a common and acceptable vocabulary that allowed the group to talk through an issue that had become rather sensitive. Perhaps most important, once group members had bought into the validity of the matrix as a model of their situation, they were able to move on to considering alternative solutions.

Deciding on which of the options to embrace presents a different set of challenges. It often appears that the upper right quadrant, High-High, is the preferable choice; however, the decision is rarely so simple because each solution is accompanied by a set of costs and benefits. Sometimes the costs and risks associated with the ideal solution are simply too great. For example, the banking planning group was reluctant to hand front-line staff free rein; however, they did indeed want these staff members to be fully aligned with the business vision. By recognizing that the autonomy gap represented a barrier to succeeding, they began to construct a path that involved things like adjusting risk management mechanisms to define authority limits in a way that reflected performance. The upper right quadrant option, High Performance, became the aspirational solution they would work toward.

2×2 Thinking is remarkably flexible on a number of levels. The scope of issue scales easily from personal decisions to large strategic conundrums. If you have any doubt about this, scan the three chapters of 2×2 frameworks in Part Three of this book. The approach is as applicable in a retail business setting as it is to designing a supply chain or addressing global trade-offs regarding the environment. The mode of application is equally effective when applied within a group setting or by an individual working alone. And the basic approach is just as powerful for analysis as it is for generating new ideas.

AT THE FEET OF MASTERS

The ability to think in a 2×2 fashion may be universal, but it is by no means easy. Although it is applicable at the individual level for tackling a single issue, it becomes increasingly challenging and subtle as we enter the realms of leadership, strategy, and intervention. These are arenas where excellent problem-solving skills and tools can have the greatest leverage.

To understand what is required to apply 2 × 2 Thinking under these kinds of circumstances, we interviewed a number of the most talented 2 × 2 practitioners in the world. Front-line consultants like Hubert Saint-Onge and writers like Steven Covey, Paul Hersey, and Watts Wacker generously shared their stories and insights. We were interested in hearing about their frameworks, but more important, we wanted to understand how and why they designed them and what they did when applying them that increased their impact. Through the discussions, we gained a clearer picture of the deep structure underlying effective use of the seemingly innocent 2 × 2 matrix. Nested in stories like the one above, a set of master principles of practice emerged:

• *Struggle* is a necessary condition for breakthrough. It is generally only after a group has worked hard on a problem, even gotten stuck in it, that positive change and new insights become possible.

• *Timing* is critical. The same idea at the wrong moment isn't half as powerful. The most complex situations benefit from a 2 × 2 analysis if the timing is right. Assertions that it is too simplistic are always problems with timing and delivery.

• *Simplicity* in methods is desirable when mapping complex and highly charged material. Some of the best frameworks have not had a single word altered in over thirty years. Their creators have in effect become their protectors, so that people can view the ideas as stable and reliable.

• *Ownership* is essential. Groups and organizations derive the greatest value when they actively participate in development and interpretation. This includes naming the issues, the axes of the framework, and the quadrants inside it. In the banking example in this chapter, Saint-Onge chose words that would resonate with people based on a familiarity with their discussion. If they preferred different wording or believed another factor needed to be introduced, he would happily make the change.

• *Skin in the game.* It has to matter, and participants need to be prepared to be accountable for their opinions and commitments. The process is not casual and is characterized by passion and personal investment in the outcome. Without this, tension is false, and something will go wrong. That something could be innocuous and boring, leading to dissolution of an effort, or it could be explosive and damaging, as when a key activity is dropped or someone feels betrayed and loses faith.

The intangible element, the *energy* of processes, is ultimately more telling than structures, tools, and matrices. Don't get hung up on the 2 × 2 form. Use it as a convenient medium and device to achieve important ends. 2 × 2 modeling brings focus and tension, often making issues clearer. It creates the context; the rest is up to you. Like the framework introduced by Peter Drucker looking at Doing the Right Job versus Doing the Job Right, if you are working on the right material and act with integrity, you are much more likely to succeed.

THE PROBLEM-SOLVING MIND

In 1997, Garry Kasparov fought and lost the chess match of the millennium to IBM's Deep Blue. Kasparov brought to the contest perhaps the greatest human chess mind ever to exist. Deep Blue had been modeled on masters and could evaluate 20 billion moves in the three minutes allowed per move. Kasparov could have won, he said afterward, but he played the game wrong, trying to outcompute the fastest computational game machine in history. A rematch of sorts, against Blue Junior, occurred in 2003 at the New York Athletic Club. This time Kasparov did what he thought he should have tried at the previous encounter: confuse the computer with unusual, even suboptimal and odd, moves. Although this worked spectacularly in the first game, the match ended in a 3–3 tie.

Whatever the outcome, the episode helps to illuminate the process of superior problem solving. Kasparov could never match the ever increasing processing speed of computers. Deep Blue software engineer Joe Hoane observed that chess geniuses like Kasparov "are doing some mysterious computation we can't figure out."[1] Computation, however, may not be the best way to describe this. As a master problem solver, his exceptional skill is a combination of three uniquely human aptitudes: organization, visualization, and experimentation. Taken together, they make it possible to invent and solve problems in holistic and idiosyncratic ways that are at once lateral and judgmental:

- *Organization.* In a manner closer to what a great artist does than conventional science, we are able to deconstruct situations and rapidly reconstruct them into new perspectives, problems, and approaches. When Kasparov sees an appealing way to reframe the situation, he settles on it and models a set of possible next steps and outcomes. In a way, he is thinking both literally and metaphorically at the same time and is being guided by both perspectives. If, for a moment, the setup on the board reminds him of his favorite tragic opera aria or a touching moment spent with his mother on a mountaintop thirty years ago, he can incorporate the inspiration into the next move.
- *Visualization.* The metaphoric capacity to envision whole, complex situations and scenarios allows us to see a vast array of possibilities quickly. The best problem solvers naturally do this generative outpouring of options, seemingly unperturbed by the reality constraints and pressures of the moment. They are hardly unaware or insensitive. Rather, they are demonstrating a higher

capacity for holding pressures and worries in abeyance while they invest themselves fully in a lateral search for best answers.

In training CIA agents, the ability to remain open to all possibilities in spite of mounting evidence is considered a prerequisite for doing investigative work. If you get it wrong at the beginning, recovery is almost impossible.

Major intelligence failures are usually caused by failures of analysis, not failures of collection. Relevant information is discounted, misinterpreted, ignored, rejected, or overlooked because it fails to fit a prevailing mental model or mind-set.[2]

- *Experimentation.* Before committing to any path, great problem solvers conduct many mind experiments, asking a thousand what-if questions and imagining the outcomes. There is little fear in exploring and modeling possibilities, and there is even less attachment to the parade of ideas generated. It's all part of the process.

Kasparov intuitively understands his limitations and knows what humans can do better than machines, even one programmed to detect patterns and think in fuzzy fashions. The machine is necessarily rule bound, while the master problem solver *makes* rules. Great problem solvers define and redefine rules. An important by-product of this, perhaps the most critical differentiator between the best and the rest of us, is the ability to shift logical levels. Alfred North Whitehead first made the observation that complex problems need to be solved at a different and higher logical level from where the problem was created.[3]

It's a cold day, you're late for work, and your ten-year-old car won't start again. A same-level approach is to find the problem and fix it. But it's cold, and you're late! A different-level solution is to take a cab, or stop driving to work, or to move closer to the office.

A company receives another piece of negative feedback from another unhappy customer. A same-level approach is to apologize and try harder. A different-level solution is to examine the entire set of relevant business processes or involve customers in redesigning the solution.

Look closely at the mental strategies of Kasparov and great leaders like Gandhi and Winston Churchill, and you will see a high level of organizing, visualizing, and experimenting taking place. By searching for answers while maintaining an open mind, they pursue the most important and interesting tensions in situations, following them to a conclusion that might be the answer they were looking for—or merely the jumping-off point for further development. Embracing tension and contradiction seems to be part of the game, and often great problem solvers go out of their way to find it or even create it. Think of the Socratic method and how knowledge is teased out of the pupil. And what could be a more masterful application of contradiction and tension than Gandhi's use of nonviolence as a powerful means of protest? Faced with the choice of militantly opposing British rule in India or working through the system nonviolently, Gandhi chose neither . . . and both. His strategy of militant nonviolence changed the rules of the game to overthrow the existing order.

It is true that there are many ways to solve problems and a range of styles and approaches to choose among for different situations. However, it is a willingness and ability to see both sides of issues and rapidly and creatively tackle them that provides the common edge. The connection between 2 × 2 Thinking and great problem solving is manifested in structure and attitude. The 2 × 2 structure is decidedly open and reflective, enabling rapid iterations of organizing, envisioning, and experimenting. The attitude is exploratory and embraces tension and contradiction as central organizing principles. The process of seeking out and exploiting core tensions moves us toward the problem and ensures we are tackling real and relevant issues. Fortunately, the core meta-frameworks and methods necessary for 2 × 2 Thinking can be learned and applied. The process starts with recognizing alternative approaches, and challenging one's habitual response to problems.

STRATEGIC, ORGANIZATIONAL, AND INDIVIDUAL APPLICATIONS

Drawing on over two decades of business and consulting practice, we have often been dazzled by someone using a 2 × 2 matrix to solve a business problem. Sometimes it was a well-known model, familiar to all involved, like the BCG Grid, or an assessment of risk and reward. Even more frequently, it was the spontaneous creation of someone in the room, as in the opening example in this chapter.

While researching this book, we were asked a rather difficult question: Which in our opinion is the best 2 × 2 framework? As parents, this felt too much like being asked to say which of our kids we loved the most. Surprisingly, however, a small number of remarkable frameworks did come to mind, not necessarily because they were the best but because they were striking and intuitive illustrations of the three categories of 2 × 2 frameworks we explore here. In subsequent discussions and presentations, we have found retelling the story of these three frameworks to be the easiest way for people to quickly grasp the structure, breadth, and relevance of 2 × 2 modeling. After offering an example, we encourage listeners to try out the approach by thinking about their own circumstances. As readers setting out on the 2 × 2 learning journey, we invite you to do the same.

Strategic Frameworks

In 1965, Igor Ansoff introduced the Product-Market matrix (see Figure 1.2), and with this, he helped to launch the modern practice of business strategy.[4] The two most essential strategy levers for any business are the product or service it delivers and the markets it sells into. For each of these, there are two basic states: current and new. There are today's customers and there is the rest of the world that could become customers. We can sell more of our current offering, or we can modify it. By combining these two sets of possibilities, companies can effectively model strategic choices in a manner that is both instructive for analysis and decision making and easy to communicate to others.

The four strategy options that result from this simple analysis are stunningly clear and helpful. According to Ansoff, the easiest and first choice is to sell more of the same to existing customers. Businesses should choose Market Penetration when a new product has been received warmly and there is lots of demand left to tap. Strategy options defined in the upper left and lower right quadrants are a little harder to implement, but are absolutely the correct steps to take under appropriate conditions. For example, when a product has proven its value in one market, the most natural thing to do is introduce it elsewhere, exploiting experience and testimonials from the last market. Or a company can sell new products to satisfied and loyal customers, drawing on the trust that has been established and their understanding of the needs and preferences of the customer group. The upper right category, Diversification, should be applied with great caution, and generally only when none of the other three alternatives

Figure 1.2. Product-Market Matrix

is available. Cost and risk tend to be higher when the product is unproven and the market unknown.

The logic of this analysis is easy to see. Consider Sony, one of the world's best-loved brands. Founded by Masaru Ibuka and Akio Morita in 1946, Sony Corporation has grown into a global supercompany by introducing a steady stream of innovative electronics products. These include the first magnetic tape and tape recorder, the transistor radio, the Trinitron TV, the Walkman, the CD, and the MiniDisc. The founders were well matched as a team. Ibuka focused company engineers on world-beating product design and development while Morita planned and led market-entry strategies that grew the company and its reputation.

In Ansoff's terms, Sony's opening strategy fits into the lower left box, perfecting products and selling them to a growing Japanese audience. Moving from tape recorder technology in 1950 to transistor radios in 1955, the company successfully expanded its portfolio by selling new products to an existing base of loyal customers. Before long, it was a well-established brand name in the domestic market. By 1960, Sony had opened its first overseas operation in New York City, entering Ansoff's lower right box, Market Development. The rest, as they say, is history, as the company's succession of leaders has continued to develop the company, remaining true to the vision and values of the founders while improvising through bumpy patches.

Probably the most controversial and rocky decision was the entry into the entertainment content business, first with music in 1988 with the acquisition of CBS Records and then movies in 1989 when Sony purchased Columbia Pictures. Compared with the string of consumer electronic products that had been their mainstay for over three decades, this move represented a departure from the familiar pattern. Entertainment value is very different from electronic products you can touch. And although moviegoers were certainly aware of the Sony name, they did not view it as an entertainment company. In Ansoff's schema, this was an upper right box, Diversification strategic approach, and as predicted, the road was rougher than with prior business projects.

Your business may be smaller than Sony's, but the same sets of forces and issues apply. What is the basis for your business's existence? If you work for a government organization or are self-employed, the question is still highly relevant. Now think about developing the business based on the current source of value. Should your organization be shifting to new and better offerings in order to retain customer loyalty? Is it timely to consider expanding into different markets to find some new customers who need the current offering? Perhaps the existing group of customers doesn't need more of your services, and others do. And finally, is it advisable to consider the riskier Diversification approach? Maybe the company is doing this now without fully recognizing the exposure.

Organizational Frameworks

What is the most crucial issue facing organizations in the future? According to knowledge management expert Ikujirio Nonaka, it is balancing the need for speed in planning and execution with the need to develop the economies of scale and scope that lead to long-term competitive advantage.[5]

To Nonaka, scale and scope refer more directly to knowledge and capabilities than size. Nonaka's career has been devoted to studying how knowledge is replacing other resources as a business's most important asset and how it is created, deployed, and shared within firms. Much of the knowledge that creates competitive advantage is tacit: it exists mainly in the heads of workers, not in spreadsheets, databases, or training courses. Workers at all levels develop tacit knowledge as they practice craft skills and learn to recognize patterns in the business problems they encounter.

Deep knowledge assets get expressed as advantages in economies of scale or scope. A great deal of the competitive advantage of a retailer aggregator like Wal-Mart or a services business like a large consultancy comes from the interdependent knowledge assets that exist within the firm's workers and are embedded in daily work processes. But as knowledge has increased in importance, so has speed. Firms are pulled toward what Nonaka calls "an economy of speed." The business environment has become more dynamic, and firms must now be more agile and flexible. One popular way of becoming quicker has been to unbundle the firm by creating webs of interconnected companies through outsourcing and partnering. In this way, firms can downsize and remove layers of hierarchy, becoming faster at decision making and execution.

The danger in this approach is that firms can get too lean. Solving complex issues is rarely a matter of simply choosing one option or the other, leading Nonaka to conclude that the ability to synthesize knowledge and seek transcendent solutions is the hallmark of today's successful firms.

The 2 × 2 matrix in Figure 1.3 depicts the dilemma of Speed (succeeding today) versus Scale and Scope (investing to succeed tomorrow). Typically, firms cycle through the four strategic options in accordance with shifting business phases and demands. Finding balance between the two driving forces eventually becomes a necessity for all firms.

Nonaka's work is not academic speculation; it is as hard as the news in this morning's paper. Many leading firms embody aspects of the upper right quadrant. Wal-Mart is able to open new stores and introduce new products and services at a pace much faster than its rivals, while at the same time using information technology to operate with lower costs than its competition. Cisco became the largest manufacturer of networking equipment in the world by retaining vital functions while partnering to attain speed and scale in other areas. To keep pace with cutting-edge engineering, Cisco has purchased a steady

Figure 1.3. Economies of Speed and Scale Matrix

stream of start-up companies with promising technologies. New companies are integrated quickly, with special attention given to recognizing and rewarding staff efforts. Capital-intensive processes in areas such as manufacturing, logistics, and distribution are treated as noncore and better suited to best-of-breed strategic partners. Companies such as these are succeeding by focusing on achieving the two contradictory aims of efficiency in scale and the advantages of speed.

It is worth reflecting for a moment on the balance between Speed and Scale and Scope in your own organization. Is the right amount of attention and resources being given to each? Does the firm possess the basic competencies to do these things well?

Individual Frameworks

We often begin business strategy sessions with a new client by asking team members to draft their personal dialectic. The instruction is simple and straightforward: create a 2 × 2 matrix that expresses a real and important tension in your life. Once they have done this, we ask them to name the ends of the two axes, and the four quadrants contained in the matrix. As an example, we share one of our own (see Figure 1.4).

The tension here is between spending time on activities that are meaningful and developmentally useful (work that makes a positive difference in the world and jazz piano are two goals that come to mind) and the ability to do them reasonably well. This sums up Alex's priority setting. He tries to say no to low-value demands and opportunities, while actively expanding the limits of what he can take on. His greatest challenge is recognizing limits and setting realistic

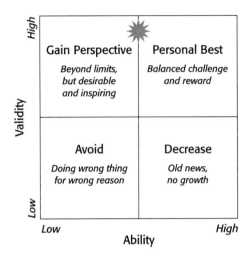

Figure 1.4. Alex's Core Dialectic Matrix

expectations to avoid frustration. The star at the top of the matrix in Figure 1.4 is the spot he aims for: working on rewarding projects that represent creative stretch yet are achievable.

When clients discuss their personal dialectics, the comments are always of a similar tone:

- People are surprised at how easy it was to complete the task.
- Creating the matrix was eye-opening twice: once while developing it and again when talking about it with peers.
- When the matrix is completed in a group, people feel more connected, open, and accepted by the rest of the team.

These kinds of experiences illustrate just how relevant and applicable the 2 × 2 approach is to personal problem solving. It is not surprising, therefore, that many of the most useful and powerful frameworks are found at this level.

Perhaps the easiest Individual 2 × 2 framework for people to relate to is one created by Stephen Covey in his classic book, *The Seven Habits of Highly Effective People* (Figure 1.5).[6] Our days are filled with activities, yet for most of us, there is never enough time to do the things that matter most. So many of the things we do are what Covey classifies as Urgent—tasks that we believe must be done. Other things are Important, and we recognize that they hold a special place in achieving our goals and living a satisfying life. So what prevents us from making better-quality choices about how to spend time and live our lives?

This is not a simple or trivial question, but it most certainly is a compelling one. Life is about choices. When we shortchange one set of goals, it is because

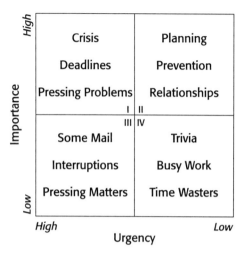

Figure 1.5. Time Management Matrix

we are choosing to say yes to other things. We have all heard and possibly experienced firsthand the lamentations of people in their later years confronting premature ill health or loneliness. How many parents have we heard say, "I was so busy while the children were growing up; I wish I had spent more time with them"? Who among us is not interested in gaining control over our life and achieving more of our goals? Changing the balance requires awareness and a willingness to take greater responsibility for our lives.

To help people take greater control, Covey asks questions like these:

"How do you spend your time?"

"Is there enough balance between Urgency and Importance?"

"If you could make time for one Important but not Urgent agenda item, what would that be, and how would this improve your life?"

We have posed these questions to groups many times, with the same immediate and beneficial impact. That is why this particular 2 × 2 framework ranks so high on our list. Within minutes, people understand how it works and are gaining personal value that far exceeds the small amount of effort it has taken to apply it to their own experience.

TRANSCENDENCE

2 × 2 Thinking is inherently and profoundly transcendent in nature. Two people face an identical problem differently: one sees an insurmountable problem, while the other perceives options and opportunities. Systems thinker Jamshid

Gharajedaghi calls these two approaches either-or versus both-and. Confronted by tough choices, the either-or reaction is to feel trapped and obliged to pick one or the other. The both-and response draws us automatically to a new and different perspective, where it is possible to search for ways to reframe the problem or use conflicting factors in the solution. (Chapter Seven contains two of Gharajedaghi's matrices: Differentiation and Integration, and Similarities and Differences.)

After watching a rerun of a Time-Life special, "Great People of the Millennium," Phil had this conversation with his guitarist brother, Jeff, and his father:

PHIL: Jeff, who is the greatest man of the last millennium?

JEFF: A thousand years?

PHIL: Yeah.

JEFF: Easy. It's Bird [meaning Charlie Parker, the legendary bebop saxophonist].

PHIL: No, man, seriously. I'll give you a hint. Newton was second; Galileo was third. [My dad chips in: "What about Henry Ford?"]

JEFF: You're talking about money? And gravity? That's what you mean by great? Bird wasn't about gravity. He was about (pause) . . . transcendence.

Reflecting on this later, Phil observed that the line, "Bird wasn't about gravity," was as true as anything he'd ever heard. To jazz fans, Charlie Parker was the perfect mix of freedom and discipline. He was never constrained by the form of a song, but he was always mindful of it and showed it respect. Composers heard new, hidden meaning in their own works, and fellow musicians and listeners were inspired. His uncompromising musical integrity, combined with creativity and virtuosity, lifted the music to a new, transcendent plane where player and listeners were momentarily transformed.

The transcendent quality is at the center of great problem solving, and it is the one characteristic consistently mentioned by the experts we interviewed. It is apparent in the opening story in this chapter about the bank, where the planning group needed to let go of the problem momentarily in order to see options. We find it in other important works as well. Bill Russell, the outstanding basketball player with the Boston Celtics through the 1960s, writes about experiencing *flow* at times of peak performance, when it felt as if time slowed down and team members communicated as if by telepathy. They found a way to transcend the physical level of the game to perceive a larger set of choices. Martin Seligman, in his seminal work on learned helplessness, points to the connection between depression, pessimism, and the perception that there are no choices.[7] The either-or mind-set cannot surmount negative circumstances and spirals downward, while the both-and outlook does the opposite. Seligman's subsequent work on learned optimism in effect teaches transcendence.[8] A recent study on luck comes to a similar conclusion, finding that people make their own good and bad luck through their outlook. So-called lucky people are open to new experiences and capitalize on serendipity, while unlucky people experience life more narrowly, turning away from novelty before positive results can occur.[9] Their either-or mind-set precludes luck by cutting it off at the knees.

The structure of the 2×2 matrix creates the possibility of seeing beyond the restrictive either-or perspective by placing conflicting items in dynamic relationship to each other. Consider Ansoff's Product-Market matrix or Covey's modeling of Urgency and Importance. The answer might still be one or the other factor (perhaps Urgent but not Important), but one cannot easily ignore the other three possibilities. This momentary transcendence is the doorway into both-and reasoning and an important first step toward more successful problem solving.

CHAPTER TWO

Form, Method, and Mastery

2×2 Thinking
as Dialectical Process

To learn about change you can study Hegel,
But it's plain to see if you toast a bagel.
You put it in a toaster that's electric.
The bagel heats up; everything gets hectic.
Then it pops up, and that's a dialectic.
—Jack Lucero Fleck,
from *Dialectics for Kids,* "Everything Changes Bit by Bit"

At first, 2 × 2 modeling appears rather straightforward and obvious: pick a couple of variables influencing something that matters, like profitability and time, place them on a standard *x-y* grid, and you're done. Right! But as most readers know, this is unlikely to produce anything of insight or value. The bare essentials of matrix building have been attended to, but all the detail and nuance are missing. It is like equating fine cooking with a well-stocked kitchen or medical treatment with a lab coat and a doctor's office.

Although the requirements of the form have been met, key ingredients are missing: these are the knowledge-intensive, hard-fought lessons of experience that guide us in making critical choices. The lessons are expressed as method—steps, procedures, and guidelines—and mastery—a deeper level of wisdom that comes from direct contact and watching great practitioners up close. The greatest source of insight into this process comes from the philosophical domain of study called dialectics. We draw extensively on dialectics in making sense of high-impact 2 × 2 modeling and problem solving.

From the Greek *dialectiké*, the origin of the term *dialectic* is literally the art *(techne)* of philosophical discussion. The meaning has shifted since the days of Heraclitus and Socrates to embody a set of beliefs about the nature of change and the structure of thinking and discovery processes. Nothing exists in isolation; nothing occurs or exists independent of other events and systems. Facts, issues, and processes need to be examined within a larger context by exploring their logical opposites, internal tension, purpose, and history. The dialectical perspective pushes us to search for meaning beyond the level of obvious, visible evidence, focusing on the dynamic relationship between things and how they evolve.

The benefits for problem solving and design are significant. Dialectical thinkers are better and faster at framing, exploring, and resolving problems. If you believe there is a single right and wrong approach to most things, you are probably not a dialectician. Dialectical thinkers are able to wend their way through complex and difficult challenges because they are less likely to ignore messages that trouble them. They see both-and potential rather than either-or forced choices in situations (see Chapter One). If you naturally ask what-if questions to generate alternative views, you are likely to be a dialectical thinker. Dialectical thinkers free themselves up to quickly create and sort a larger list of possible problem statements and solutions. They like to put things in perspective and are suspicious of easy, simple answers to complex problems.

Dialectical method is ultimately about transcendence. This means getting beyond the initial view of a problem or situation to gain a new, more helpful perspective. In business and social contexts, this often involves influencing the feelings people have about an issue that stand in the way of progress. To do this well and consistently, you need form (the 2 × 2 matrix), method (a process), and mastery (principles and competency).

FORM: THE HUMBLE 2 × 2 MATRIX

The starting point is the 2 × 2 matrix itself and understanding why it works. When Blaise Pascal, father of probability theory, sought a rationale for pursuing a religious path, he applied his exceptional intellect to create the argument contained in Figure 2.1. Either God exists or not. We can live a religious life, acting as if God existed, or we can live hedonistically without moral restraint. If God does indeed exist and we have lived an unruly life (God forbid), the price is eternal damnation. The opposite, living piously in a godless universe, isn't really very bad at all, he surmised. By applying 2 × 2 logic to the issue, he was able to present one of the most compelling non-faith-based arguments for following a religious path. A creative blend of theology and mathematics, this formulation is considered by many to be the first example of what is now called decision theory.[1]

The use of intersecting *x*- and *y*-axes (used in all 2 × 2 modeling) is basic to statistical methods, ranging from the *t*-test to multivariate factor analyses. Statistics concerns itself principally with the classification, quantification, and measurement of relationships. By comparing different states of possibly related items on a simple matrix grid, we are able to note and test patterns, converting quantitative into qualitative value, or numbers to meaning.

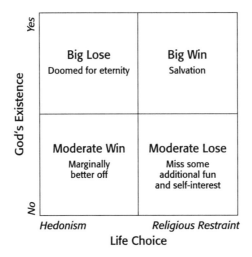

Figure 2.1. Pascal's Dilemma

Two characteristics make the form so powerful: simplicity and limits. *Simplicity* makes the 2 × 2 matrix intuitive to apply and easy to communicate to others. There is no need to waste time with elaborate explanations of the method itself. The form is obvious. And yet it is capable of supporting and expressing the most complex sorts of material, from economic forecasts in supply and demand calculations to negotiation strategies modeled with the use of Game Theory and the Prisoner's Dilemma.

Limits are imposed through the selection of a single issue, which is then precisely and dynamically defined through the choice of two prime, opposing forces. With limits come focus and tension, essential aspects of the 2 × 2 problem-solving process.

Together, simplicity and limits render the humble 2 × 2 matrix natural, adaptive to many situations, highly scalable, and as useful at the individual level as it is for addressing national policy considerations.

The 2 × 2 matrix is a tool, much like primary colors and elemental shapes such as circles and lines. Although the form is there for all of us to use, some apply it better than others, just as some of us are better at painting or manipulating shapes and building things. To improve our success in using the 2 × 2 matrix, we need to add method and mastery.

METHOD: A UNIVERSAL PROBLEM-SOLVING APPROACH

When Plato described Socrates' logic as dialectical, he was referring to the intensely honest and courageous investigation of important subjects, including, or perhaps especially, the self and reality. The Socratic method as used to

Table 2.1. Examples of Form, Method, and Mastery

Domain	Form	Method	Mastery
Cooking	Ingredients, pots, pans, stove, kitchen	Recipes, cookbooks	Touch, creativity, scalability
Construction	Building materials, equipment	Blueprints, building methods, and codes	Taste, design, beauty, strength, ideal trade-offs
Medicine	Equipment, drugs, hospital	Procedures, manuals, protocols	Diagnostic accuracy and speed, healing ability
Scientific research	Equipment, labs, substances, projects	Scientific method, test procedures, formulas	Sixth sense, patience, accumulated knowledge
Teaching	Curriculum, classrooms, instruction, roles of teacher and pupil	Pedagogy and androgogy	Insight, timing, sensitivity, ability to inspire
Parenting	Roles, responsibilities	Theories, methods, principles learned from books, courses, TV	Intuition, trust, anticipation, inspiration
Music	Instruments, songs, performance halls	Lessons, technique	Virtuosity, interpretation, ability to move listeners

adroitly elicit curiosity and promote learning is the practical application of this form of dialectic.

The definition of dialectical method took firmer shape around the start of the nineteenth century thanks to the efforts of the philosopher G.W.F. Hegel. Building on the conceptual work of Immanuel Kant, Hegel observed the importance of contradiction for progress—how forces seemed to elicit their complement and vied with each other for dominance, ultimately resolving in some fashion. "Contradiction," he wrote, "is the root of all movement and vitality, and it is only insofar as it contains a contradiction that anything has impulse and activity."[2]

With dialectical reasoning, Hegel created an intellectual method to address issues and raise the quality of logic and discourse among his contemporaries. According to Hegel, the thesis and antithesis of an important issue are pursued in tandem until their resolution is found in the synthesis.

You begin with a single idea, which he called the thesis. Consider, for example, the impact of scientific methods in areas such as medicine, agriculture, and psychology. In prescientific time, people made sense of events in the natural world with explanations based in folklore, religion, and superstition (*thesis*). As scientific tools and methods improved, the old beliefs fell into disrepute (*antithesis*). In time, science hit its own limits, encountering problems that could not be solved. On occasion, scientific solutions created entirely new problems as secondary effects of themselves; consider pollution levels, treatment-resistant germs, and urban sprawl. Resolution of the tension set up between the two points of view (the *synthesis*) presents us with new possibilities that draw on both traditions. Today we see increasing openness to blends of naturalistic and scientific orientations. In medicine, for example, this is taking the form of integrated Eastern and Western practices, drawing on science-based cures while promoting balanced living, natural foods, and exercises like yoga and forms of meditation.

Friedrich Engels and Karl Marx applied Hegel's dialectical formula to the analysis of power structures and forms of economic and political organization. They concluded that tensions between owners of value (*thesis*) and creators of value (*antithesis*) would ultimately lead to more egalitarian and fair structures (*synthesis*).

According to Hegel and his contemporaries, the process does not end after a single cycle. Each resolution of tension typically contains its own contradiction, sparking a new round of investigation. Thus goes the dialectical process.

In Chapters Four and Five, we provide two levels of dialectical problem-solving method. Chapter Four is a nuts-and-bolts tutorial that describes exactly how to go about constructing a powerful and original 2 × 2 matrix in response to a problem situation. This is a primer that takes the reader from issue definition through to choosing and testing the two essential dimensions that form the matrix. Chapter Five moves up a logical level, placing 2 × 2 Thinking within the context of organizational problem solving and strategy formulation.

2 × 2 Thinking offers a different approach to qualifying issues. Problems that stick around suggest there are underlying factors in need of exploration and development rather than elimination. Properly and squarely viewed, problems such as these become opportunities. Dialectical thinking helps to quickly surface and resolve core conflicts and dilemmas, ensuring that attention is directed toward the areas needing understanding and management. Chapter Five illustrates the power of this approach with the case of strategy formulation at Fujitsu Corporation's North American Retail business.

MASTERY: WISDOM IN ACTION

A young colleague of ours and his fiancée recently enrolled in an eight-session Latin dance course. Both novices and with their wedding two months away, they recognized an opportunity to acquire a lifelong skill that would pay off in the short term at their wedding. The first class was all about the fundamental structure and basic dance moves (*form*). Over the next few weeks, they learned a myriad of combinations (*method*), gaining confidence and a bit of flair through repetition and feedback provided by the two expert instructors (*mastery*). By week eight, they felt they could recognize and appreciate mastery when they saw it . . . , and they understood how much work it would take to achieve it. Suitably inspired by the experience, they are on their way!

Mastery is a combination of talent, dedication, effort, and experience. It generally takes time, risk, and sometimes failure. There is the well-known story of Thomas Watson refusing the resignation of one of his young managers at IBM who had made an error that cost the company $10 million. Watson's response was, "No way": IBM had invested $10 million in the man's development, and he was unlikely to make this kind of mistake ever again.[3]

Mastery is why we pay more for the top performer to do essentially the same job a junior person could do and feel that we are getting a good deal. Who wants a twenty-something medical specialist operating on them or a junior law associate handling a complex business transaction? Certainly they should be part of the team, but we want seasoned professionals on the job when the stakes are high. Mastery is hard to transfer, which is why mentoring and coaching are so important for certain kinds of learning. Mastery is composed primarily of what Ikujiro Nonaka and Hirotake Takeuchi, coauthors of *The Knowledge-Creating Company*, call tacit knowledge: personal and difficult to express and pass on formally.[4] (See the framework write-up in Chapter Seven for a fuller description of this point.)

Mastery in deploying 2×2 modeling is no small thing, and true to Nonaka and Takeuchi's notion of tacit knowledge, it is indeed a challenge to capture it in a few words and pictures. You learn the craft as you use it. We suggest keeping in mind the five mastery principles set out in Table 2.2 as you apply 2×2 Thinking. Periodically, it is worth performing a quick process audit to ensure that the principles are reflected in your approach.

Principle 1: Creative Tension

Tension results from unresolved opposition between forces. Archery is a good example. Pulling back on the string intensifies tension between the two ends of the bow. When the arrow is released at the optimal point, it flies forward with full force. Add aim, and the archer hits the target.

Apply the same thinking to the now famous Balance Theory of Supply and Demand (featured in the film *A Beautiful Mind*). Pricing is dynamically set by respecting the naturally opposed forces of availability of something (the push of Supply) and the need for it (the pull of Demand), as measured by price and quantity. This same tension exists in Steven Covey's Urgency versus Importance formulation. Calculation of Urgency versus Importance is most valuable when time is scarce, forcing attention to pressing but ultimately mundane tasks, perpetually

Table 2.2. Principles of 2 × 2 Mastery

Creative tension	Tension is the prime source of problem-solving energy. Ensure there is real and relevant tension between the two dimensions, as in Risk versus Reward and Urgency versus Importance.
Opposition	Opposition between forces is either direct or complementary. Direct opposition is Hot versus Cold or On versus Off. Complementary opposition is Size versus Speed or Growth versus Profit. Recognize the nature of opposition, and work with it.
Iteration	Nothing exists out of a context. As one tension resolves, new ones set up at a different logical level. All solutions need to be viewed as part of a continually evolving set of dynamics.
Integrity	Every step demands courage and honesty, beginning with naming the core dialectic, through to acknowledging and building on what emerges. Find direction with courage and integrity.
Transcendence	Learning requires unlearning, and resolution of basic tensions often means neither winning nor losing. Stay open to new possibilities.

postponing more significant life or business priorities. Remove the time pressure, and the exercise loses its tension and ultimately its purpose. Find the tension, and purpose and value return. A different 2 × 2 model, perhaps one that contrasts Importance with Cost or Capability, might be more relevant and capable of generating useful insights.

Dialectical axiom: Ensure that creative tension exists between the two axes to provide the energy and aim necessary for success.

Principle 2: Opposition

Hegel observed that opposition is the source of forward movement. Tension is born of such difference and struggle, seeking out resolution at a new and higher level. The key to harnessing this power lies in selection of the core dialectical struggle and identification of the competing forces. Get it wrong, and you're wasting your time.

As applied to problem solving and design, we have identified three legitimate forms of opposition and one artificial one that we call the false dialectic. Our primary concern is that the forces be independent of each other (statistically orthogonal). The simple test for dialectical opposition is the possibility of four plausible options resulting from combinations of high and low conditions of the two forces.

- *Direct opposition.* This is the purest form of opposition and accounts for approximately a quarter of the frameworks included in this book. Examples are

Drucker's Getting It Right (Right Job versus Doing the Job Right) and Covey's Urgency versus Importance. These dialectics are the most glaring instances of apparent either-or tension. The test for direct opposition is the ability to place the two dimensions on a single continuum. For example, Urgency and Importance are instances of priority, ranging from immediate to long term; Right Job and Doing the Job Right are aspects of work.

  • *Complementary opposition.* This category refers to opposition between factors that are qualitatively different yet interdependent in a relevant way. They could never exist as the polar ends of a single scale, unless the scale is of a generic nature like *focus,* which doesn't count. Ansoff's Product-Market matrix and the BCG Grid (Market Growth versus Competitive Positioning) are examples of complementary opposition.

Although the two factors are not strictly opposites, they create a dynamic field of interaction seeking resolution. Taken together, they succinctly account for a significant amount of variation possible in a situation. This is important because the selection of these factors serves to constrain and direct problem-solving efforts. The insight or energy generated is proportional to the amount of leverage represented by the dialectical dimensions that are chosen.

Many dialectics of this type can be broken apart to create two directly opposed matrices (the first type of opposition), yielding different and often more granular insights. Ansoff's classic strategy formulation separates easily into two new matrices, one profiling Markets and the other Products. As Figure 2.2 illustrates, by contrasting Existing Markets (Yes versus No) and New Markets (Yes versus No), we are able to map the four market strategy options available to a firm.

Figure 2.2. Market Options Matrix

• *Reflexive opposition.* Another form of opposition occurs when a single cat-egory is used to represent both of the dialectical dimensions, viewed from two or more perspectives. The Prisoner's Dilemma and Johari Window (both found in Chapter Six) are examples. In the Prisoner's Dilemma, parties must choose a collaborative or competitive strategy without knowing what the other's choices will be. The Johari Window compares Self-Knowledge with what Others know or don't know about the Self. These matrices are properly viewed as a variation of direct opposition.

• *False dialectic.* False dialectics occur when change in one factor (a depen-dent variable) results from changes in the other (the independent variable). When investment leads to growth all the time, the relationship is not dialecti-cal but causal. Viewed graphically, these false dialectics yield a diagonal plot line from the lower left to the upper right of an *x-y* grid. When set in a 2 × 2 matrix, they tend to define only two plausible options: low-low and high-high. False dialectics have their place as valuable analytic and modeling tools; how-ever, for this purpose, it is important to understand the differences to avoid null and frustrating exercises. Tom Stewart's modeling of Knowledge Intensity in Fig-ure 2.3 is an example of a useful analytic matrix that presents a false dialectic.

Dialectical axiom: Ensure that opposition between forces is real. Under-stand it, and exploit it.

Principle 3: Iteration

The buildup and release of tensions are best understood within the context of the complex sets of processes and relationships that surround the issue in ques-tion. No problems exist in isolation or should be studied separate from their nat-

Figure 2.3. Knowledge-Performance Matrix

ural context. This might appear to render the exercise of dialectical 2 × 2 modeling paradoxical and contradictory—we isolate to integrate—however maintaining this perspective is critical for drawing full value from the process. By setting limits and selecting critical dimensions, we add focus and energy to our efforts, knowing full well that some exclusion and distortion will result. Critics of 2 × 2 modeling will challenge (often with validity) that reality is more complex than any two variables, however carefully they are selected. Of course, it is! At every step, therefore, the process must remain true and accountable to real-world constraints and reality testing.

When allowed to flow naturally and freely, most problems progress in a cyclical manner, oscillating from side to side, with each resolution (*synthesis*) constituting a new starting point (*thesis*). Charlie Fine, MIT professor and author of *Clockspeed,* observes this perpetual pattern in market and organizational behavior, likening it to Watson and Crick's double helix (Figure 2.4): "Business genetics features the industrial equivalent of the double helix—a model based on an infinite double loop that cycles between vertically integrated industries inhabited by corporate behemoths and horizontally disintegrated industries populated

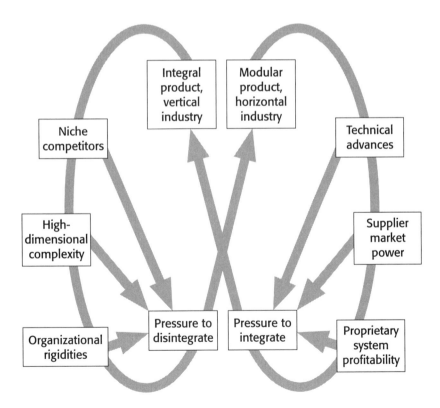

Figure 2.4. The Double Helix

by myriad innovators, each seeking a niche in the wide open space left by the earlier demise of the giant."[5]

Consider the following example of an iterative, cyclical application of 2 × 2 modeling to solve a personal planning dilemma. In a recent lunch conversation we had with a colleague in the midst of a career transition, he asked, "So, given my options, what do you think I should do?" Being trained consultants, we of course responded with questions, which thankfully in this case happened to be the most helpful response: What excites you most? What are you really best at? Do you want a satisfying experience or financial security? How marketable are you at this moment, and are you prepared to wait for the ideal fit? In serial fashion, we built several 2 × 2 matrices, leading eventually to his choosing a different direction from the one he had been favoring. Although entrepreneurial activity was appealing to him, his strongest skills lay in coaching and facilitation. He realized that his deepest satisfaction came from guiding others in their business deliberations rather than managing a business himself. On the question of financial pressures, he saw that the urgency to decide was in fact artificial, driving him toward a shortsighted choice he might later regret.

The application of 2 × 2 logic and method to a real and urgent problem at once enriched and grounded the discussion. We suspect the same conversation might have felt superficial if the circumstances had been hypothetical.

Dialectical axiom: Return regularly to the natural context of the problem to maintain perspective and urgency. The value of 2 × 2 Thinking is directly proportional to the timeliness and importance of the topic. Go directly to the heart of the matter; address essential rather than peripheral points.

Principle 4: Integrity

2 × 2 modeling is characterized by discovery and unpredictability. The two axes set the tone and challenge level for the ensuing search. When a process is conducted with integrity and openness, results are often surprising. Referring to his work on large-scale systems change, a long-time colleague of ours, John Cotter, inscribed on his stationery, "When you dance with a bear, *you* don't decide when to stop." The same can be said of 2 × 2 modeling, where investigation of unanticipated outcomes is often the most rewarding path.

When Royal Dutch Shell developed a scenario of a possible world oil embargo in the 1970s, it could have trivialized and skirted the unpleasant finding. Instead, it readied itself for such a situation, and several years later when the scenario became reality, was the best prepared of the major oil companies, with ample supplies and backup facilities to maintain operations. For a number of years, GE enforced a disciplined assessment of its competitive market position for all of its businesses. Priorities were determined by contrasting market attractiveness with GE's relative strength in that marketplace. If it could not occupy one of the top two spots in an industry that was demonstrably desirable, the unit was sold, disappointing some executives, but increasing earnings by 559 percent through the 1990s.[6]

Dialectical axiom: Stay open to what emerges, building on interim findings. As in the example of our colleague engaged in career planning, the greatest gains are made when the process is characterized by openness, integrity, and courage. One observation leads to another insight, which eventually sheds important light on the central topic.

Principle 5: Transcendence

Dialectical thinkers write about transformation rather than adaptation. Change creeps along slowly until something entirely new suddenly appears on the scene. Quantitative change leads to qualitative change once a threshold is reached. The butterfly is not a caterpillar with wings, and steam is not merely heated water but a new state. In human experience, love and trust are of a different order from the series of events and experiences leading up to them.

The whole purpose of dialectical, 2 × 2 Thinking is to attain a transcendent perspective, creating new options or moving beyond negative or stuck feelings that render progress impossible. (Self) consciousness is critical in achieving transcendence, which is always an active process demanding effort and imagination. This is why 2 × 2 modeling is so effective in team design efforts and for the resolution of interpersonal and interorganizational conflict. Hubert Saint-Onge, coauthor of *Leveraging Communities of Practice for Strategic Advantage,* describes this power of 2 × 2 reasoning as a function of language: "When conflicting parties agree on the definition of the axes of the matrix and start dialoguing about what to name the four quadrants, I know they are going to work things out. They now have unwittingly started to create common language for resolving their differences, which is a bridge to seeing what they have in common."[7]

Dialectical axiom: Seek out opportunities to reframe. The answer often lies in perspective, which implies letting go of some old views.

THE SWEET SPOT: ALIGNING FORM, METHOD, AND MASTERY WITH THE ARCHETYPES

Form alone is mechanical and aimless. Resorting to 2 × 2 modeling without method and mastery risks tackling the wrong issue or staying on the surface. Method without form and mastery is a frustrating and inefficient endeavor. It's like having the recipe for a cake but lacking both the proper cooking pans and that sixth sense that guides an experienced pastry chef. Mastery on its own is interesting, but most efforts are a lot easier when the tools and processes are available.

All this is most useful when the issue being tackled is suitable ground for dialectical treatment. As an analogy, it may be true that exercise is generally good for everyone, but it is not always the best response to a problem (such as marital difficulties or declining sales), and there is a wide assortment of exercise regimens available. Barry Johnson, author of *Polarity Management,* makes an interesting distinction between problems that can be solved and "polarities" that need to be managed.[8] The two defining features of polarities are that they tend to be ongoing and the polar forces or choices are interdependent. This is helpful. Chapter Three sets out the eight most interesting classes of polarity worth managing. (For a sampling of the diagnostic and modeling power of the archetypal dilemmas, try out the self-assessment guide on page 56.) When you target a real and pressing archetype with form, method, and, most important, mastery (Figure 2.5), problems become the launching pads for valuable insights and opportunity identification.

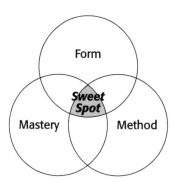

Figure 2.5. Aligning Form, Method, and Mastery

CHAPTER THREE

The Eight
Archetypal Dilemmas

Archetypes are deep, recurring patterns that help us to understand what is taking place at the observable, surface level of life. The value of archetypes lies in their applicability to everyday experience, rendering the mysterious interpretable and the mundane more essential. Carl Jung, the Swiss writer and psychiatrist, saw archetypes as universal truths, existing for all societies within a shared "collective unconscious." We don't so much create archetypes as invent stories that give a name and identity to them. Concepts such as hero, villain, virgin mother, and redemption exist in all societies, appearing locally with unique names and dramas.

Take apart any strategic dilemma, and you will find a basic struggle occurring between opposing forces—for example, Quality versus Speed, Time versus Money, Risk versus Reward. The archetypal dilemmas offer eight thematic groupings of common struggles. Each archetype is a response to a particular question or challenge. Answering that question is likely to take one down a particular road. For example, feeling torn between two choices is often a battle between one's reasoning side and one's emotions. The Head and Heart archetype outlines the essential nature of such crises. Change versus Stability is an entirely different balancing act, highlighting the need for adaptive behavior in all living systems.

The best way to apply the archetypes is as a guide or metaphor.[1] Each is a different route with underlying assumptions and structure. Sometimes there is an immediate, perfect fit; on other occasions, several of the archetypes may be relevant. Try them out, asking questions from the perspective of the different archetypes. How would you approach the problem if you treated it as a Head and Heart challenge? What are the merits of each side of the debate? Try out a couple of the others. What if this were an Inside and Outside issue (Are we sensing and meeting expectations?) or Cost and Benefit (What will it take to succeed, and is it worth it?)?

Table 3.1 of archetypal dilemmas contains a synopsis of the eight basic themes and suggests the diagnostic question that will help you to choose the appropriate one for your situation.[2]

HEAD AND HEART

The essence of the Head and Heart archetype is the need to choose between apparently incompatible yet equally essential options. Framed and labeled by Michael Macoby in *The Gamesman,* Head and Heart typifies the classic tough choices that life throws our way.[3] One of the earliest and most evocative examples of this is Abraham being asked by God in the Old Testament to sacrifice his only son, Isaac. Abraham anguishes and in the end obeys. At the last moment, God stops him; Abraham has proven his faith. Abraham's heart response is reflected in the faith he is asked to demonstrate. His head is expressed in the hesitation, deliberation, and internal bargaining. In that case, he listens to his heart and fortunately is rewarded. Reenactment of this motif is found in other religions (Christ in Christianity and Ishmael in Islam), philosophical writings such as Søren Kierkegaard's *Fear and Trembling,* and movies like *Casablanca* and *The Matrix.*

People react in different ways to similar situations. What appears to be irresolvable may in reality be a function of how one chooses to view the problem. Sometimes stepping back a few paces and reframing is what is required. Often the best path lies in integrating two competing forces. In Macoby's context, managers, leaders, and their organizations are most effective when neither head nor heart is forfeited. Macoby writes, "The detached head can neither affirm nor will. It thinks but it cannot act. . . . We use our heads fully only if our hearts are strong"[4]

Classic Head and Heart

The cash crunch of the 2001 technology meltdown forced many companies to make the toughest of business decisions: those dealing with staff retention. In many ways, layoffs and staff retention issues were core to a host of other tough dilemmas confronting CEOs as the recession lengthened. Should I continue to

Table 3.1. 2 × 2 Archetypes

Archetype	Key Question	Description	Scenario
Head and Heart	How can I choose between these?	The toughest choices are between doing what makes sense and what feels right. Achieving alignment between the two is a source of great power.	The classic example is where God asks Abraham to sacrifice his son, Isaac. His heart is obedient, but his head resists. In this case, heart prevails, and Abraham is rewarded for his faith.
Inside and Outside	How do we meet the demands being placed on us?	Systems do best when they are well matched to the demands of their external contexts. Matches of greatest interest are structure, competencies, and culture.	Under Lou Gerstner, IBM was restructured to meet the demands of a transformed marketplace.
Cost-Benefit	What is the price of getting what we want?	Efforts to predict the future involve risk and choosing the course of least pain and greatest gain.	The Cunard Shipping Company "bet the business" and succeeded in winning back the lead in ocean travel.
Product-Market	Given this starting point, what are our options?	You can change the essential offering, or you can modify how, where, or when it is presented.	The Palm Pilot succeeded where Apple's Newton could not. It quickly proceeded to expand the market and then to upgrade the product.
Change versus Stability	What do we need to do to adapt? How much change is healthy? How do we get	Systems of all sizes and nature are in perpetual dynamic tension between the forces for growth and adaptation, on the one	Creative accounting practices (Change) spurred risky experimentation, with catastrophic outcomes for companies like

(continued)

Table 3.1. 2 × 2 Archetypes, Cont'd

Archetype	Key Question	Description	Scenario
	unstuck without falling apart?	hand, and integration and stability, on the other. Too much of either is deadly, leading to chaos or rigidity.	WorldCom, Enron, and Arthur Andersen, which could no longer find balance and stability.
Know– Don't Know	What is known, what is not, and what is known about what is or isn't known?	Self-knowledge is mapped against others' knowledge. Different forms or levels of knowledge represent problems and opportunities.	Since no one would tell the emperor he wore no clothes, he became an object of ridicule. Leaders of prominent businesses sometimes become too powerful and forget that they too are governed by the laws of nature and markets.
Competing Priorities	What should I do first? What's really more important?	We are driven to shortsighted trade-offs, relieving immediate pressure and pain but postponing tackling truly important tasks.	Performance-enhancing drugs have become a recurring nightmare since the East German women's swim team used them to beat the competition in the 1976 Olympics.
Content versus Process	Are Content and Process healthy and aligned?	Content is the what, process the how. Success in most things requires a sufficient mastery of both of these qualities.	Your words are saying yes, but your eyes say no. When a company like Dofasco says, "Our product is steel, our strength is our people," it is recognizing the interdependency between the what and the how.

invest in R&D for the future or cut deeply to meet current financial goals? Should I reprice options to retain key employees? If I reduce capacity and head count now, will I be able to meet demand when the recession ends?

Hot on the heels of a seven-year run-up of growth and profitability, most executives were ill equipped for the task. Consequently, a lot of lurching resulted as businesses struggled to cope with a downturn that only deepened over time. The Head and Heart battle was a central, defining statement for companies and their leadership, with significant long-term consequences.

The Head response that some companies took was to move quickly to sell off nonessential business units, cut staff, and preserve the core of the company to be able to survive and fight again tomorrow. A sample of headlines from this period brings the memory back all too vividly:

"Nokia to Cut 1,000 Jobs as Slowdown Bites"[5]

"Nortel Layoffs, Losses, Have Industry Asking: What's Next?"[6]

"Motorola Announces a Further 4,000 Job Cuts"[7]

For many companies that acted from a purely rational Head perspective, it has proven challenging to resurrect trusting relationships with employees and strategic partners.

The Heart response was expressed as an unflinching commitment to protect the jobs of valued and loyal employees under any circumstances. Some companies, like FedEx and Southwest Airlines, were successful and have benefited from the motivational payoff of loyal and appreciative staff. Many others, like Ariba and Sun, were not as lucky and were forced to institute demoralizing waves of staff cuts as earnings and company value dropped.[8]

Some companies recognized the situation for what it truly was early on and listened to both their heads and their hearts. While no panacea, it was an improvement over the either-or approaches just described.

Hewlett Packard (HP) is a good example. Facing the need for renewal and anticipating the inevitable downturn in the computing industry, HP took a series of alternately Head and Heart steps. First was the Head decision to replace Lew Platt as chairman and CEO with an outsider, Carly Fiorina, who brought a more contemporary and countercultural vision. A series of well-timed staff rationalizations reduced overhead costs; the head was leading, but in a planned, balanced way. Simultaneously, the company reasserted its heritage of invention and formulated a bold e-Inclusion and socially responsible agenda, positioning HP as the global leader that cares. Staff involvement in shaping the recent merger-acquisition with Compaq again demonstrated a thoughtful blend of heart with head. In a rough and declining market, HP did

not lose its ability to think and act strategically, nor did it sacrifice its humanity or creativity. (See Figure 3.1.)

INSIDE AND OUTSIDE

 Systems do best when they are well matched to the demands of their
external contexts. Domains of greatest interest are structure, competencies,
and culture. Lawrence and Lorsch's modeling of organizational complexity sets the standard for this archetype, proposing that an organization requires
no more or less complex a structure than what is demanded by the external
environment.[9]

Aging bureaucratic organizations typify the problem of too much structure,
rendering agility a near impossibility. Structures evolve as legitimate mechanisms for addressing problems and opportunities. Too often, however, old structures are maintained in addition to new ones as organizational politics and
loyalties influence strategic thinking.

High-growth entrepreneurial companies, in contrast, often find themselves
with too little structure. Racing as fast as possible to respond, there is often little time and competency to build new structures that are needed. Everyone is
already working double time, and investing in anything that doesn't help fight
back the wolf at the door today feels superfluous.

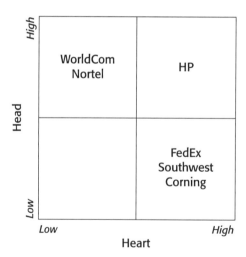

Figure 3.1. Head and Heart Matrix

Classic Inside and Outside

IBM has successfully tackled this archetype several times in its history, most recently in its transformation from a hardware company to a professional services firm. When Lou Gerstner assumed the role of chairman and CEO in 1993, IBM was oversized and tied up in red tape. Overly decentralized decision processes, duplication of functions, and territorial defense of nonperforming businesses were contributing to a worrisome decline in business and doing little to meet the needs of customers. Compaq was on its way to displacing Big Blue as the number one PC seller. In contrast to a net income of $7.7 billion in 2001, the company had lost money in the years between 1991 and 1993, reporting a net loss of $8.1 billion in 1993.[10]

With the help of Abby Kohnstamm, a former American Express marketing executive, Gerstner refocused the company on its customers, in the process streamlining the organization and aligning it with the needs of the external market. Hardware was becoming a commodity, and customers wanted reliable service and support from a smart, trusted technology partner. IBM retooled itself to become this.

In a marketplace where virtually all of its direct competitors suffered extreme declines, IBM has maintained revenues and grown more profitable, achieving an estimated 8 percent share of the $420 billion technology services business market.[11] Deepening its commitment to leading in the services area, IBM announced in the fall of 2002 that it would spend over $1 billion on services-related R&D. (See Figure 3.2.)

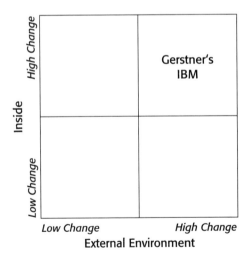

Figure 3.2. Inside and Outside Matrix

COST-BENEFIT

The history of civilization can be viewed as an ever-improving ability to manage risk.[12] As Peter Bernstein describes in *Against the Gods: The Remarkable Story of Risk*, it was not until the Renaissance and the emergence of probability theory that prediction and risk management ceased to be based on superstitious beliefs and started behaving more like a science.[13] Mathematicians like Pascal, Fermat, and Bernoulli paved the road for predictions based on projections that take into account both what is known and what is likely to happen. In an increasingly complex world, a blend of structured quantitative and qualitative methods is essential. Modern banking, health care, insurance, and business financing would be impossible without them.

There is an element of this in most 2 × 2 formulations, which are, after all, attempts to predict the future and choose the course of least pain and greatest gain. The BCG Grid used for portfolio management is a good example of this, as is the calculation of Risk and Reward. One's readiness to invest further into something depends ultimately on two things: the attractiveness of the payoff (the benefit) and the likelihood that a defined amount of further investment (risk or cost) will produce success.

Classic Cost-Benefit

Ocean liners ruled transatlantic travel and trade at the turn of the century. Regarded by many as symbols of national pride and identity, shipping lines vied fiercely for dominance in speed and grandeur to attract prestigious passengers and lucrative mail contracts. After several years of being outdone by opulent and record-breaking German liners, the British shipping company Cunard sought to reclaim dominance with a duo of greyhound superliners, the *Lusitania* and *Mauritania*. Aiming to best the competition in every dimension, these were to be the largest moving objects ever constructed (794 feet long) and able to sustain a cruising speed of 24.5 knots on the open seas, swiftness never before achieved by a liner.

The venture was a bet-the-business decision, with many unknowns to keep even the calmest strategist up at night. The biggest gamble concerned selection of the ships' propulsion system. The speed target was right at the upper limit deliverable by the existing reciprocating engine technology. An emerging experimental design, the Parsons marine turbine, could theoretically produce ample power with less weight and better fuel consumption. Doubtless, the turbine engine was a risky option given that none had ever been constructed at the size required. And moving parts would have to be machined to perform at 8/100-inch tolerance, or risk catastrophic failure.[14]

After a year's testing on scale models, the Parsons design was chosen. Ultimately, the risk of investing in this unproven technology paid off royally. The *Mauritania* reached the previously unheard-of speed of 27 knots on trial runs; subsequent to this success, every new liner was fitted with turbines. Within a month of service, the *Mauritania* claimed the transatlantic speed record and retained it for the next twenty-two years, longer than any other vessel in history. Not only was the new design faster, it allowed for easier and less costly maintenance, resulting in more time in the water and a longer life. (See Figure 3.3.)

PRODUCT AND MARKET

 What should we change in order to maintain or increase success? Business leaders have two fundamental levers they can resort to: the product or service itself and the customers the products or services are sold to. Igor Ansoff provided the classic representation of this in 1965.

What are the available options? You can sell more of the same within a current market (*market penetration*), sell a new product within this market (*product development*), sell the same product in new markets (*market development*), or pursue new paths on both the market and product front (*diversification*). Market penetration and market development are low risk and high reward under favorable conditions. Diversification, that is, entering a new market with an equally new offering, is considerably more challenging and risky, but sometimes it is the competitive route that must be pursued to stay in the race.[15]

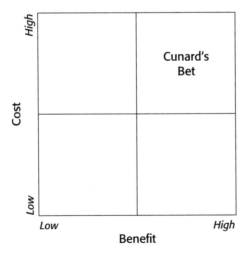

Figure 3.3. Cost-Benefit Matrix

The power of this archetype lies in the way it isolates and focuses directly on two primary elements of a competitive strategy. There is value that lies in the product or service itself, and value in key attributes associated with the experience of consuming this value. That's all. Yet the amount of variation that is possible within these parameters is limitless.

Classic Product and Market

The PDA (personal digital assistant) market provides a vivid story of winning and losing product-market decisions taken over a ten-year period. In August 1993, Apple beat the competition in the race to bring a small, convenient, affordable planner to market. Dubbed the Newton, it arrived with great fanfare at a $700 price point and proceeded to quickly underwhelm and disappoint. There were only a few problems, but they were significant ones: script deciphering was inadequate, uses were limited, data portability was inconvenient, and visibility wasn't great. In Geoffrey Moore's *Crossing the Chasm* terms, the product performed well enough for techies and some early adopters, but it was not yet ready for mass market adoption.[16]

Because it had already invested heavily in product development, Apple's response was to promote the Newton aggressively in all markets. It treated product problems with market solutions. After suffering considerable losses, Apple finally pulled the product out of the marketplace in 1988 with its pen between its digital legs. The lesson taken by many at the time was that consumers were not ready for PDAs; perhaps, they thought, a computer and a PDA overlapped too closely.

In March 1996, US Robotics launched the Palm Pilot. Essentially the same device as the Newton, this company had ironed out the product design and functionality barriers to adoption. In strategy terms, it brought a superior product to the same market (*product development*). Strong sales of the Pilot as an executive and professional productivity device quickly established the Pilot as the dominant hand-held device (*market penetration*). Customers not only purchased this product, they helped to design and update it by joining a rapidly growing developer community that had expanded from 2000 in 1997 to over 250,000 in 2002. Competition from Handspring, HP, and Compaq only helped to establish the PDA as a must-have for any serious businessperson. Adjusting price on the older low-end models has helped extend the market downward to include students, musicians, tradesmen, and administrative staff; the same product was now being successfully offered to new markets (*market development*). Over 20 million Palm Pilots have been sold, and the product has maintained roughly a 40 percent share of the PDA market. As a final step to capture more sales, PDA software and functionality is being bundled into cellular phones, offering the convenience of carrying one integrated, multifunctional device (*diversification*). With partners such as Kyocera and Sony, the Palm operating system drives the majority of mobile hand-held devices sold today. (See Figure 3.4.)

CHANGE AND STABILITY

 Systems of all sizes and nature are in perpetual dynamic tension between the forces for growth and adaptation, on the one hand, and integration and stability, on the other. Too much of either is deadly, leading to chaos or rigidity. A simple illustration of this is the mechanical operation of a thermostat or a carburetor. Moving above or below certain levels triggers corrective action, keeping the system under control within predefined limits.

Complex, human organizations experience this same tension, with the added challenge of needing to constantly reset limits to match evolving conditions. Start-up entrepreneurial companies focus on Change, while maturing companies tend to invest more heavily in developing Stabilizing structures. Ultimately, organizations must do both of these well. Systems and complexity theorists view this as the core competitive competency distinguishing good from great companies.

It is particularly difficult to maintain this balance in large, complex organizations with distributed responsibilities, since it is often unclear whose job it is to notice and respond to change management problems. Senior management and human resources are the most likely places to look, but it is rarely anyone's first priority, which creates its own set of problems. This is complicated by the

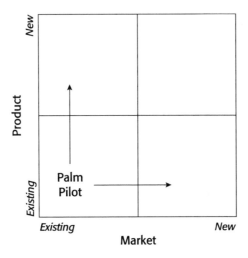

Figure 3.4. Product and Market Matrix

inherent nature of this archetypal process. Once the trend toward either Change or Stability is under way, it is difficult to put in the stops until it has gone at least a little too far and is experienced as problematic.

Classic Change and Stability

Companies easily lose their balance with a little encouragement from the marketplace. Remember convergence? Not too long ago, the telecommunications sector was in the enviable position of steady growth and high margins (*stability*), based on a strong value proposition in an industry with hefty barriers to entry. Then along came WorldCom and a host of radical service aggregators, and things changed. Feeling pressure from Wall Street analysts to have an Internet strategy, companies like AT&T and BCE embarked on ambitious acquisition sprees (*change*). The strain of overinvestment proved too much for most, creating integration problems and suboptimal performance. Now the analysts are rewarding focused financial results, leading those same companies to return to their core businesses.

Once, accounting firms were stodgy, boring defenders of conservatism and caution (*stability*). Indeed, their clients depended on this characteristic. Yet some of these very same firms played a major role in starting the stampede to "creative" accounting. Up to the dramatic implosion of Enron, Arthur Andersen, WorldCom, and others in 2002, the trend toward loose corporate governance practices and accounting (*change*) was affecting most large corporations to some degree. Companies that tried to buck the prevailing trend paid for it in their stock price evaluation. The reaction in the months following these disclosures has been extreme efforts to stabilize, which themselves will need to be corrected over time.

The most dramatic examples of Change and Stability challenges in the corporate sphere are cases of imminent disaster. Although many end in failure, some are able to turn things around in time and learn something in the process. Such was the case with Borland Software. In 1999, at the peak of Silicon Valley exuberance, Borland was floundering. A highly successful builder of software developer tools through the 1990s with a user base of 3 million, it had lost its bearing and was about to replace its executive team for the fourth time in three years. Profit was down, Wall Street analysts had pretty much written the company off, there was enough cash for only three or four more months, and staff were fleeing as quickly as possible. When the board hired Dale Fuller, an experienced Silicon Valley ninja (ex-Apple, ex–successful start-up), he didn't have much time to make a difference.

Tackling core problems of capital, competitive focus, and discipline simultaneously, the status quo was turned upside down. Demanding fourteen-hour days from his senior staff and himself, the company achieved a striking set of changes and results. The transformed organization did not work for everyone, and four hundred of the eleven hundred staff were let go. In parallel with the intense change process under way, stabilization was also occurring. All projects and products were aligned with a single theme (networking), revenues and profitability were again respectable, and customers were witnessing a visible return to the core product and service offerings Borland had long been known for.[17] (See Figure 3.5.)

KNOW AND DON'T KNOW

The emperor has no clothing and consequently makes a fool of himself without knowing it. Knowledge management experts point out that organizations typically don't know what they know, and as a result, they are unable to access and share resources well. The Johari Window framework (see Figure 3.6) provides the classic version of this archetype, where Self-Knowledge is mapped against Others' Knowledge of the Self. Under most conditions, it is preferable to expand the area of Openness, where self-knowledge and Others' perceptions are aligned. In this state, we learn from the free flow of feedback, and we disclose enough of our views to allow those around us to trust our motives. What they see is in sync with what they get. Each of the remaining three options contains some danger, caution, and opportunity for improvement. The blind spot (Self doesn't know what Others know about the Self) can be eliminated through openness to honest and helpful feedback. Think of the

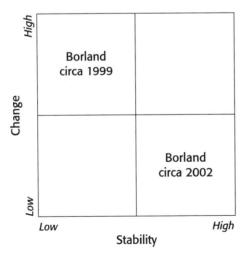

Figure 3.5. Change and Stability Matrix

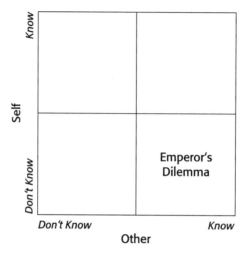

Figure 3.6. Know and Don't Know Matrix

embarrassment the emperor might have avoided if only his subjects felt safe enough to clue him in to what was hanging out.

Classic Know–Don't Know

What do Jean-Marie Messier, Bernard Ebers, and Kenneth Lay have in common? Each encountered career-threatening and company-devastating experiences in 2002 that were as preventable as they were devastating. Propelled by pride, overly successful, and increasingly secretive, they engaged in behaviors that blew up in their faces, taking down the fortunes of many others with them.

Feedback is a two-way street. When codirectors and shareholders tried to challenge and influence Messier, the golden boy leader of Vivendi, he engineered their removal. The court case against Lay and other executives at Enron has revealed a parade of colleagues and advisers who tried to convince Lay's executive team to moderate outrageous and flagrantly exploitative practices. In time, people stopped trying, resigned to the inevitability of their actions and what lay ahead. And Ebers believed it was okay to risk $366 million of World-Com's money to "adjust" a personal loan situation.

At a more mundane level, we can all relate to those uncomfortable situations where someone's personal style or a particular characteristic is highly off-putting, yet no one is willing to let the person know about it. Bad breath and boring stories come easily to mind. Without ever knowing the problem, these poor souls are left hurt and wondering what they did wrong.

Table 3.2. Archetype Table of 2 × 2 Frameworks

Archetype	2 × 2 Frameworks
Head and Heart	Gartner Group's Magic Quadrant contrasts Ability to Execute with Completeness of Vision
	Brown's Portfolio Analysis compares Business Quality to Mutual Value
Inside and Outside	Harbison and Pekar's Alliance Drivers matches Capabilities of the firm against the degree of Globalization within an industry to determine the need for strategic partners
	Stewart's Human Capital contrasts Difficult to Replace with Value to Customer
Cost-Benefit	Generic Risk and Reward contrasts the value of a Reward against the Risk involved in its attainment
	Generic Cost-Benefit contrasts the effort and Cost of attaining something with its Benefits
Product-Market	Ansoff's Corporate Strategy Matrix contrasting Products against Markets
	Hamel and Prahalad's Beyond Customer-Led contrasts Customers with Needs
Change versus Stability	Gharajedaghi's Differentiation and Integration compares Integration with Differentiation
	Collin's Good to Great compares Culture of Discipline with Entrepreneurial Ethic
Know–Don't Know	Luft and Ingham's Johari Window compares Self-Awareness with Others' Awareness of the Self
	Flood and Drescher's Prisoner's Dilemma compares options to Cooperate or Defect in a non-zero sum game
Competing Priorities	Covey's Urgency and Importance compares what is Urgent with what is truly Important
	Martin's Virtue Matrix contrasts Intrinsic Social Value with Instrumental Business Value
Content versus Process	Hersey and Blanchard's Situational Leadership compares Relationship and Task behavior
	Ackoff's Means and Ends examines the degree to which the Means and the Ends of different parties are aligned

COMPETING PRIORITIES

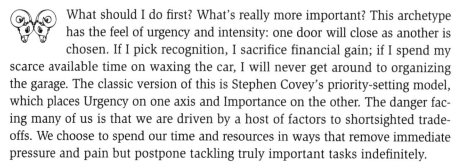 What should I do first? What's really more important? This archetype has the feel of urgency and intensity: one door will close as another is chosen. If I pick recognition, I sacrifice financial gain; if I spend my scarce available time on waxing the car, I will never get around to organizing the garage. The classic version of this is Stephen Covey's priority-setting model, which places Urgency on one axis and Importance on the other. The danger facing many of us is that we are driven by a host of factors to shortsighted trade-offs. We choose to spend our time and resources in ways that remove immediate pressure and pain but postpone tackling truly important tasks indefinitely.

Moreover, this archetype almost always hides a small lie we find hard to admit and deal with. The solution involves facing all the relevant circumstances and framing options in a manner that more fairly surfaces alternatives and consequences.

Classic Competing Priorities

In the 1976 Montreal Olympics, the East German women's swim team won all but two of the events. Prior to 1976, East Germany's women had never won an Olympic swimming medal. Subsequent investigation revealed extensive use of performance-enhancing drugs, much of it apparently unknown to the athletes themselves. With this, the era of drug taking and testing in international sports was launched, and the world now wonders with every outstanding performance whether drugs have played a role and who will be caught and punished for abuses.

The dilemma facing competitors is overwhelming and not always crystal clear. How important is winning? What are the long-term health costs of drug taking, and am I prepared to pay the price? What constitutes a drug? Is it the fact that it is banned? What if it's "natural" or can't be detected? And how do we feel about gene doping, the revolutionary performance-boosting method that is currently impossible to detect and extremely dangerous? (See Figure 3.7.)

The adage that you can't have your cake and eat it too focuses us on a false dichotomy. Choosing one option or another is often a shortsighted approach, preventing us from dealing with the real issue and recognizing critical interdependencies between opposing forces. As Covey maintains, you can address both what is Urgent and what is Important if that is your intent.

CONTENT AND PROCESS

 Content is the what and process the how. Success in most things requires mastery of both of these qualities. Organization structure and methods are process considerations. Product functioning, chemical

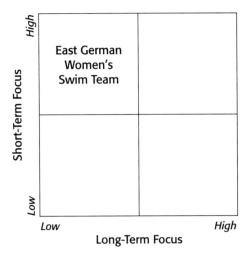

Figure 3.7. Competing Priorities Matrix

formulas, and professional trade expertise (such as plumbing) are typically content. At Procter & Gamble, toothpaste is content, while product storage and distribution and logistics are process. In small group dynamics, content refers to the substantive, topical focus, while process refers to interpersonal dynamics like power and inclusion.

The unit of analysis provides the context for determining content and process. The content for any system lies in its primary purpose. It is the what. How this is supported and achieved generally fits into the process category. Looking at Procter & Gamble once again, product design and materials are core content, while assembly and distribution are supportive, and thus process. For the Procter & Gamble division or strategic partner responsible for logistics and distribution, this work represents content. Process in their case consists of internal planning, staffing, and control functions necessary for effective delivery of distribution and logistics.

Classic Content and Process

The observation that words may lie but our bodies and our actions present the true picture of one's feelings has a long history. Cultural references to this are many, from Shakespeare's warning in *Othello*, "I am not what I am," to the nasty wolf dressed up as Grandma in "Little Red Riding Hood" (in spite of his sweet words, the big, sharp teeth give him away). Communication specialists claim that 80 percent or more of what gets communicated is nonverbal, reinforcing the importance of process in human communications. This cuts both ways, invalidating truth as easily as revealing falsehood. This is why lawyers carefully dress and rehearse witnesses before presenting them to a judge and jury. The nonverbals of JFK made a nation want to believe and trust him, while the shifty gaze and discomfort of his adversary Richard Nixon had the opposite effect. Try a simple experiment: turn down the sound on your television the next time you watch a show, and see how much of the meaning you miss. Odds are that you will be able to follow the plot line fairly well. (See Figure 3.8.)

Often the most important characteristic of the process-content relationship is alignment. Russell Ackoff describes this as tension between Means and Ends, examining the extent to which collaborating parties hold similar or opposing views.[18] As in human communications, the ideal condition is a well-matched set of Process and Content orientations. When this is not possible, we are able to accept a wider range of Process styles in others when we believe that we share similar ends. The common threat of Nazi Germany forged an unusual alliance of countries like Britain and Russia; these relationships quickly ended once the common end no longer mattered.

A MODERN PARABLE:
APPLYING THE ARCHETYPES

In 2001, most of the world's consulting firms were reeling from a dramatic downturn in business after a decade of unabated growth and prosperity. Not only were clients reluctant to spend as much as in previous years for their ser-

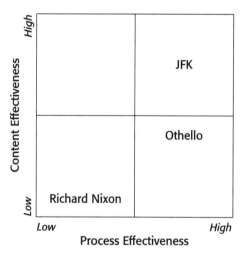

Figure 3.8. Content and Process Matrix

vices, there was growing cynicism about the profession as a result of high-profile cases of poor judgment and conflict of interest. Deep soul searching and strategizing within each of the major firms might have unearthed the following archetypal analyses:

- The problem is really Head and Heart. We need to terminate all nonperforming activities, no matter what their history or who heads them up. We can't afford to be soft and mushy about this. It's time for clear, decisive action.
- This is all about Inside and Outside. Our competencies no longer match what our customers need. If we don't invest in reskilling and cutting the parts that are noncontributing, we're finished.
- It's a classic Product and Market mismatch. We're making the wrong offerings to the right markets. Our customers still want to do business with us, but not for more of last year's solution.
- It's really a problem with managing Change and Stability. Business was so good that we stopped updating and renewing our competencies and relationships. Now that times are tough, we don't have enough new ideas and programs to develop. The business model that made us successful in the past has become an obstacle.
- It's all about Content and Process. Our message to customers is stale and losing credibility. First the threats of Y2K failed to materialize, and then the horrors of conflict of interest practices materialized!

Of course we know all of these contain at least some of the story. None is wrong. The archetypes each surface another perspective, another door into solving the problem. Ultimately, we solve the problems we recognize. By quickly trying each one on for size, there is the chance of getting a better fix on what is needed and what we can do about it.

The self-diagnostic guide in Exhibit 3.1 is a simple way to apply the archetypes to your own situation.

Exhibit 3.1. Organizational Dilemmas Self-Assessment and Scoring Guide

Organizations are faced with numerous challenges. This is a given. Knowing which ones are most crucial is an important first step to managing them effectively. This quick self-assessment guide helps you to prioritize dilemmas and focus attention on the ones that are most instrumental in determining the success of your business.

Step 1: Assessment

Rate the extent to which each of the following statements describes your organization's current strategic reality:
1 = Strongly Disagree, 5 = Strongly Agree.

A	It's hard to know which option is right. There are compelling arguments on each side.	1	2	3	4	5
B	It's not clear how much to invest—that the rewards merit the risk.	1	2	3	4	5
C	We lack a full understanding of external demands. It's unclear that we have the right skills and structure to meet the needs.	1	2	3	4	5
D	We need to change and learn in order to keep pace, but there is a lot of pressure to stablize things so customers and staff know what they can depend on.	1	2	3	4	5
E	It's hard for us to know whether to change the what (content) or the how (process).	1	2	3	4	5
F	We're not sure what will give us the greatest advantage—modifying what we do (the product) or who we do it for (the market).	1	2	3	4	5
G	We don't have a clear picture about some important aspects of our own organization. This may be about capabilities or how we are regarded by customers or other companies.	1	2	3	4	5
H	We seem to be facing a set of competing priorities, pulling us between short-term and long-term interests.	1	2	3	4	5

Step 2: Ranking

Transfer your ratings to the chart below.

	Your Rating		
A		Head versus Heart	The toughest choices are between doing what makes sense and what feels right. Achieving alignment between the two is a source of great power.
B		Cost versus Benefit	Efforts to predict the future involve risk, and choosing the course of least pain and greatest gain.
C		Inside versus Outside	Systems do best when they are well matched to the demands of their external contexts. Matches of greatest interest are structure, competencies, and culture.
D		Change versus Stability	Systems of all size and nature are in perpetual dynamic tension between the forces for growth and adaptation, on the one hand, and integration and stability, on the other. Too much of either is deadly, leading to chaos or rigidity.

	Your Rating		
E		Content versus Process	Content is the what, process the how. Success in most things requires a sufficient mastery of both qualities.
F		Product versus Market	You can change the essential offering or modify how, where, or when it is presented.
G		Know versus Don't Know	Self-knowledge is mapped against others' knowledge. Different forms or levels of knowledge represent problems and opportunities.
H		Competing Priorities	We are driven to shortsighted trade-offs. We remove immediate pressure and pain, but postpone tackling truly important tasks. The solution involves facing the full set of circumstances and framing options in a manner that fairly surfaces options and consequences.

Step 3: Analysis

Focus on the categories with the highest rating to find new insights into organizational dilemmas.

PART TWO

2 × 2 PRACTICE

CHAPTER FOUR

Designing 2 × 2 Matrices

Making Intuition Explicit

In the life cycle of every conflict,
there is a point when it's large enough to be recognized,
but small enough to be resolved.
—Daniel Dana

Choosing the right 2 × 2 matrix is as much an art as a science. The obvious danger is overreduction: simplifying complex realities in unhelpful ways. A useful matrix cuts to the essence of what is being investigated and presents an accurate and enabling map of the territory in question. Keep in mind that perspective, timing, and communication are as important as the framework itself. You need the right model applied at the right time.

UNDERLYING DESIGN LOGIC

2 × 2 Thinking is most helpful when you have arrived at an impasse. If the next step in a process is self-evident and noncontroversial, a 2 × 2 approach is likely to be superfluous. Take a simple example. It's Thursday night, and the family is trying to decide what to have for supper. One of the kids proposes ordering in pizza; no one objects, and it's settled. The issue is straightforward, consequences of the choice are insignificant, and no one is opposed.

Now let's push the example. Pizza is proposed, and not everyone wants it. A quick 2 × 2 exercise takes us to the heart of the matter and helps to create options and then sort them. Discussion reveals that health and cost are the decision drivers for those opposing pizza. Completion of a matrix built around these factors identifies pizza as a low-cost but not terribly healthy choice for dinner.

Salad is low cost and high health, as is whole wheat pita bread filled with avocado and veggies. Finally, gourmet seafood is rated high on both criteria.

The supper matrix doesn't instantly solve the problem, but it does make the issues clearer, helps in generating alternatives, and suggests criteria for reaching a decision. Perhaps the family decides to splurge and sacrifice the cost criteria in the interest of meeting the health goal. Maybe they decide to get the pizza this time and settle for salad or pita sandwiches tomorrow. The 2 × 2 matrix provides a framework for these considerations.

Now consider a more serious example. A woman is chronically in debt on her credit cards. Worse, she is putting her family into a monthly crisis when she has spent money on superfluous items and it's time to buy necessities. Sitting down with a financial consultant, she discusses some of the reasons for her behavior, and they go over her monthly expenses in great detail. The adviser then asks her to put all of her expenses by category onto a 2 × 2 matrix. On one axis is Necessity—yes or no—and on the other is Wants—high or low. She discovers that nearly 20 percent of her spending is on the low-low side—things that are merely nice to have. The model becomes a constant reminder of the trade-offs, helping her to prioritize spending decisions more effectively.

Keeping examples such as these in mind, let's explore the underlying structure and design dynamics of 2 × 2 modeling.

Initiation

A situation has reached a turning point of some sort; a decision is needed or is about to be made. The turning point is characterized by a new, higher level of complexity, causing reflection, pause, and, often, discussion. Sometimes the issues are clear, explicit, and consensually viewed. Often they are not, and even the opinion that there is an issue can be in dispute. Crossing this bridge is the first step.

Naming

Definition of the two axes is the most crucial part of the design process. It is critical to put names on the axes that the work team can own. The names should be specific to the company or situation. First, you identify, prioritize, and apply core issues. Through trial and error, trade-offs eventually lead to a provisional set of dimensions. These may (and often do) change over time.

Testing

Test the axes to make sure you've got it right. To add value, the two dimensions need to be relevant, different, and together cover a large amount of the topic territory under consideration. The dialectical force is sufficiently engaged when the net effect is the creation of dynamic tension in search of release. Testing includes looking for relevance and coverage, difference, and dialectical tension.

Relevance and Coverage. The object is always to get to the center of the matter, identify core driving forces, and model alternative solutions. The higher the leverage value of the driving forces is, the greater the potential impact of the modeling effort. As an example, consider a company trying to decide whether to acquire a new competency by developing it internally versus purchasing or contracting for it externally. Factors to consider include cost, time, geography, and culture. In most cases, the list of contributing factors is long, so the challenge is to find ones that are essential and will bring new insight.

Some quick experimenting might lead you to contrast Core to Value Proposition with Difficult to Grow (Figure 4.1). Now we have four major options meaningfully organized, and criteria for making the best decision.

As circumstances shift, factors such as Time and Cost may loom larger than Difficult to Grow and replace it as the second axis. An effective approach is to consider a series of critical factors such as these in quick succession. Imagine that the company in question is General Motors, and the competency in question is the design and manufacture of alternative fuel-based vehicles. Like all the other major auto companies, GM invested in early fuel cell R&D during the 1990s, but results were limited. Recognizing the magnitude of the challenge, GM entered into a series of strategic alliances to learn and move efforts along more quickly. Political and competitive pressures continue to make this a more important issue each year. As Toyota and Honda take the lead with early well-regarded models, GM will need to invest more in order to own more of the knowledge, leadership, and, in time, profit.

Figure 4.1. Competency Acquisition Matrix

If we replaced the *x*-axis with *Cost* (Figure 4.2), we would find that Partnership is more affordable and shares the risk with other smart players while aligning interests. Applying Cost as the *x*-axis creates a new perspective on the four alternatives, with Strategic Partnership moving to the upper right quadrant, Contract moving to lower right, and Grow dropping into the lower left spot. When Time Pressure (Figure 4.3) is used as the *x*-axis, options are shuffled once again. As compared to the original matrix in Figure 4.1, Grow returns to the upper left, and Contract and Strategic Partnership switch spots.

Difference. The two dimensions of the matrix must be unique and separate from each other for maximum payoff. This ensures dynamic tension while helping to generate four viable options for serious consideration. When this is not the case, you tend to end up with two possible quadrants and two null ones.

Examples of false uniqueness are Temperature and Location, or Strength and the Amount of Weight one can lift. Modeling these kinds of relationships can be quite interesting and even useful; indeed, research reports are typically full of charts containing these types of data. They are less helpful from a dialectical standpoint, however, because they do not enlighten beyond the known categories. What you get out of them is exactly what goes in. In 2 × 2 Thinking, we are seeking novelty, insight, direction, and transcendence.

Dialectical Tension. Dialectical tension results when unresolved, competing forces are recognized and brought into interaction with each other. Human history reflects this, where each gain in one area is paralleled by a loss in another.

Figure 4.2. Cost-Driven Perspective Matrix

Figure 4.3. Time-Driven Perspective Matrix

The cell phone brought greater communication mobility, but also a new level of intrusion into daily lives. In theaters, schools, and other public spaces, new social protocols and modes of interaction are replacing the privacy and control destroyed by the technology. Over time, imbalances correct themselves, providing both direction and motivation.

METHOD

Constructing 2 × 2 matrices can be fast or slow, intuitive or highly structured. Obviously practice helps. Our advice is to get started and not make the process any more complicated than it needs to be. The eight steps modeled in Figure 4.4 provide a straightforward and practical approach to applying 2 × 2 Thinking to a specific problem.

Step 1: Acknowledge

This first step is to identify the phenomenon or problem that is resisting easy understanding or resolution.

The design process tends to begin outside awareness. A group or organization is tackling a problem, and progress is disappointing. At some point they recognize the difficulty and discuss it, determining that a method or framework is needed to move forward. As with most other problem-oriented processes, nothing useful can occur until there is acceptance that a gap exists. The best solution could literally fall into our laps, but if we're not open to new ideas, we would reject it. At this stage, it is critical not to be hemmed in by existing

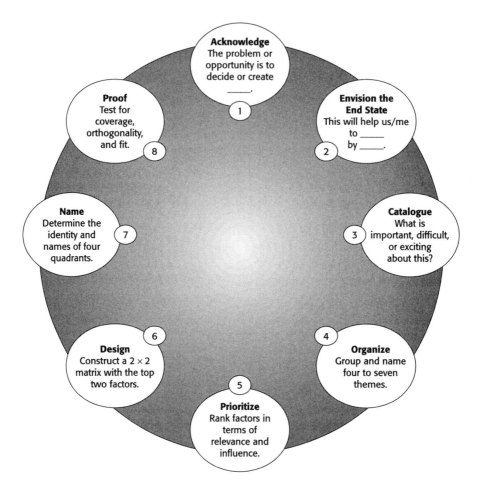

Figure 4.4. 2 × 2 Methodology

boundaries or investments. There can be no sacred cows. Any aspect of the company's products, operations, or people can be the locus of a dilemma.

ACTION: Name the problem or opportunity:

The problem or opportunity is to decide or to create _____

_____.

Step 2: Envision the End State

The next step is to envision what is important and worth knowing about this. Ask, What would be an ideal outcome?

You don't need to know how you will achieve something to know what you hope to get out of it. Forcing some statement of self-interest at the outset provides direction and creates urgency. Just as important, it sets success criteria for the whole undertaking.

ACTION: Describe the ideal outcome in a sentence:

This will help us/me to _____

by _____.

Step 3: Catalogue

The third step is to create an inventory of interesting and important aspects of the situation. Begin by listing many features of the situation in a somewhat broad and uncritical way. This helps to bring issues to life, and when pursued in a group, surfaces beliefs, hopes, and fears, which can be the key to success at later points in the process.

ACTION: Generate a good-sized list of features, completing the following phrases:

The essence of the situation is _____.

What is important is _____.

What is difficult is _____.

Step 4: Organize

The next step is to categorize the features listed in Step 3. Find the common themes among the list of important aspects generated, and place individual items in the appropriate cluster. Most lists, regardless of their size, can be reduced to a manageable number of themes, typically between four and seven. Any more than this is unhelpful. On occasion, the clustering exercise helps to generate new items or categories. This is constructive when it is leading you closer to the heart of the matter. On occasion, it represents avoidance and sabotage on the part of interests that are feeling threatened by the process. Beware of allowing efforts to be diverted for invalid reasons. In the end, only legitimate and honest issue framing will lead to new insights and useful results.

ACTION: Write each of the items from the list generated in Step 3 on three- by six-inch sticky notes. Working either individually or in a group, place items with common themes closer together. Continue this process until you have assigned all of the items to a group. Finally, name each of the clusters appropriately.

Step 5: Prioritize

The goal here is to identify the defining factors. By reviewing the work done thus far, it will be clear that points have varying degrees of relevance. Select the single most important factor influencing valued outcomes. Then rank the remaining items in the order of their importance.

ACTION: Rank factors from step 4 in the order of their relevance and influence.

Step 6: Design

Now you construct the 2 × 2 matrix. This is a critical step and may require some experimenting to get right. Don't force closure; stay open to considering variations. As you get closer to identifying the ideal axes, you will sense added tension and potential. The matrixing process takes on a life and energy of its own, which is, to a great extent, its power. Use the dimensions and the matrix shape to experiment with possible representations of the situation. Give it a voice, and listen closely, without preconceived opinion.

ACTION: Draw a 2 × 2 grid, and place the top priority item on the vertical axis for now. Name the two ends of the dimension—for example, Temperature (Hot versus Cold), Market (Fragmented versus Integrated), or Industry Attractiveness (High versus Low). Now experiment with several of the top remaining factors for the horizontal dimension. After selecting the second dimension name the two ends as you did with the first factor.

Step 7: Name

This is the time to name the four quadrants in interesting and helpful ways.

The most creative and interesting part of working with 2 × 2 modeling is deciding what goes inside the matrix. This is the step with the largest amount of latitude for expression and interpretation. The two axes are what they are and must accurately and fairly reflect the territory and intent they describe. Selecting the two dimensions is science; naming the four quadrants is art. If you doubt this, check out several of the frameworks in Chapters Six through Eight of this book. This intuitive task merits review and adjustment as the matrix is applied.

ACTION: Before naming, describe the meaning of each of the quadrants. This can be in single words, phrases, or sentences. Be terse rather than wordy. Then give a name to the quadrant that is most obvious to you. Usually one or two are easy and quick, and at least one resists labeling. They're all important.

Step 8: Proof

The final step in the process is to test for coverage, orthogonality, and fit.

Coverage: Are there important cases of the subject that are imaginable but not addressable within the matrix you have created? Orthogonality: Are there four plausible quadrants or principally two? Fit: Does the framework address the essence of the matter in a helpful enough way? If the matrix fails any of these tests, it is probably worth going back and experimenting a bit further to see what else is possible.

ACTION: Test for coverage (Are there any cases that are not well explained?), orthogonality (Are there four real quadrants?), and fit (Does the framework yield added perspective and insight?).

CHAPTER FIVE

2 × 2 Thinking in Action

Fujitsu FTXS Tackles
Level 2 Dilemmas

W atching business teams apply 2 × 2 Thinking well is as inspiring as it is instructive. A recent engagement with a North American business unit of the electronics giant Fujitsu provided just such an opportunity. Working with this organization, we saw not only how master strategists face dilemmas but how the resolution of one strategic challenge leads to the next set of issues as the company, customers, and the competitive landscape evolve.

Fujitsu is the world's third largest computer and information technology company, with headquarters in Japan and operations around the world. Founded in 1935 as a spin-off of Fuji Electric, Fujitsu developed the first computer in Japan in 1951. The company produces an assortment of hardware, software, computer chips, and other technologies, in addition to operating a variety of computer services businesses. Fujitsu is a global corporation employing 157,000 people with annual sales in 2002 of $38.4 billion.

FUJITSU TRANSACTION SOLUTIONS

Fujitsu Transaction Solutions (FTXS) is focused on retailing enterprises headquartered in North America. It designs, builds, delivers, and manages the hardware, software, and services for solutions that enable retail customer transactions. The majority of FTXS revenues come from in-store solutions such as point-of-sale systems. Long-term customers include well-known names like Staples, TJ Maxx,

Stop & Shop, and Albertsons. The authors were engaged in 2001 and again in 2003 to help FTXS evaluate its competitive position and address its business strategy.

The 1990s was not a good decade for FTXS. In spite of solid products and a globally recognized brand, Fujitsu's North American retail operations lost substantial amounts of money through the period. Reporting to Fujitsu's U.K.-based subsidiary, ICL, the North American business lacked coherence and direction. The disappointing performance was due to several factors:

- Structure: FTXS lacked sufficient autonomy and empowerment under a Eurocentric reporting structure and strategy.

- Strategy: There was an absence of clarity in the core value proposition.

- Focus: The division couldn't decide if it was in the hardware, software, or services business.

- Competitive landscape: The market was dominated by one main competitor: IBM.

- Inadequate brand strength: Even when Fujitsu had superior offerings, its marketing and the use of the ICL brand were not enough to get a strong message across.

- Commercial flexibility: FTXS was hamstrung by a lack of commercial flexibility from its European parent.

FACING THE LEVEL 1 DILEMMA

The opportunity to address these issues head-on arrived in 2000 when Fujitsu appointed a new North American–focused CEO, Austen Mulinder. Reporting to the board of Fujitsu in Tokyo, the mission was clear: stop the bleeding, and build a top brand in retail technologies and service. Restructuring occurred in October 2000, and by April 2001, the brand was relaunched as Fujitsu Transaction Solutions. Most of the former ICL service businesses in North America, including field services for automated teller machines and mobile applications, were integrated into the retail group at that time.

Although the situation seemed challenging when Mulinder took over, it would soon look even worse. He quickly discovered that losses were greater than expected and that the retail group had not won a major new account in three years. Without a steady stream of new clients to drive hardware installations and ongoing service fees, it was inevitable that the revenue situation would get worse before it could get better. Despite the urgent financial issues the group faced, Mulinder's most pressing concern was the strategy: his new company lacked any sense of a clear mission and value proposition. Without an improved offering, he knew the division would have to rely on brute-force selling efforts to improve its position.

Mulinder described his strategic challenge: "We had several jigsaw pieces that needed to fit together into a compelling strategy. I had a hardware business with associated product management; there was a field service business with field engineering, logistics, and call management; and I had an application software business." Historically, computer companies viewed this combination of products and services as a liability, diluting focus and confusing customers. But from Mulinder's point of view, he could not afford to jettison any of the parts of the business.

"My dilemma was that I needed it all, because we were about fifty-fifty in hardware and services revenue. There is a certain level of fixed costs in hardware and support people you must have in order to be credible as a partner for national or global retailers. If I chose to focus on just hardware or software or services, I would be out of business."

The solution the FTXS team conceived retained all the elements of the existing business, but creatively reframed their value to address the current and emerging set of customer needs. First, the hardware versus services issue needed to be recast. Choosing between the two businesses was the wrong way to frame things, principally because they were too interdependent to consider separately. The hardware business was important for many reasons, not least because it enabled salespeople to gain entry to the early stages of a customer's purchasing cycle. And Fujitsu had a great reputation for bulletproof products, so it was a legitimate core competency. Clearly, services were the basis for establishing ongoing relationships, and here again, the company's skills and reputation were assets.

Looking outward, the group spent time studying the evolution of the retail market. This is where they found the key to their services business. "I believed then, and I still believe," says Mulinder, "that a majority of chief information officers [CIOs] in the retail space have one overriding challenge: Wal-Mart is coming after almost every retail niche, and anyone who doesn't aggressively take costs out is in trouble. At the same time, retailers have to find ways to differentiate their value from Wal-Mart and other retailers because they won't win on cost. So the CIOs are in a real bind because the chief financial officers are telling them, 'We have to reduce costs . . . a lot.' And their CEOs are telling them, 'I need you to invest more in information technology to help us differentiate our value.' So we asked ourselves, 'How does a CIO take cost out and invest in strategic programs at the same time?' That was the dilemma we aimed to solve."

They named their solution to this level 1 dilemma the Life Cycle Strategy (Figure 5.1). Leveraging the key existing strengths of Fujitsu quality and drawing on a loyal and strongly customer-focused culture, FTXS proposed to manage a

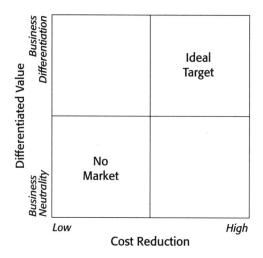

Figure 5.1. FTXS Life Cycle Strategy Matrix

client's investment in hardware, software, and services over a multiyear life cycle. They guaranteed clients that they would "Relentlessly Lower Costs" year after year by eliminating unnecessary steps and improving work processes. At the same time, they promised to bring differentiated value to the customer.

Whereas before they had felt pressured to focus on either hardware, software, or services, the new strategy made a virtue of being in all of these businesses. "We repositioned FTXS as a one-stop shop to manage all the technology in a retail store's life cycle regardless of its source, while aggressively selling Fujitsu products designed with a life cycle cost reduction perspective," says Mulinder. "The only way to do that is to have hardware product management capability, software capability and multivendor call management, field engineering, and logistics capability."

The new strategy brought clarity of focus and an unambiguous sense of urgency. The team set about configuring all the competencies required to deliver on the promise. Staffing was cut by a third, and the number of vice presidents was trimmed by more than half. Mulinder assigned each member of the new executive team clear and measurable objectives related to the value proposition. Core processes and systems were developed to drive the cost base down. Most significant, the senior vice president of client operations, Doug Wallace, implemented an innovative and unique centralized call management model and worked with customers to drive costs out of technical support so that FTXS could deliver on its relentless cost reduction promise. "We were clear that we needed to change the rules of the game to beat IBM and become the dominant force in the market, and we set about achieving that aim by turning the conventional operational wisdom on its head," says Wallace. "This change in thinking created the opportunity to dramatically lower our cost base and then to share these gains with our customers."

With a new value proposition in place, the multiyear sales drought was about to end. By September 2003, more than ten major retailers had switched from IBM, NCR, and Wincor, and had chosen Fujitsu point-of-sale (POS) equipment and software or services as its standard. Strong-performing brands like Nordstrom, Marshall's, Ross Dress for Less, Payless ShoeSource, and ChevronTexaco had become Fujitsu customers. In 2003, the company pulled strongly into the black. Revenues were up in the first half of the year by 35 percent, and profits were even higher. An analysis of the retail direct business in 2003 showed that nearly 80 percent of the revenue from its retail store customers came from new accounts added since the start of 2002. FTXS's order book and sales pipeline are full, indicating this success will continue into the future.

The life cycle–based Relentless Cost Reduction/Differentiated Value Strategy was working its magic on two fronts: customers immediately saw the payoff for them and staff felt positively challenged to fulfill the commitment; they understood the rationale and appreciated the chance to perform minor miracles to earn the trust and loyalty of customers. As an added bonus, the FTXS team found that the top-performing retailers seemed most swayed by the new value proposition. As they won these fast-growing customers, their own growth took off.

FTXS's story to this point is interesting for two reasons. First, they successfully identified the core dilemma facing retailers and created an innovative strategy that met it based on their current capabilities, without any significant new investment. The new strategy used the same business assets—hardware, software, services, and people—that the company already had. As Mulinder says, "We went from having no discernable value proposition to having one that was well differentiated and successful, but the components didn't change." This trick, akin to turning a tired old car into a supercharged racing machine, is at the core of good dilemmas-based design. Instead of defining a set of either-or choices, with extreme trade-offs such as hardware versus services, the group focused on core issues. In this case, they developed a transcendent solution—the life cycle strategy—that has proven itself in the marketplace and moved the company from one order of problem—marketplace survival, to a better one—growth enhancement.

Second, the experience is a primer on how effective leaders reinvigorate organizations in crisis. When he took over, Mulinder and his team were under extreme pressure to produce revenue. Nevertheless, at exactly that moment, he chose to shift critical attention from selling to developing a new value proposition. Paradoxically, when the needs of the business are most urgent, effective leaders often step back and focus valuable attention on issues of long-term importance. Leaders lead. They don't run around putting out fires and tasking their organizations with chasing ill-conceived strategic goals. Mulinder describes his balancing act between immediate revenue and long-term value this way: "I struggled over whether to invest my time in developing a value proposition that was differentiable and sustainable versus simply going out and selling what we had. We did the strategy work that needed to be done, and once I had something everyone could align on, I turned 180 degrees and went out selling it full time."

FINDING THE LEVEL 2 DILEMMA

The FTXS Relentless Cost Reduction strategy was the perfect response to the situation the company faced two years ago. Caught squarely between a rock and hard place, it converted the constraints of pricing and quality into a launching pad for a transcendent solution. But like all other strategies, it had flaws. For one, it was theoretically unsustainable to fulfill both promises of the strategy. No less an authority on business strategy than Michael Porter has established that low cost and differentiated high value are inevitably options, not a matched set. Ron Brunt, one of the architects of the strategy, echoed this thought when he told us, "We continually have to ask whether the customer is willing to see us as the right vehicle for both innovation and cost reduction."

In fact, the FTXS contribution to date has been slanted more toward cost reduction than value. Fortunately, cost reduction was a significantly better offer than most competitors could muster. In a business in which customers are highly price sensitive, FTXS crafted a strong value proposition that moved the sales discussion from initial costs to total cost of ownership over time.

The second problem was more fundamental. Even if FTXS was fully successful in its venture, it was unclear that there was a long-term viable and profitable business in the part of the retail market that it was chasing. Margins continue to shrink as the basic feature set is commoditized. Continuous innovation is required to capture new areas of value in retail. By succeeding with the current plan, they could be ensuring a limited time horizon in which to grow and be profitable. Something needed to be changed in the business model once again. This was the starting point for our second engagement with the team.

THE TEAM GOES TO WORK

Just as Mulinder had chosen to focus on the important task of building a strategy rather than the urgent task of revenue when he took over the division, he now chose to create a sense of urgency and change while his team was on top.

We were invited to deliver a workshop with nine FTXS executives to accelerate the process of identifying and modeling the new core dilemma. Applying the principles and methods described in the book, we turned our full attention to articulating the company's level 2 dilemma. The five-phase model in Figure 5.2 describes the steps we followed. The following sections present the major tools we used and highlights of the work completed by the executive team. Details of the plan created in Step 3 are not included due to competitive sensitivities; nevertheless, the process description remains rich and illustrative of the value of tackling core dilemmas in this systematic manner.

Step 1: Issues and Challenges

The purpose of this step in the process was to identify the range of issues and feelings surrounding the current situation. The main question driving this phase was, "What's happening, and why is it important?" Three complementary processes were employed to identify and validate the most pressing business issues: symptom identification, perceptual industry maps, and explanatory metaphors.

Symptoms Identification. It is important to begin at the beginning. The story needs to be told before any assumptions or decisions are made. Viewed from the perspective of a consultant assisting a team, our first task was to engage in naturalistic observation and modeling (our mantra was, "Listen, listen, listen"). We conducted interviews to gather a range of perspectives about the situation.

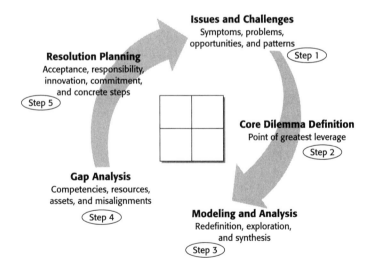

Figure 5.2. 2 × 2 Thinking in Action: A Five-Phase Model

The team developed a list of positive and negative symptoms that reflected the crossroads the business had reached. On the positive side, team members were pleased with progress, confident about maintaining sales momentum, appreciative of executive and staff efforts, and optimistic about the potential opportunity to integrate offerings with other Fujitsu businesses. Concerns included insufficient funding re-investment to sustain their differentiation, a lack of salespeople who excelled at selling the full value proposition to new accounts, and the continuing presence of IBM as the perceived low-risk choice for conservative retail CIOs. There was a general sense that strategic partnerships were important in order to flesh out their offerings, as was the ability to forge close and trusting relationships with their clients.

Perceptual Industry Maps. A perceptual map positions industry competitors, products, or customers on a 2 × 2 matrix where the axes reflect considerations that are critical to the current analysis. Perceptual maps are commonly used in marketing studies to identify opportunities and areas of weakness. At the same time as generating insight, they are often quite provocative, forcing one to question assumptions.

Figure 5.3 is a map we created for a publishing client interested in assessing opportunities in the food magazine marketplace. By plotting existing magazines on the basis of their Editorial Focus and Health Consciousness, the client was able to identify an underserved opportunity space. Matching this with demographic analysis provided the understanding needed to launch a unique offering to a well-defined market segment.

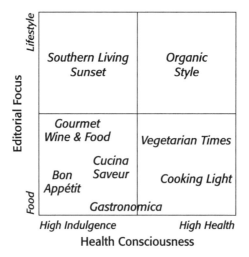

Figure 5.3. Health Magazine Marketplace Matrix

We found that the retail electronic transactions market space is complex and highly competitive. It is dangerous to make assumptions. Customers want it all, but mostly, they demand reliability and cost-effectiveness. Solutions are sprawling combinations of interdependent hardware and software components, service providers, networks, and partners. The value proposition for change must be compelling for a company to be willing to switch provider. It's too much hassle otherwise.

Drawing directly on the interview data, we constructed a set of hypothetical industry maps and presented them to the group. Three of these illustrate the method and shed light on the FTXS challenge:

• *Customer value analysis.* Based on the economic profiling work of Bradley Gale (see the CVA framework in Chapter Six) and using the input of the sales team members in the workshop, we constructed a matrix that contrasted customer perceptions of FTXS and its competitors in retail services. Prominent among these were IBM, NCR, and Wincor. We compared competitive offerings on two dimensions, Quality and Price (Total Cost of Ownership, a common measure in the computer industry) (Figure 5.4). Two possible conclusions were reached. First, although FTXS's offering is strong, only existing customers know this. Additional investment in communicating their successes would be necessary to speed up sales growth and cycle times in sales. Second, they should either withdraw from customer opportunities and segments where their offer is viewed less positively or invest to improve the offer.

Figure 5.4. FTXS Customer Value Analysis Matrix

• *Core strategy competitiveness.* In launching the Relentless Cost Reduction campaign, FTXS raised the bar on efficiency. The Life Cycle model provided a platform for process improvements years into a contract. It also promised innovations to help clients differentiate from their competitors. Staples, the office products giant, is one of FTXS's largest customers. According to Brian Light, who served as Staples' CIO through 2001 and is now executive vice president of Staples' Business Delivery, "Our goal is to put anything and everything on autopilot, and that includes how our in-store technologies are installed, integrated, and serviced. We wanted our own in-store technology provider to slash cost and hassle—and Fujitsu has done just that."

The core strategy competitiveness map in Figure 5.5 uses the FTXS strategy as a grid to plot some of the key competitors. IBM and NCR are the two largest players in the POS field, and each brings competitive strengths that need to be countered. This industry map is powerful because it suggests barriers that must be overcome in winning significant new customer accounts. It also points out that FTXS will do best when a client's need for cost reduction is the main driver. As one participant observed, "When we lose a sale, it is not because of our strategy. It is because the customer sees IBM as the safe choice. When the customer really digs into our model, we win."

• *Likelihood to buy.* The Likelihood to Buy map in Figure 5.6 is inspired by the work of Simon Majaro (see the framework in Chapter Six). Two key drivers of customer purchasing decisions are the Product (whether it is unique or me too) and the Producer's reputation in the area in question. In effect, the Prod-

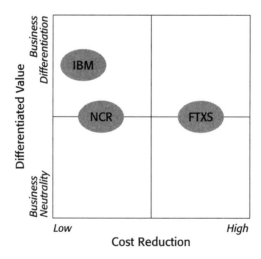

Figure 5.5. Competitive Perceptual Map

Figure 5.6. FTXS Likelihood to Buy Map

uct question is about differentiation, and the Producer dimension describes trust. As a relatively new brand in this market in North America, Fujitsu was in the process of establishing its reputation. The point of differentiation was the way in which it partnered with customers to drive down operating costs rather than the initial cost of its hardware. This map dramatically demonstrates the gap between their success with existing customers and the relatively low awareness of this beyond that group of companies.

Explanatory Metaphors. The metaphor exercise asked participants to draw and explain their image of the current business challenge. The rationale for this was twofold. Drawing elicits unconscious thoughts, which can be pivotal to understanding and improving a situation. Also, the use of metaphors legitimizes the discussion of important but sensitive subject matter. When this exercise is applied successfully, trust levels tend to rise, and several of the images prevail within the group as meaningful shorthand points of reference. All of this did indeed occur for the FTXS executive group.

Metaphors that the members of the team drew included a high-wire walker suspended over Niagara Falls, a bicyclist who must continue peddling forever (Figure 5.7), a fight between unequals (three participants chose the David and Goliath metaphor), and an orchestra that can't afford new instruments. All of these examples highlighted issues that were front of mind for managers in the company: the challenge of competing against a well-funded gorilla (IBM), the need for investment capital to sustain competitive differentiation, and the fact that people within the division were working hard just to keep pace with customer demand; there was no time for important work, only urgent work.

Figure 5.7. Cyclist Metaphor

The metaphors suggest some of the costs and limitations of the current strategy. It has been successful in gaining market share and bringing a level of financial stability to a business that was losing money. But if it were to end there, the leadership believes the division would eventually fall behind once again. With so much effort going into winning and delivering to new retail customers, there is little left to capture the bigger market opportunities that are apparent to the executive team.

Step 2: Core Dilemma Definition

Definition of the core dilemma lies at the heart of the work and therefore merits extra effort. Indeed, it is usually the case that struggle and some level of discomfort are beneficial to this task. Agreement reached too easily is usually a sign that something is amiss. At this point, we needed to convert the issues identified in step 1 into two-headed dilemmas. For example, a challenge of limited investment might be translated into the conflicting values of short-term profitability and long-term development. With the FTXS executive team, the work was completed in two steps. First, a comprehensive set of dilemmas was generated. Then working with this list, the central dilemma was defined.

Dilemmas Generation. By this point in our process, the meeting room walls were filled with words and pictures drawn on large sheets of flip chart paper. We were approaching our Rubicon, where we would need to leave behind the range of interesting threads of issues in order to focus on one central dilemma. It is critical that the group is engaged in a meaningful and informed way at this stage. Tension comes from the need to focus without abandoning the insights contained in the remaining dilemmas that were identified.

The first step is generating a comprehensive set of dilemmas. Group members were given some individual time to draft their own proposals, completing the statement, "We have to manage the tension between _____ and _____." Not surprisingly, heated discussions were sparked while creating the list of dilemma statements. In effect, members were revealing their true thoughts about what is right and wrong about the business. This level of discourse and challenge is vital, and although it is somewhat time-consuming, seeds of future agreement and commitment are being sown.

A diverse set of dilemmas was produced that captured the many facets of the FTXS challenge. After some reflection, the dilemmas were grouped to indicate six areas of tension (Table 5.1).

Core Dilemma Definition. The centerpiece of the process is articulation of the core dilemma. This is the stake in the ground to which the planning group and the process will return many times. The core dilemma sets the course for the ensuing work by firmly establishing primary forces in conflict.

Sometimes the core dilemma emerges quickly and effortlessly; in other cases, there is heated debate. As in the prior exercise, the value here far exceeds what is produced on paper. Debate is instructive and helps to move the process along. Although it is essential to agree on the central dilemma, it is not necessary to eliminate other top contenders being considered. We suggested to the group to proceed with the top choice and keep track of the three to five dilemmas rejected at this time. They are also part of the puzzle and may be returned to later in the process.

Discussion at FTXS ranged over a number of recurring themes, including the ideal customer profile, the economics of the business, the strategic offer (whether value or volume), and conflict between short- and long-term business interests. This last dilemma drew the most attention and emotion, and ultimately the group settled on a version of this. The core dilemma became the tension between Profitability and Growth (Figure 5.8).

Profitability is necessary and certainly desirable. However, the timing and trade-offs involved in attaining Profitability can have a serious impact on business viability. When the business was losing money, as it had not so long ago, profitability became the key goal and measure of legitimacy. With this goal achieved, the leadership team needed to broaden their concerns to include investment and sustained profits.

Growth challenges the team to look beyond the existing set of offerings and customers. Where is the business headed? Is there long-term survival without growing? And what core competencies are needed to sustain growth? In the technology field, growth rarely occurs without investment, as one generation of solution is quickly replaced by the next.

Table 5.1. FTXS: Six Domains of Dilemma

Marketing and Knowledge		
Demand Creation	versus	Capability
People	versus	Processes
Right Customers	versus	Compelling Offers
Solutions	versus	Relationships
Long-Term Opportunity		
Build for Tomorrow	versus	Sell Today
Potential to Increase Shareholder Value	versus	Potential to Dominate Markets
Annuity Revenue	versus	Short-Term Sales
Focus and Targeting		
Right Customers	versus	Accessibility
Retail Focus	versus	Horizontal Focus
Systematic	versus	Opportunistic
Understanding Evolving Needs	versus	Innovation
Sales Activity	versus	Making Money
Customer Driven	versus	Market Driven
Business Model		
Life Cycle Management	versus	Point Solutions
Value	versus	Volume
Investment	versus	Revenue
Survival and Sustainability		
Staff Survival	versus	Business Growth
Customer Focus	versus	Managed Processes
Greatness	versus	Survival
Investment		
Parent Company Contribution	versus	Business Growth
Partnering	versus	Parent Investment
Right Customers	versus	Speed of Growth

Figure 5.8. FTXS Level 2 Core Dilemma

The tension between these two forces was recognized as significant for the FTXS business. Furthermore, it appeared that if they could resolve this dilemma, the majority of other issues would be addressed.

Step 3: Modeling and Analysis

Defining the core dilemma is at once a powerful act of affirmation of what is of central importance, and a process of letting go of the host of other issues clamoring for attention. The core dilemma becomes the lens through which insight is intensified and strategic options are created. This is accomplished in two somewhat paradoxical steps. The first, Archetypal Dilemmas Modeling, involves actively reframing the situation, viewing it as a case of one or another classic type of problem. In the second step, Implications Analysis, the group constructs the response to the tension represented by the core dilemma.

Archetypal Dilemmas Modeling. Sometimes we solve problems best by momentarily directing our attention away from what we believe to be the most critical and pressing factors. Obviously this is not something you want to do for very long; however, reframing the problem statement can open important windows into a situation.

We do this in our approach by considering a number of classic, archetypal variations of the dilemma at hand. What if this were a case of *x* or *y* dilemma? Chapter Three contains a full description of the eight archetypal dilemmas. In this situation, we agreed that three of the archetypes were highly relevant yet different enough from the statement of the core dilemma to merit experimentation. The payoff was immediate, as pieces of the eventual plan began to fall into place.

The three archetypes were:

- Product versus Market. You can alter your offering (Existing and New), and you can alter the customer markets you sell into (Existing and New).

- Cost versus Benefit. Everything comes with a price. Where is investment likely to deliver the biggest payoff, and what level of risk are we facing?

- Change versus Stability. Systems are in constant tension between forces for adaptation (Change) and integration (Stability). It can be catastrophic to lose the balance in dynamic markets.

The Product-Market dilemma (Figure 5.9) succinctly depicted a set of the major strategic options and their logical sequence. The lower left quadrant represents the current opportunity to increase sales in the existing market. To accomplish this, the organization needs to deliver on commitments and intensify marketing and sales efforts. FTXS has the opportunity to expand beyond

Figure 5.9. FTXS Product-Market Dilemma

this level of success by improving and expanding on its offerings. The upper left quadrant describes this option. Step 3 is described in the lower left quadrant, and involves expanding the target customer markets, leveraging the competencies and track record they have developed together with the enhanced offering features. The upper right quadrant, new products to new markets, represents strategic territory to avoid. Additional insights were gained by applying a Cost-Benefit analysis.

For the past couple of years, the FTXS executive team had correctly assumed that success would need to be achieved without any significant investment. The Cost-Benefit perspective forced the group to reclassify its primary goal from survival to sustainable growth and to model the riskiness of different courses of action. Organic growth without investment places the franchise at risk: competitors willing to invest aggressively could copy and surpass them in their own strategy. Investment that merely followed the lead of others was also risky, since the best they could hope for was to equal the competition while spending a lot more money. The preferable scenario was to build on FTXS and Fujitsu strengths in meeting emerging customer needs in a unique and hard-to-replicate fashion.

Change and stability compete daily in the IT industry. The pace of change and rate of new product introductions is so fast that competitive advantage is fleeting at best. Any strategy must always address the next wave of change in addition to the current one.

The current next wave of change in the IT industry is being defined by technologies such as wireless and grid computing, as well as emerging values such as self-service. In retail, the mobile device, whether it's a phone, a smart card, or an in-store scanner, will handle an ever greater number of transactions. For FTXS, this means taking an expansive view of what "retail" and "transaction" mean. It would be dangerous to concentrate overly on existing business (stability) while the whole POS paradigm (scanners, self-service, anywhere mobile commerce) is changing.

Implications Analysis. By this point in the process, the business challenge is well understood, and the group has identified many aspects of the solution. It is time for integration and design. The Core Dilemma is the creative canvas, defining the key tension and the parameters within which the solution needs to work.

Until fairly recently, profitability was the focal point for the FTXS business. Phase 0 (P0) is off the grid in Figure 5.10, indicative of the business unit's dismal performance. Growth was not even a consideration until Phase 1 (P1), when steady sales within the retail market became possible. This is the current reality. As satisfying as the moment is to the team, ongoing success in markets this competitive is in no way guaranteed.

The organization has developed an impressive set of competencies and an operating platform that is highly competitive. The retail sector experience has

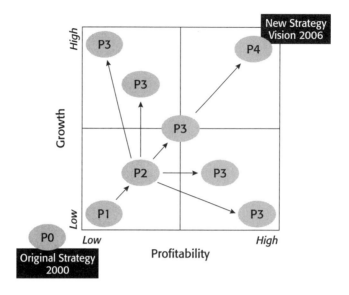

Figure 5.10. Core Dilemma Options

allowed it to build a hard-to-replicate expertise in managing transactions. Expanding that capability with new offerings that leverage the next phase of technology development, coupled with the life cycle cost reduction orientation, will make the value proposition even more appealing. Phase 2 then becomes a period of building a more stable business within the existing base of prospects and customers, improving growth and profitability.

Beyond mere stabilization of the current strategy, the company faces a range of options that aim to manage the trade-offs and transcend the dilemma of growth versus profitability. It could choose to advance quickly to the right side of the matrix and squeeze the current franchise for short-term profits. The danger in choosing this path is the difficulty in remaining competitive as technology and practices shift. The opposite extreme is to postpone profitability to invest in the creation of a more robust and flexible set of future offerings.

The group modeled several opportunities, labeled P3 in Figure 5.10, in order to create a strategy and growth plan that would respond to the Core Dilemma and emerging competitive environment with a robust value proposition. Because elements of the strategy are highly proprietary and still evolving as we write this, we cannot go into detail on the nature of those plans. Nevertheless, we will highlight the general steps in the next stage of the process.

The goal of any strategy at this point is to elegantly resolve the major issue areas that the group identified as initial dilemmas in step 2. At a high level, FTXS aims to manage the tension between offers and customers (marketing), the conflict of building for tomorrow while selling today (long-term opportunity), and the strategic dilemma of market focus. Attending to these dilemmas provides the platform for refining both the strategy and divisional business model.

In phases 3 and 4, FTXS will have internalized the new strategy and put it into practice, preparing itself for further investment and accelerated growth. The current strategy, conceived in 2001, brought the company great success in 2003. The new strategy should pay off in 2005 and 2006 and beyond.

Step 4: Gap Analysis

Dilemma-based strategy formulation unleashes creativity, energy, and optimism. As in the case of the FTXS business group, agreement on an exciting and empowering plan is extremely motivating. And yet no real progress is possible without a sober and grounded assessment of the gaps and barriers that stand in the way of accomplishing the new agenda. The first step toward this is a careful and candid analysis of the gaps. The major gaps tend to be in such categories as human, financial, technological, and market power.

Gap analysis begins with a review of the new dilemmas-based strategy itself. For each implied action, the group considers critical requirements and capabilities. The output is captured in a straightforward four-column table that highlights key success factors and their associated requirements. Table 5.2 contains several of the more important items identified by the FTXS strategy team.

Table 5.2. Gap Analysis

Key Success Factors	Means	Benefit	Cost
Prove ability to deliver cost reduction and new strategic concept	Customer testimonials, white papers	Internal and external belief, conviction, and sales	⬛$⬛
Scalability of cost reduction capability	Systems and operational processes	Improvement over costs base Added functionality	⬛$⬛
Expanded technology suite	Engineers, operations	Add sizzle (harder to duplicate or replicate)	⬛$⬛
Identify and acquire key technology enablers	In-house partners, middleware, technology strategy workshop	Drive costs down, added intelligence, differentiate	⬛$⬛
Ability to articulate value proposition	Replicate what few can do through mentoring and practice	Consistent story, improved win ratio	⬛$⬛

Step 5: Resolution Planning

The final step in any significant planning undertaking is ensuring sustained follow-through. Good ideas and intentions need to be cast in the shape of a plan with objectives, time lines, budget, and responsibilities. It was fortuitous in our work with FTXS that the company was at the start of its annual budget and planning cycle. The leadership team understood the value of acting on the plan as well as the cost of not following through. Timing allowed them to ensure follow-through in a planned and supported way.

Prime responsibility fell to Austen Mulinder, the president and CEO, with clearly defined support roles for Doug Wallace, senior vice president of client operations, Tim Hester, vice president of business planning, and Ron Brunt, chief architect. At the end of the consultation, the recommendations were being tightly integrated into the year's business plan as well as a multiyear proposal to the parent company. Initial feedback was positive, and a more detailed proposal is on the way.

EPILOGUE

Sometimes to succeed a company must be prepared to cannibalize recent victories . . . before others do it to them. The willingness to challenge and build on their level 1 strategy was critical to FTXS's ability to continue to leverage the company's assets and advantages.

The notion of level 1 and level 2 strategies provides a dynamic framework for planners. Each new strategy, no matter how successful, carries within it the seeds of its own demise. Over time, its vulnerabilities bring it into conflict with opposing forces, requiring a fresh assessment of enabling and constraining factors. Strategic advantage lies in embracing the uniquely relevant Core Dilemma for that business and exploiting it to release the organization's full creative potential.

PART THREE

2 × 2 FRAMEWORKS
INVENTORY

CHAPTER SIX

Strategic Frameworks

Customer Needs Frameworks
Beyond Customer Led
Discontinuity and the Life Cycle
Customer as Value Manager
Customer Value Analysis

Strategic Context Frameworks
Scenarios
Gartner Magic Quadrant
Portfolio Analysis
Problems and Solutions
Dialectical SWOT Analysis: Strengths,
  Weaknesses, Opportunities, and Threats
Market Tipping

Strategic Options Frameworks
Corporate Strategy

Generic Strategy
E-Business Opportunity Matrix
Global Product Planning
Generic Network Strategy

**Marketing and
Communications Frameworks**
Mass Customization: The Four Approaches
Attentionscape
Managing Customer Loyalty
Likelihood to Buy

Risk Frameworks
Revenue and Profitability
BCG: Product Portfolio Analysis
Uncertainty-Impact Matrix
Entrance and Exit Strategies

S trategy is the art and science of competing more effectively than one's competitors. The visible strategic act of corporate leaders is making choices that advance the goals of the firm in the best possible way. The more intense the competitive landscape is, the tougher the choices become. Great strategy making is, of course, more complex, subtle, and multifaceted than this.

The key question the strategist seeks to answer is "How do we compete more effectively?" The archetypal strategic dilemma involves resolving the tension

91

The Archetypal Strategic Dilemma

Core Question: How do we compete more effectively?

Key Issue: Value proposition

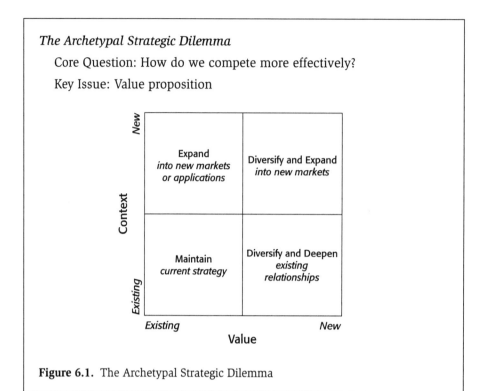

Figure 6.1. The Archetypal Strategic Dilemma

between Context and Value (Figure 6.1). Context is the who, why, where, and how of value creation; Value is the what. The job begins with defining the fields of inquiry in ways that naturally give rise to the right sorts of dialogue, learning, and, eventually, choices.

Leaders establish constraints that frame future decisions. When Lewis and Clarke arrived at the fork in the Clearwater River on their long, arduous journey in 1805, the deliberation was framed as, "Which way should we go?" and not, "Should we go on?" Gandhi, in the early 1900s, chose the path of nonviolent protest, inspiring a nation and overpowering the endurance of the British Empire. First, he defined the strategic arena as how to achieve independence for India, and then he focused the issue as a choice of means: Would there be violence or not? Saul Alinsky, the ingenious 1960s guerrilla lawyer and advocate for social justice and change, laid strategic traps for uncooperative institutions. When disenfranchised residents in Harlem were refused credit from the local bank, he organized legions of supporters to tie the bank in nonproductive knots, lining up all day to deposit and then withdraw pennies at a time.[1] He defined the battlefield as an issue of access and then gave the bank problems much greater than that represented by fair access. He applied this social jujitsu time and again to champion the causes of his clients.

More often than not, effective definition of strategic issues and options is built on a dialectical foundation. Lewis and Clarke were torn between the leader's vision and the navigator's expert but incomplete advice. India, under Gandhi's guidance, pursued the tension between the right to self-determination and rule, and the maintenance of civility and progress. Alinsky played one interest (high-value clients, risk aversion) against another (community power expressed through system jamming and escalating embarrassment).

Viewed in this way, making tough strategic choices is really the final step in a more complex process. Gaining leverage lies in planning and controlling that process, arguably the most important thing a leader can do.

A BRIEF HISTORY OF STRATEGY

Modern business strategy practices can be traced to the work of Alfred Chandler and Igor Ansoff in the early 1960s.[2] Form follows function was the way Chandler framed strategy in his book *Strategy and Structure*. The *how* should derive from the *what* and *why*. Ansoff's seminal book, *Corporate Strategy*, focused on the strategic problem of a firm and presented a framework and language for strategic decision making. The now famous Product-Market matrix (see page 135) defined growth and diversification options in a way that planners could easily apply and communicate to others.

A generation of business leaders took the strategy credo to heart, and planning departments began to appear everywhere, creating detailed multiyear blueprints for their corporations. General Electric's strategic planning office employed over two hundred senior-level staff in 1983 when Jack Welch disbanded it. Mintzberg's empirically based study of executive behavior, reported on in 1983, described what was really going on, emphasizing the dynamic, reality-informed, and iterative nature of strategy.[3] A more apt metaphor for strategy, it seemed, was course correction, and zigzagging rather than perfect planning processes yielding long-term blueprints.

The term *strategic thinking* replaced *strategic planning* in the late 1970s to reflect this need to sense and adjust to external reality on an ongoing basis. The best strategy making is done in context, on the fly. Mintzberg's leaders built strategy on the move. They thought strategically, grabbing moments in the hall, on elevators, and in conversations. Reflection and action define an ongoing learning process that is periodically expressed as strategy.

Competition shifted to warp speed in the 1990s, driven by the Internet and globalization. New rules were being written daily, as all semblance of predictability and permanence seemed to disappear in a shrinking and real-time world. Direct and inexpensive access to competitive intelligence, coupled with the rise of new inter-enterprise business models, redefined competitive practices. Being strategic replaced the development of long-term strategy, and businesses found it more helpful to refer to strategic contexts within which rolling three- and six-month plans were implemented.

Strategy making is recognized now as a dialectical dance between competing goals and modes; form and function shape each other; the organization is the strategy. Agility, an aspect of form, is recognized as key to strategic effectiveness; market share and profitability compete for primacy, and growth and stability oscillate in self-correcting loops.

STRATEGY IN THE 2 × 2 CONTEXT

Strategy is inherently dialectical in nature, and so it is no surprise to find a wealth of important and useful strategic 2 x 2 frameworks. The frameworks in this chapter are organized into five categories:

- *Customer needs.* Customers are the ultimate arbiter of any strategy. Businesses have devised elaborate surveys and focus group methods to help them get inside the customer's head and understand her experiences and motivations. The frameworks in this section address the challenge from an assortment of useful and creative angles.

- *Strategic context.* Business success is as much a function of external factors as the actions undertaken by a firm itself. Strategic context includes such considerations as the nature of competition and the timing of an offering.

- *Strategic options.* The essence of strategy lies in defining a value proposition and creating the competitive plan. This group of frameworks helps to generate a rich set of possibilities and sort them in an efficient and meaningful way.

- *Marketing and communications.* Brand development and positioning are critical competitive factors, determined largely by how a firm presents itself and communicates its value. Businesses need to know how they are perceived in the marketplace and what they are seen to stand for.

- *Risk management.* With competition and reward comes risk. Businesses must get clear about the value of the prize, the costs involved in trying to succeed, and the possibility of failure. This set of frameworks helps to make risk decisions more explicit and rational.

CUSTOMER NEEDS FRAMEWORKS

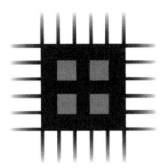

What is in the minds and hearts of our customers? How do they view us? How will their needs evolve? Who else might become customers?

The success and renewal of a firm's value proposition begins in the market-place with customers. In the past decade, power has been migrating steadily away from firms to customers, riding on the wings of readily available knowl-edge. Proactive customers know what they want, and they seek out suppliers who will deliver to their satisfaction. Paying attention to customers' needs and experiences is common sense and good business. The cost of acquiring a new customer can easily be several hundred dollars. Retaining customers doesn't need to be an expensive undertaking, with the added bonus of learning more about how to do your business better.

Beyond Customer Led
Gary Hamel and C. K. Prahalad

The public does not know what is possible, but we do.
—Akio Morita, Sony cofounder[4]

As much as anything, foresight comes from really wanting to make a difference in people's lives.
—Gary Hamel and C. K. Prahalad[5]

To Hamel and Prahalad, innovation and the ability to challenge one's own prac-tices and assumptions are necessary core competencies for the successful 21st century corporation. Successive waves of organizational improvement tend to play within existing boundaries and do little to shape markets in helpful ways. Corporate restructuring and reengineering are two major sets of initiatives that lower costs and improve efficency but ignore core issues of value definition and renewal. Hamel and Prahalad's work represents a healthy and invigorating re-action to hierarchical strategic planning, encouraging everyone to be more pro-active in recognizing opportunities, innovating, and making their own work more meaningful. Their message is delivered in award-winning *Harvard Business Review* articles like "Strategic Intent," books like *Competing for the Future* and *Leading the Revolution,* and the work of Strategos, the strategy consulting firm that Hamel heads.

The Two Dimensions and Their Extremes. The Beyond Customer Led matrix (Figure 6.2) explores the two dimensions of Needs and Customers:

> Needs. Businesses pride themselves on understanding their customers and their evolving needs. Most methods, however, provide insight into those needs that customers recognize and can express as a wish or a gap. The Needs dimension defines this condition as one end of a continuum, with unknown, unarticulated needs as the counterpoint.

> Customers. Two classes of customer are important to a business: those it currently serves and those it does not.

The Four Quadrants. Companies can meet the known needs of existing cus-tomers, or they can venture further into new and promising areas of potential and future needs. The Beyond Customer Led matrix identifies four possible need groups:

• Upper left: Unarticulated-Served. A satisfied customer today may become frustrated or uninterested if his unexpressed but felt needs are not addressed.

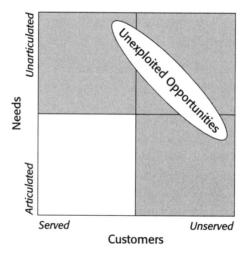

Figure 6.2. Beyond Customer Led Matrix

This set of needs represents a rich opportunity for reinvention, value extension, and learning.

• Lower left: Articulated-Served. This is the known world of customer needs. Although it is crucial to care for these signals, there is limited innovation potential here, and companies need to be careful not to lose sight of what is evolving in their efforts to be responsive.

• Lower right: Articulated-Unserved. Offerings developed and perfected for existing customers can be extended to new customers in different markets. Like the upper left quadrant, this space describes a prime and natural strategic opportunity zone.

• Upper right: Unarticulated-Unserved. Getting inside the heads and experiences of unaddressed customers is the last frontier of customer need identification. As remote as this may sound, it is exactly what proactive and visionary companies like Honda have done to fuel their remarkable expansion over the past two decades.

Example: The Chrysler Minivan. In the 1950s, U.S. automobile production accounted for two-thirds of the world total. By the 1970s, that number had been cut to 23 percent due directly to the growing strength of its offshore competitors in Japan and Europe. The oil crunch of the 1970s added to the problem, leaving thousands of gas-guzzling sedans sitting in Detroit plant parking lots while consumers flocked to buy fuel-efficient cars from overseas.

In the early 1980s, Hal Sperlich was working at Ford to develop what would become the now ubiquitous minivan. When he couldn't convince Ford this was a good idea, he left to join Chrysler. The rest is history.

The North American automobile companies were losing market share for a number of good reasons. Built for volume production, their assembly lines and factories were costly and inflexible. A disaffected workforce was more concerned with protecting labor gains than making their companies innovative and more competitive. Probably most worrisome, competitors' cars were outperforming theirs, using new lean manufacturing methods that were almost impossible to apply in older car plants.

The cost structure and underlying business model of the North American companies made innovation nearly impossible, yet this was precisely what was needed to revitalize the sector. When Sperlich launched his campaign within Ford, it ran afoul of both the strategic thrust and the company executives, eventually leading to his being fired. "[Ford] lacked confidence that a market existed, because the product didn't exist. The auto industry places great value on historical studies of market segments."[6]

Demographics painted a clear picture of the coming period. Relatively affluent and growing North American families needed larger interior car space. They just didn't know they did because nothing like the minivan yet existed. The minivan provided that extra bit of space that made trips to the cottage more comfortable, hockey equipment easier to cart around, and home repairs less painful (Figure 6.3).

The Beyond Customer Led matrix shows how unarticulated needs can be used to inform strategic vision and ultimately help redirect investments. "In 10 years of developing the minivan we never once got a letter from a housewife asking us to invent one. To the skeptics, that proved there wasn't a market out there."[7]

Sperlich's innovation and Chrysler chairman Lee Iaccoca's vision and courage were instrumental in pulling Chrysler out of a desperate decline. When the MPV model was launched in 1983, it sold more than half a million units, helping right Chrysler and overnight creating a new car category.

Context. Beyond Customer Led is ideal for strategic planning and product-service reinvigoration. This is a simple and powerful way to tap creative thinking within a firm and in dialogue with partners and customers. It is also a useful device for auditing future plans once they have been developed by asking questions from the perspective of each of the four needs groups—for example, Will these plans meet the known needs of existing customers?

Method. There is a highly intuitive feel to applying this framework as a tool. The process works best as a creative search exercise, responding to a set of questions which elicit content for each of the quadrants. Once this is done, patterns in needs and opportunities can be identified. This tool works well for individuals and teams:

• Step 1: Make incremental improvements. Looking at the lower left quadrant, ask the following questions: How well are we responding to the articulated

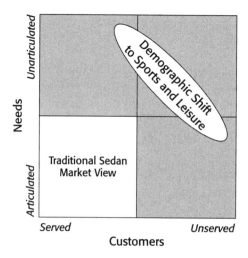

Figure 6.3. Minivan Market Matrix

needs of our customers? Are there innovative ways we could improve on meeting their needs?

• Step 2: Anticipate needs of existing customers. Looking at the upper left quadrant, ask the following questions: What do we know about our current customers that suggests additional needs we are not addressing? How will our customers' situations change over the next five to ten years? What needs will these changes create that we might respond to?

• Step 3: Meet known needs of new customers. Looking at the lower right quadrant, ask the following questions: Which of our offerings have the greatest portability to new settings and customer segments? Which new markets are most attractive and well suited to our offerings?

• Step 4: Explore needs of noncustomers. Looking at the upper right quadrant, ask the following questions: Which new markets are most appealing to us? What would be useful to know about them? How might we go about learning more about their needs? What needs exist beyond the obvious ones?

• Step 5: Review. Having answered these questions, step back from the matrix and look for patterns of opportunity. What are the most unusual ideas? Which ones are the best fit with your firm's competencies?

References

Hamel, G. *Leading the Revolution.* Boston: Harvard Business School Press, 2000.

Hamel, G., and Prahalad, C. K. "Strategic Intent." *Harvard Business Review,* May 1989.

Hamel, G., and Prahalad, C. K. *Competing for the Future.* Boston: Harvard Business School Press, 1994.

⊞

Discontinuity and the Life Cycle
Geoffrey Moore and Paul Wiefels

You may think you're in the high-tech business—software, hardware, networking, services, biotech, whatever. In fact, you're in the discontinuous innovations business. Which means you're in the most risky business on earth.
—Paul Wiefels[8]

Dramatic improvements in end-user capabilities, then, are the accelerator that drives technology adoption, just as paradigm shock is the brake.
—Geoffrey Moore[9]

The technology adoption life cycle, developed at Harvard University in the 1930s, originally described the pattern and rate of acceptance of new seed potatoes in the U.S. Midwest. Shaped like the typical bell curve, it elegantly mapped how a new technology grows from an experimental notion to a widely used commodity. As a technology matures and becomes less risky, different groups of customers, each with a distinct set of characteristics and needs, adopt it. The earliest adopters are technically oriented, with genuine interest in the product features. Later buyers tend to be pragmatic and conservative, and care most about business benefits resulting from the technology's use.

Geoffrey Moore expanded on the cycle in his 1991 book, *Crossing the Chasm*, describing what occurs when the technology is discontinuous and disruptive. In these cases, as was true for many of the Internet companies in Silicon Valley when Moore wrote his book, successful movement through the cycle involves bridging a set of gaps. Color TVs and laptop computers are continuous technological improvements, drawing on preexisting infrastructures and user skills. Wireless computing and electric cars are discontinuous and demand greater patience, investment, and learning while the technology becomes fully functional and supported by manufacturers, servicers, and standards. Not all new technologies successfully cross the chasm between the early experimenters and the more risk-averse majority buyers.

The book became a marketing bible for information technology companies during the supercharged 1990s, and Moore's Chasm Group was called on to guide hundreds of entrepreneurial ventures through the technology adoption life cycle. Discontinuous technology is by definition a risky business, and Moore's modeling offered structure, principles, and method to convert innovation into profitable business. Begin by understanding where your technology fits in the adoption cycle, focus on the right customers for the stage you are at, and deliver value that responds to current needs and interests. Strategy and communications change dramatically as a technology matures and one audience is replaced by the next.

The Discontinuity and Life Cycle framework (Figure 6.4) is the core tool employed by the Chasm Group for strategic diagnosis and market planning, integrating the cycle with market forces and customer types. Although this framework describes the world of discontinuous technologies, the method and lessons are relevant for most businesses involved in launching new products.

The Discontinuity and Life Cycle matrix is a highly integrated planning tool that communicates three sets of information: the technology adoption life cycle, the customer audiences being served, and the forces driving and restraining market adoption. At first glance, the picture may appear complex; however, each of the three sets of information is valid, relevant, and intuitively clear. The key to deciphering the map is to follow the life cycle, which moves in a clockwise direction starting in the upper left quadrant.

The Two Dimensions and Their Extremes. Two kinds of discontinuity shape the technology adoption life cycle: Paradigm Shock and Application Breakthrough. It is helpful to think of these forces as variations of Cost (Paradigm Shock) and Benefit (Application Breakthrough):

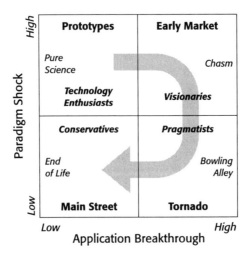

Figure 6.4. Discontinuity and Life Cycle Matrix

Paradigm Shock (Pain). Paradigm Shock measures the amount of adjustment required by end users and infrastructure providers to use the new
technology. When this is too high, as it often is in early phases, people are
more reluctant to invest. Electric cars are expensive and demand considerable investment and learning on the part of owners, mechanics, and gas
stations in order to perform adequately. This pain dampens enthusiasm
and the willingness to purchase, save for the most enthusiastic buyers.

Application Breakthrough (Gain). Application Breakthrough is the gain
derived through use of the new technology. Potential users become motivated to sign on as the ability to benefit rises. Often there is a noticeable
threshold that must be reached before a larger mass audience recognizes
the merits of the new technology and pursues it. Faxes and cell phones are
examples. In the case of electric cars, the benefits of ownership need to
outweigh the costs for the technology to move to a state of mass adoption.

The Four Quadrants. The four quadrants in this model help to organize and
align key elements of a marketing strategy:

   • Upper left: Prototypes. Life cycles begin here, built on ideas with potential
rather than practical things. At this stage, pain and adjustment tend to be high,
and tangible benefits are low. This is the world of pure science and prototypes,
where users are tech-savvy enthusiasts.
   • Upper right: Early Market. A limited Early Market is led by one or several
visionaries who recognize the potential of the new technology and support its
development through funding and leadership. The first application breakthroughs

are made in this phase, attracting the interest of more pragmatic customers. The challenge of this period is to demonstrate the potential value of the innovation in a convincing enough manner to recruit customers willing to experiment with it in their organizations. The Chasm, which lies between the Early Market and the Bowling Alley, can last for an extended length of time, effectively blocking mainstream adoption. Anticipating and planning for this time lag is critical.

• Lower right: Bowling Alley. New technologies must be proven in smaller niche-like environments before broad uptake can occur. This is like targeting specific bowling pins, with momentum and impact increasing as successive pins are knocked over. To accomplish this, the supplier must gain a full understanding of the specific issues facing the target business and deliver a complete end-to-end solution. This is an incremental strategy phase, where success with one or two players in a segment leads to additional competitors' getting on board. If one or two industries can be won over, interest and credibility rise, and infrastructure requirements for mass adoption begin to be met.

• Lower left: Main Street. Maturation of basic infrastructure and the emergence of standards fuels what Moore calls the Tornado. In Tornados, demand accelerates significantly as the product moves from niche to generic. Buyers tend to be technical as companies recognize the benefits and want to integrate the new technology as quickly as possible. The key to winning in Tornados is being part of the dominant solution or platform, staying focused on the core offering, and meeting the demand in a reasonable enough time frame.

Example: Winners and Losers in the PC Industry. The early years of computing were dominated by IBM, which at one point accounted for almost 80 percent of computer-related revenues worldwide. As the computing paradigm switched from mainframes to minis and PCs, a new generation of hardware, software, and services companies entered the scene, redefining the market. Out of this competitive chaos, two companies emerged as winners: Microsoft in software and Intel in the microchip market. In 1993, Intel took 50 percent of the total profit earned by the top 150 high-tech companies in Silicon Valley and by 2003 had a market value approaching that of IBM. Microsoft's market value is roughly twice that of IBM.

Organized first around the DOS operating standard and subsequently around the now ubiquitous Windows, the pair has dominated the computing world and benefited disproportionately from waves of innovation and the ever-growing number of users. How Microsoft and Intel achieved this success and continue to exercise such influence is made apparent by the discontinuity and life cycle analysis (see Figure 6.5).

Until the late 1970s, computing was principally the domain of specialists and hobbyists. Computers were expensive, large, and complicated. Interacting with them required learning elaborate programming languages. Prototypes of faster,

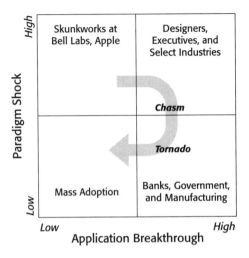

Figure 6.5. Wintel Adoption Cycle Matrix

smaller computers were being tested, but materials, design, and usage barriers kept all but the keenest enthusiasts away.

This all began to shift in the 1970s with the introduction of smaller minicomputers and desktop personal computers. The revolution was under way as visionaries at Bell Labs, Apple, and a few other places designed personal computers that were functional and held the promise of applicability to a wider audience. At the core of the new machines was a small, affordable microprocessor that enabled miniaturization and an operating system that was more intuitive and human-friendly.

To get through the first Chasm organized around the DOS operating system, the Wintel coalition contained a host of strategic partners, including Lotus for its spreadsheet software, MicroPro's Wordstar word processor, HP for printers, Conner for hard disk drives, and Novell for a network operating system. As these firms came together to deliver a complete working system, the Bowling Alley strategy quickly accumulated the energy needed to launch a Tornado that would lock in whole markets to the new systems and standards, with Microsoft and Intel at its center. The key to unleashing the Tornado was the flood of applications that independent software developers created to support the common platform. The move to Main Street occurred once technical and cost barriers had been removed and the infrastructure was solid.

The cycle was repeated again in 1991, but more quickly, when the Windows operating system was introduced. This time, fewer partners were included in the core coalition. Intel remained with its 486 and Pentium chips, as did HP, but Microsoft took the opportunity to integrate its own word processing package,

Word, and spreadsheet application, Excel. One of the lessons of Tornado marketing is that markets want to deal with the fewest number of vendors organized around standard offerings. The outcome, as we know, is that the Microsoft Office suite of applications quickly became the desktop standard, much as Windows was the dominant operating system.

Margins compressed as these products matured and found their way onto Main Street, but market size increased exponentially. In successive mini-waves of innovation, additional partner functions have been integrated into the core set, like Novell's network operating system. However, by providing a standard, they have been able to preserve their role, adding improvements and cutting costs to stay ahead of the competition.

Context. The framework is applicable to strategy and marketing efforts of businesses where innovation and technology development are central to success. Each phase of the technology adoption life cycle has a unique set of requirements and opportunities, and it is dangerous and wasteful to be working from the wrong starting point.

Method. The object is to gain market acceptance in the quickest and most effective manner. While accuracy of analysis is important, the first critical task is to align the business leadership team around their assessment of the phase of development of the technology category to which the innovation belongs:

• Step 1: Diagnose. Determine where the technology category lies on the technology adoption life cycle.
• Step 2: Move out of the twilight zone. At any point, the market adoption process is at risk of losing steam and being marooned. New technologies cannot survive these for very long, and it becomes a priority to break loose. The two levers are reducing Paradigm Shock and increasing Application Breakthrough benefits.
• Step 3: Move to the next stage. Strategies exist to advance successfully to the next stage. For example, Early Market entry requires finding visionaries and defining high-payoff development areas, while Bowling Alley entry depends on careful segmentation and understanding industry-specific challenges.

References

Moore, G. *Crossing the Chasm: Marketing and Selling High-Tech Products to Mainstream Customers.* New York: HarperBusiness, 1991.

Moore, G. *Inside the Tornado: Marketing Strategies from Silicon Valley's Cutting Edge.* New York: HarperCollins, 1995.

Wiefels, P. *The Chasm Companion: A Fieldbook to Crossing the Chasm and Inside the Tornado.* New York: HarperBusiness, 2002.

⊞

Customer as Value Manager
Alex Lowy and Natalie Klym

> It's a new imperative; businesses need to design their processes in ways that allow customers to drive value creation.
> —Natalie Klym[10]

What does it mean to develop a customer-driven fulfillment network? The concept of the customer as value manager (CVM) comes from a multimillion-dollar research project into the future of supply chains conducted by Digital 4Sight in 2000. It explored how companies use information technology to support sales and let individual customers design those parts of the product or service experience that matter to them. There are great variations in the degree to which customers want to play an active role in processes related to product design, configuration, sales, delivery, and support. Some prefer to act through intermediaries; others want to buy on-line. Some care about product configuration; others are concerned with fast delivery. The model encourages companies to think in terms of enabling customers to access only those parts of the supply chain that add value for them (Figure 6.6). When we view customers as value managers, we present them with an individualized supply chain that perfectly fits their needs. Ideally, we isolate and emphasize supply chain capabilities to meet customer needs rather than the needs of mass production.

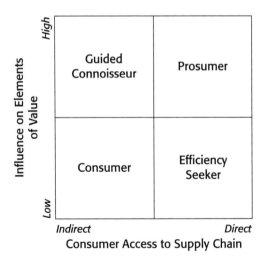

Figure 6.6. Customer as Value Manager Matrix

The Two Dimensions and Their Extremes. The CVM model differentiates customer groups by the degree to which they actively participate in offering design and by the way they access supply chain activities:[11]

Influence on Elements of Value. Influence refers to the degree to which customers want to have a voice in the design and customization of products and services.

Customer Access to Supply Chain. Customers interact directly (using information systems) with supply chain activities or through intermediaries. Consider the case of a company selling business furniture. Customers might prefer to purchase through an intermediary such as an architect, space planner, or retailer, or they might choose to buy directly from the company.

The Four Quadrants. The model segments buyers by their purchasing preferences rather than by demographic or economic characteristics:

- Upper left: Guided Connoisseur. The Guided Connoisseur is a serious customer who is experienced in dealing with intermediaries—architects, space designers, retailers—and expects a high level of choice and customization. One way to reach the Guided Connoisseur is through on-line tools that can be shared by them and their chosen intermediary. This is commonly done in the building industry.
- Lower left: Consumer. The Consumer segment is happy to buy standard products through existing channels. In our corporate furniture example, this might represent a corporate customer who lets a space planner make all furniture decisions.
- Lower right: Efficiency Seeker. The Efficiency Seeker wants to control the buying experience and is prepared to accept a limited role in designing product specifications. This might be an executive in a fast-moving start-up who wants to be able to go on-line to manage his account and is more concerned with convenient financing, quick delivery, and service than in an expanded selection or product customization.
- Upper right: Prosumer. The Prosumer is a sophisticated customer who wants both high customization and direct access. This buyer is comfortable dealing through the on-line channel and doesn't want the transaction overhead of retailers and agents.

Method. Follow these steps to conduct a Customer as Value Manager analysis:

- Step 1: Assess the offering. Make a short list of the critical features of your product or service offering viewed from the customer's perspective. You may include elements such as style, price, delivery terms, selection, and financing.

• Step 2: Assess customers. Make a list of your major customer groups and identify individual customers within these groups. This will help you think about where to place them on the matrix.

• Step 3: Diagnose. Place customers into the four quadrants based on the extent to which they need to influence and manage value. Refer to the list of features identified in step 1 to evaluate customer preferences.

• Step 4: Design. Define strategies to provide customers with their preferred form of access.

Reference

Tapscott, D., Ticoll, D., and Lowy, A. *Digital Capital: Harnessing the Power of Business Webs.* Boston: Harvard Business School Press, 2000.

⊞

Customer Value Analysis
Bradley Gale

Winning customers by providing superior quality attracts customers who are inherently more loyal. . . . By contrast, customers who instinctively buy on price, or are trained to buy on promotions, tend to wander from supplier to supplier looking for the one who is most desperate.
　—Bradley Gale[12]

Are your customers satisfied with your current offerings? Do you know why they are satisfied? Is it because of your price or your value? And even if they report that they are deeply satisfied, under what conditions would they switch to a competitor's product or service?

These are questions that marketers find difficult to answer. Customer satisfaction surveys are helpful, but only fill in part of the picture. Customer Value Analysis (CVA) is a powerful tool that reveals how specific product attributes contribute to customer perception of value and the buying decision. It enables one to focus on the aspects of product or service that are most likely to increase customer acquisition, retention, and profitability.

The branch of economics that is concerned with how consumers make decisions is called utility theory and has its roots in the work of economist Jeremy Bentham in the late eighteenth century. Modern Customer Value Analysis is the result of work done by Bradley Gale and others at AT&T in the 1980s. A generally satisfied customer, they found, does not necessarily produce repeat business or improved financial results. The CVA principles and method described in Gale's 1994 book, *Managing Customer Value*, were created to get at the critical drivers and interdependencies influencing customer buying decisions (see Figure 6.7).

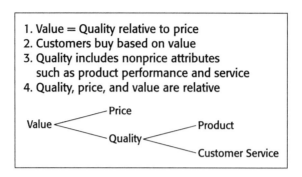

1. Value = Quality relative to price
2. Customers buy based on value
3. Quality includes nonprice attributes
   such as product performance and service
4. Quality, price, and value are relative

Figure 6.7. How Customers Choose Among Competitors

Customer Value Analysis is built on the proposition that customers choose among suppliers based on perceived value. Value (Figure 6.8) is a combination of price and quality. Lowering the price or raising the quality of a product will improve its overall perceived value relative to competitors' products (provided, of course, that such information is communicated convincingly to potential customers).

Customer Value Analysis is a two-step process. First, measure how customers perceive the quality and price of your products versus those of your competitors. Then plot these data on a Customer Value Map. Firms that are perceived to be lower in price and higher in quality than competitors are poised for market share gains. Conversely, a low score in either or both of these measures is cause for concern. The fair value line indicates where quality and price are in balance. Gale uses the terms "Customer-Perceived Price" and "Customer-Perceived Quality" (or "Market-Perceived Quality") to reflect that the profiles are determined principally by gauging customer perceptions.

The Two Dimensions and Their Extremes. The Customer Value Map explores two key dimensions: Customer-Perceived Price and Customer-Perceived Quality:

Customer-Perceived (Relative) Price. Customer-Perceived Price reflects all relevant components of price. For homes, this might include financing costs, maintenance, local real estate taxes, and expected appreciation, as well as the initial purchase price. If you were shopping for steaks, purchase cost would be the only relevant price.

Customer-Perceived Quality. Perceived Quality includes all product attributes other than price. Different attributes are relevant in each product category. Home buyers might consider location, materials, style, size, landscaping, and other factors. In the steak example, quality perceptions might focus on such attributes as color, marbling, freshness, brand, government inspection, and convenience of purchase.

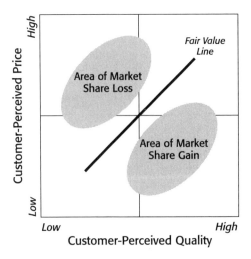

Figure 6.8. Generic Customer Value Map

The Four Quadrants. Each quadrant (Figure 6.9) corresponds to a general relative value and suggests a particular action. The fair value line sits at a different angle for different product categories. For example, in luxury goods, a small quality improvement may justify a large price differential. However, for commodities, consumers may be indifferent to quality differentiation, suggesting a more horizontal fair value line:

• Upper left: Worse Customer Value. Customer preferences shift in economic downturns, and higher-priced products often find themselves in this position. The recession of 2000–2003 contributed to the demise of the Concorde as wealthy travelers decided to cut back on its pricey transatlantic flights in favor of cheaper air travel.

• Lower left: Commodity Value. Goods in this quadrant are commodities with little differentiation between vendors. As a result, the products tend to sell on price. Many raw materials and agricultural products are sold as graded commodities. The price a seller of copper receives is typically the same as the price every other seller receives.

• Lower right: Better Customer Value. Products in this category are perceived as value leaders; costs are competitive, and the products possess the quality attributes that customers value most highly.

• Upper right: Unique Value. This quadrant is populated by upscale goods and services that offer Unique Value. Examples include high-margin products such as custom jewelry and entertainment experiences for which close substitutes are not available.

Figure 6.9. Customer Value Map Quadrants

An area chart of customer value, sometimes called a defection-acquisition index (Figure 6.10), is used to gain insight at a more granular level into factors influencing customer decision making. Each horizontal bar represents an attribute or feature, such as style, service, or image. Ratings to the left of the bar indicate that a company is perceived as performing worse than its competition, making it vulnerable to customer defection. Ratings to the right indicate it is perceived as better than the competition, suggesting opportunities for customer acquisition.

In addition to targeting product and service investments into areas that will have the greatest impact on ability to win and retain business, the area chart also is useful in identifying areas of potential investment or cost savings. For example, if it is expensive to improve feature 1 but relatively easy to improve feature 3, the firm could gain the most customers for the least dollars by focusing its investments on feature 3. This type of modeling is also sometimes referred to as performance impact analysis.

Example: Denim Jeans. Let's use a hypothetical example based on recent events. In the denim jeans market of recent years, Levi's has consistently lost market share, falling from $7 billion of revenue in 1996 to $4.2 billion in 2001. It lost business on the high end to more stylish and innovative competitors such as Calvin Klein and fashionable upstarts such as Diesel. Conversely, it lost low-end business to companies such as Arizona Brands. For much of this period, Levi's was heavily dependent on U.S.-based manufacturing and couldn't compete on price with offshore competitors. In such a situation, one can well imag-

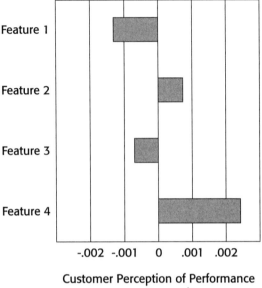

Figure 6.10. Area Chart of Customer Value

ine that existing Levi's customers might respond positively on a traditional customer satisfaction survey, but still purchase a different brand. A customer value analysis can provide insight into the situation.

The key components of quality in a pair of jeans might include materials, cut or styling, availability, peer group approval, and advertising. The hypothetical CVA analysis in Figure 6.11 shows that although Levi's is lower priced than many competitors, it is still on the wrong side of the fair value line. Merely cutting the price is unlikely to right the fair value equation. Instead, Levi's needs to change the product or the perception of the product, or some combination of the two. Deeper analysis of customer value on a feature-by-feature basis may reveal that Levi's invests too much on some attributes of the product and not enough in others.

Method. An in-depth CVA implementation requires marketing research skills and familiarity with statistical analysis techniques described in Gale's book. Many consulting companies specialize in Customer Value Analysis as a specific offering. For a general introduction to the method, we suggest trying the following exercise. If customers are not easily available for surveying, have your sales teams rate the products and those of the competition.

Figure 6.11. Customer Value Map for Levi's Jeans

• Step 1: Define. Develop a list of competitors and products to which you wish to be compared.

• Step 2: Research. Develop quick market-perceived price and quality profiles by asking customers what attributes they consider in making a purchase. Then ask customers to weight the attributes by distributing 100 points among them. Create the price and quality ratios (the method is described immediately after step 3).

• Step 3: Summarize the implications. Using the market-perceived quality ratios, identify and discuss the defection and acquisition implications of your analysis.

Creating a Quality Profile. There are three steps to creating a quality profile:

1. Determine the attributes of product quality that influence purchases.

2. Survey customers to determine how your offering is perceived relative to that of your competitors.

3. Weight the scores to derive a quality ratio.

The simplest way to determine the components or attributes of quality is to ask a group of survey subjects what they believe they are. Then ask them how you and your competitors rate on each attribute of quality. (It may also be useful with some products to gather information from secondary sources such as research firms to objectively define product performance. For example, if you were comparing motorcycles, you might factor in objective data about performance and handling or warranties.) Next, ask them to weight each quality attribute by dividing 100 points among all of the attributes based on their relative importance in the overall purchasing decision. A market-perceived quality ratio is then created by multiplying each competing product's score by the weight of the factor.

Table 6.1 contains a sample quality profile. Company A surveys handbag buyers to find out which features are most important to their purchasing decisions. It discovers that there are three key features: materials, style, and brand image. Company A also finds that although purchasers rate it above competitors in terms of materials and brand image, they rate it at the same level with competitors on style. This is important because style is the product attribute that customers rate as most influential to their buying decisions. The overall weighted ratio is 115.375 (a score of 100 indicates relative parity with competitors), indicating the company is well positioned versus competitors in terms of perceived quality.

Creating a Price Profile. Perceptions about the costs of purchasing and owning a product can be as important as actual price in influencing purchases. This is especially true in the case of expensive products such as cars, where the anticipated costs of maintenance, financing, and the gain or loss through resale value figure prominently. To capture this information, price profiles are calculated based on customers' perceptions of the cost of components that constitute the total price of a particular good (Table 6.2). Weighting these components produces a market-perceived price ratio, similar to the quality ratio.

Table 6.1. Customer-Perceived Quality Profile

Quality Attributes	Importance Weighting	Company A	Competitors	Market-Perceived Quality Ratios	
				Ratio Company A/ Competitors	Weight Times Ratio
Materials	25	8	6	1.33	33.25
Style	50	9	9	1	50
Brand image	25	9	7	1.285	32.125
					115.375

Table 6.2. Customer-Perceived Price Profile

Price Attributes	Importance Weighting	Company A	Competitors	Ratio Company A/ Competitors	Weight Times Ratio
				Market-Perceived Quality Ratios	
Purchase Price	100	8	8	1	1
					1

Once price and quality ratios are completed, the outcomes are plotted on a Customer Value Map that compares perceived quality and price points for a company and its competitors. Points on the map correspond to each company's relative performance in terms of overall quality and overall price. At any point on the fair value line, a company should neither lose nor gain market share.

Reference

Gale, B. T. *Managing Customer Value: Creating Quality and Service That Customers Can See.* New York: Free Press, 1994.

STRATEGIC CONTEXT FRAMEWORKS

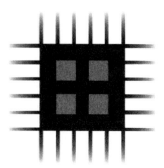

What external trends and factors need to be considered? How will they affect choice of strategy? What impact will they have on implementation?

Strategy is relative. Like moves on a chessboard, the wisdom of a decision depends entirely on the placement of the other pieces as well as what is in the minds of the other players. Understanding the external context is always important, but it is most useful in two critical phases of strategy development: as input before a strategy is formulated and as consideration during implementation.

There are many different approaches to context analysis. One can focus on the future, the market structure, competitors, trends, and other features of the competitive landscape. Often firms contract this task out to a consulting or research partner to ensure they receive an unbiased view. However, you can also learn a great deal simply by sampling different strategic context models. Each of the frameworks in this section offers a different way to profile the competitive landscape and is worthy of consideration. After reading a framework summary, invest five minutes to see what it tells you about your strategic needs.

⊞

Scenarios
Adapted from Global Business Network

Scenarios are not about predicting the future, rather they are about perceiving futures in the present.
—Peter Schwartz[13]

The future is unknowable and therefore risky.[14] Traditional planning methods work well enough when the time frame is the next quarter or perhaps one to two years into the future. But beyond that, projections based on current reality are dangerously unreliable. Reality rarely unfolds in a linear fashion, and unpredictable events—wars, revolutions, scientific breakthroughs, stock market booms, natural disasters, and others—spoil the best-laid plans.

Scenario planning aims to reduce longer-term risk by creating imagined futures based on an appreciation of key forces driving social, economic, political, and technological change. Companies, governments, and other large institutions create scenarios to make judgments about the future viability of current strategies and to explore areas of long-range concern that would never show up in a typical planning exercise. Many of the most useful scenario planning efforts adapt readily to the 2 × 2 form. We'll examine two of them in this section.

Scenario planning emerged as a serious business method at Shell in 1960s and 1970s where Pierre Wack led a group that developed scenario methods and anticipated the oil price shocks of 1973. Later, Wack, working closely with Willis Harman, Peter Schwartz, and other scenario developers at the Stanford Research Institute, refined the methods. Schwartz himself took over scenario planning at Shell, where he had the opportunity to improve the technique further, anticipating issues such as the fall of the Eastern bloc countries. In 1987, he and a group of visionary thinkers and writers, including Jay Ogilvy, Stewart Brand, Lawrence Wilkinson, and Napier Collins, formed the Global Business Network, a firm specializing in scenarios. Today, the technique is widely used in government, academia, and corporate planning exercises.

The goal of scenario planning is not to create the one right scenario. Rather, it is to create a set of viable options—robust scenarios that may hew closely to the future as it unfolds. Parts of each of the scenarios are likely to become manifest over time. To be useful, modeling needs to push limits so aspects of the scenarios are radical enough to encompass wild card events.

Choosing axes is the most critical step in scenario matrix development. Each axis must represent a dynamic force that is likely to be a defining feature of any future reality. Well-chosen axes create four plausible futures that help assess the risks of particular positions and strategies. Defining the axes frequently begins with asking questions that could have a great impact on the institution's future, such as, "What happens if economic growth slows down or increases greatly?" "Will social attitudes become more liberal or more conservative?" "Will raw material prices be stable or fluctuate greatly?"

We look at two examples here that illustrate the range and impact of the method: one on the future of automobiles and the other on libraries.

Example 1: The Future of Automobiles

This example was developed by the Global Business Network in the 1980s while working with an automotive company. The work influenced Detroit's thinking about the increasing appeal of sports utility vehicles (SUVs) and spurred development of other multifunction vehicles.

The Two Dimensions and Their Extremes. This matrix (Figure 6.12) explores two key dimensions: Fuel Prices and Societal Values:

Fuel Prices. Fuel Prices are a key driver of economic activity in almost all industries, particularly transportation. They range from low to high.

Societal Values. Societal Values provide a complex and nuanced measure of social conditions that might drive car-buying patterns. Traditional Values describe a conservative society in which religious, social, and personal values are relatively stable. In this vision, nuclear families would become stronger, gender roles would be well defined, and traditional practices in all fields would remain dominant. Inner-Directed Values describe a society that places greater emphasis on self-fulfillment and less fidelity to social norms. In this vision, people would be more likely to tackle anything new, from exotic religious practices and extreme sports to experimental social practices and nontraditional brands. Values, combined with fuel prices, spawned four plausible yet vastly different scenarios.

The Four Quadrants. Values, combined with Fuel Prices, spawned four plausible yet vastly different scenarios:

• Upper left: Engineer's Challenge. Under this scenario, North America falls prey to the kinds of continuing high fuel prices that were first experienced during oil embargos in the 1970s (returning again in 2003). The challenge for auto companies becomes how to build innovative, fuel-efficient cars while appealing

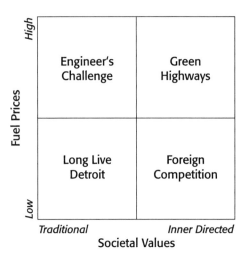

Figure 6.12. 1980s Automotive Scenario Matrix

to a customer base whose taste and values reflect an earlier period when car design was driven by style and power, not efficiency.

- Lower left: Long Live Detroit. In this scenario, the domestic car industry in North America would benefit from the combination of permanently low gas prices and a customer base that stuck close to traditional brands. Firms would build the types of cars (gas-guzzling muscle cars) that were popular in the 1960s. While muscle cars continue to come and go, this clearly was not the dominant scenario.
- Lower right: Foreign Competition. A lack of traditional brand loyalty, combined with low fuel prices, would enable Japanese and German firms to capture an ever-increasing share of the U.S. market. Sportier cars, light trucks, and vans would proliferate as tastes splintered and markets fragmented.
- Upper right: Green Highways. This is the eco-dream quadrant. High fuel prices make the return of inefficient automobiles unlikely. Inner-directed values drive customers to focus on the more sober aspects of car ownership, such as pollution control, fuel efficiency, and the effect of automobiles on the environment. As a result, automakers vie with one another to produce more eco-friendly vehicles.

At the time this set of scenarios was being developed, the two upper quadrants seemed quite likely. The world had become accustomed to higher oil prices in the 1970s, and there was little expectation that we would have sustained energy deflation throughout the 1990s, but that is what happened. Gas prices in real terms were far lower in the 1990s than in the two previous decades. At the same time, people in North America moved right on the horizontal axis, becoming more inner directed overall. The lower right quadrant turned out to model the automotive future more accurately than the other three. By the end of the century, light trucks, vans, and SUVs dominated car sales, and foreign firms had racked up impressive gains in market share.

Example 2: Librarian Scenario

The basic structure of the Librarian Scenario matrix was developed by Lawrence Wilkinson of the Global Business Network.[15] It was adapted by Tom Wilson of the University of Sheffield to explore the future of library services and its impact on the job prospects of librarians.[16]

The Two Dimensions and Their Extremes. The matrix explores two key dimensions: Social Contract and Locus of Concern (Figure 6.13):

Social Contract. The degree to which society is likely to share common values (Coherence) or to fragment into conflict among interest groups (Fragmentation) defines the extremes of the Social Contract. In fragmented

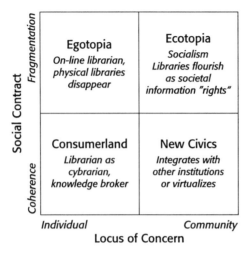

Figure 6.13. Librarian Scenario Matrix

societies, central authorities exercise control over the behavior of individuals. In Coherence scenarios, shared values makes such control unnecessary.

Locus of Concern. The Locus of Concern represents the long-standing struggle between the Individual and Community. It asks, "Will the key locus of concern for citizens be the well-being of the community or themselves?"

The Four Quadrants. The four quadrants illustrate the possibilities:

• Upper left: Egotopia. In Egotopia, Community is disintegrating. Individuals are connected by the Internet and do much of their work there. Since Individuals have less stake in the community, social infrastructures decline. Under such a scenario, physical libraries are likely to disappear, replaced by on-line librarians who provide open market services electronically.

• Lower left: Consumerland. A strong social contract supports the need for shared physical and on-line public libraries. But the librarian focuses on serving individuals, not groups. In this vision, the librarian is a "cybrarian," brokering knowledge to the members of society.

• Lower right: New Civics. The New Civics envisions a strong Social Contract combined with strong Communities. In this future, the library remains an important community component that might integrate with other institutions in order to perform its mission better.

- Upper right: Ecotopia. In Ecotopia, libraries are a right, not a luxury. This is envisioned as a more socially responsible future in which communitarian values prevail. Although social cohesion is low, support for institutions of business and government remains high. Corporations focus more on meeting social goals, and citizens exercise power to clean the environment and fund needed services.

Under all four scenarios, physical libraries were considered likely to decline and on-line services would grow. Also, there would be a demand for librarian services under all four scenarios. In some, such as New Civics and Ecotopia, this appears to be greater due to the commitment to maintaining physical libraries, but overall, the scenarios demonstrated a continuing demand for fee-based and public library services.

Method. Scenario planning can be an intensive process, involving many people and lasting several months. In his book *The Long View,* Peter Schwartz provides an overview of the scenario planning process that is adapted here:[17]

- Step 1: Focus. Identify the focal issue of your decision. Scenario development works better by looking inside out, examining the kinds of major decisions you'll be grappling with this year and in the future. Identify some key decisions that have to be made and will have big repercussions on the firm, such as, "Should we build the new facility?" or "Is it wise for us to enter the European market?"
- Step 2: Examine key environmental forces. What are the local factors—such as information about suppliers, customers, and competitors—that influence the success or failure of decisions chosen in step 1? What will be the key determinant of success for the decision in step 1?
- Step 3: Identify driving forces. Examine the economic, social, political, demographic, and technical driving forces that are external to the firm. These range from high certainty (demographics) to low certainty (political upheavals) forces. Typically, additional research is required to support your conclusions at this step.
- Step 4: Prioritize issues. Take your macro (step 3) and micro (step 2) lists, and rank them by importance and uncertainty. If working in groups, suggest giving each person three votes, and use the votes to establish priorities.
- Step 5: Build the scenario logic. The ranked factors provide the raw material for creating the axes of your 2 × 2 matrix. Work as a team on the meaning of the two axes, and pay special attention to factors that may be combined or integrated. Language is critical at this stage. Global Business network consultant Nicole Boyer says, "The planning team must own the language describing the axes and each quadrant. The story has to feel right for it to make an impact on an organization."

- Step 6: Flesh out the scenarios. Describe in some detail (one to four pages) what the world would look like if any of the four scenarios came to pass. What would be the impact on the use of your product or services, commodity prices, shopping habits, government policies, or other areas of life that would affect your business? Look again at the key drivers in steps 1 and 2, and visualize how they might play out under each scenario.

- Step 7: Consider strategic implications. Scenarios enable you to test strategies for risk. Boyer asks, "Are your strategies robust in all four quadrants? Do you die? Do you thrive? You may have strategies that are moderately risky in all scenarios, or you may have a big bet that is very risky in most of the scenarios. If all the scenarios are equally likely, would you bet your company on only one of them?"

- Step 8: Create measures and signposts. Once a solid set of scenarios is developed, ask, "What are the key measures that tell us if the future is unfolding according to one of the scenarios?" Look for simple indicators that might provide useful information. For example, if one of your scenarios is increasing community fragmentation, how would you measure that? Household formation? Parent-Teacher Association attendance? Divorce rates? These indicators provide an early warning system for future strategic choices.

References

Ringland, G. *Scenarios in Business.* New York: Wiley, 2002.

Schwartz, P. *The Art of the Long View.* New York: Doubleday, 1992.

van der Heijden, K., and others. *The Sixth Sense: Accelerating Organizational Learning with Scenarios.* New York: Wiley, 2002.

Wilkinson, L. "The Future of the Future." *Wired* (special edition), 1995, pp. 77–81. [http://www.wired.com/wired/scenarios/build.html].

Wilson, T. "The Role of the Librarian in the Twenty-First Century." Keynote address for the Library Association Northern Branch Conference, Longhirst, Northumberland, Nov. 17, 1995. [http://www.shef.ac.uk/~is/wilson/publications/21stcent.html].

⊞

Gartner Magic Quadrant
Gartner Group

Leadership is the capacity to translate vision into reality.
—Warren Bennis[18]

Major information technology buying decisions are among the most expensive and fateful that executives make. They must choose suppliers that understand their business, stand behind the product, and can provide needed services. The investments are typically long term, so they must choose a vendor that will be around in the future—one with the vision and foresight to survive in the cut-throat technology marketplace.

Gartner Inc., founded in 1979 in Stamford, Connecticut, is the leading research firm providing insight and advice to corporations on technology markets and products. Gartner associates serve as independent counsel on strategic business issues and often are called before the U.S. Congress to discuss the technology issues driving the economy.

The Gartner Magic Quadrant (Figure 6.14) describes the relative positioning and future prospects of firms in technology hardware, software, and services. Producers take Gartner's ratings seriously and devote significant marketing resources to building the case that they are material for the upper right—the Leaders quadrant.

The Two Dimensions and Their Extremes. The Magic Quadrant measures firms' offerings by contrasting two business values: Ability to Execute and Completeness of Vision. Long-term success in information technology requires both. Completeness of Vision is most important when a product category is new and customer needs are evolving rapidly. Ability to Execute becomes more important over the longer term as companies require support and customized solutions to meet specific needs.

Ability to Execute. Ability to Execute reflects the discipline and resources—human, financial, intellectual—needed to get the job done. In addition to

Figure 6.14. Gartner Magic Quadrant

core competencies, firms rated high on Execution display financial strength and the right strategic alliances along the value chain.

Completeness of Vision. Completeness of Vision focuses on creativity and inventiveness. It measures a firm's ability to lead and influence the direction of technology development and implementation practices in their market.

The Four Quadrants. Combinations of the two dimensions define four possible competitive positions:

- Upper left: Challengers. These companies execute well and often dominate large segments of the market. However, they are not fully in step with emerging market directions or capable of setting the industry agenda.
- Lower left: Niche Players. These are often smaller competitors with credible technology or firms focused on smaller market segments. Firms in this quadrant are judged not to excel at either innovation or performance.
- Lower right: Visionaries. Visionaries understand where the market is going but do not have all the capabilities necessary to execute the vision. Companies in this quadrant are notable for their breakthrough ideas but are challenged to develop the broad competencies needed to support and sustain customers.
- Upper right: Leaders. Leaders execute well today and are positioned for the future. These are companies with excellent customer service, dynamic solutions, and strong value delivery. Gartner recognizes firms that can adhere to a well-articulated strategic plan, align their vision with industry trends, and are flexible in reacting to market forces.

Example: Supply Chain Software. The matrix is a regular feature of the Gartner Group's research reports on software and hardware technology. Each Magic report includes market analysis, vendor inclusion criteria, and comments from Gartner's army of analysts. Page 124 contains two examples of what a completed matrix looks like. (While names have been deleted, each dot represents a real company evaluation.) The quadrant in Figure 6.15 compares supply chain management (SCM) software vendors. SCM software is typically bought in a suite that may include applications for demand planning, manufacturing planning and scheduling, distribution transportation planning, and other processes. A firm needs to meet stiff criteria, including a global presence and broad product offering, to be considered for inclusion in the Magic Quadrant. As a result, new entrants are often excluded. In this example, only two firms are ranked above the midpoint on the Ability to Execute dimension. Since Gartner maps are issued frequently, each one is a current snapshot, and it is not uncommon for companies to change their position on the map over time.

In new markets, few products or firms meet all the criteria for leadership. The Portal Software example (Figure 6.16) is a map of the emerging company

Figure 6.15. Magic Quadrant for Supply Chain Software

Figure 6.16. Magic Quadrant for Portal Software

portal software industry in 2000. At that time, the market was still quite small, and few products or companies had proved they could adequately meet customer needs or implement and service their products. Gartner rightly identified that no companies ranked high on Ability to Execute.

Context. The Gartner Magic Quadrant offers a relatively simple and powerful way to model industry competitors. It is well suited to corporate strategic planning exercises in any field where technology changes increase the risks of vendor selection.

Method. Follow these steps to conduct a Magic Quadrant analysis:

- Step 1: Define the problem. In a sentence, articulate the business issue you intend to confront.
- Step 2: Create a matrix. Focus the dimensions of the axes with a list of key issues relating to the specific problem at hand. For Completeness of Vision, consider the number of new products, research and development, technology, and standards. For Ability to Execute, consider financial viability, track record, management quality, investor relations, impact of government legislation, and production systems. Then define your own list of additional key issues for each axis.
- Step 3: Assess. Place all relevant industry players on the matrix according to your first instinct. Then with an associate, debate and review each company until you are satisfied that the placement is fair and accurate. The more people who validate the matrix, the more reliable it will be for decision making.
- Step 4: Follow up. Update the matrix following major announcements by players and new entrants. Over time, you will gain a better understanding of industry trends and organizational strategies.

Reference

The Gartner Group [http://www.gartner.com].

⊞

Portfolio Analysis
Nancy Brown

Unfortunately, not all business is good business.
—Nancy Brown[19]

Not all customer accounts are worth pursuing or maintaining. Companies understandably have a difficult time rejecting business, but this is sometimes precisely what they should do. This applies to existing accounts as well as those in the sales pipeline. The Portfolio Analysis matrix provides a useful structure and set of criteria for assessing the relative value of customers (Figure 6.17).

The Two Dimensions and Their Extremes. The Portfolio Analysis matrix explores two key dimensions: Business Quality and Mutual Value:

Business Quality. Business Quality is considered Excellent if the relationship is profitable and growing and the client is satisfied. It is Poor if engagements are unprofitable, missing milestones, draining resources, or the client is dissatisfied.

Mutual Value. Mutual Value is a measure of the interdependence between service provider and client. Mutual Value is Symbiotic when the client and service provider are able to produce new, positive results that they could not have achieved separately. For example, Motorola recently outsourced its human resource department to Affiliated Computer Services (ACS). Gaining critical mass and a marquee client enabled ACS to bring its business process outsourcing (BPO) offering to market faster and to add functionality, increasing its competitiveness. Motorola gained access to best-in-class human resource and process management practices from ACS and was able to remain focused on its core competencies. It also retained a royalty on other BPO engagements that ACS sells. Beneficial Mutual Value to the service provider could also mean expanding into new vertical industries, establishing recurring revenue streams and creating an offering that can be replicated. Mutual Value is considered to be Nonexistent when service is rendered primarily as a low-cost alternative.

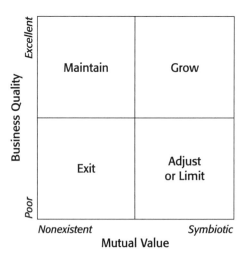

Figure 6.17. Portfolio Analysis Matrix

The Four Quadrants. Careful consideration of Business Quality and Mutual Value produces four strategic options:

- Upper left: Maintain. Work of this nature is worth doing for the money but contributes little to long-term strategic development. Cash cows tend to be in this quadrant. Some of these businesses will eventually need to be cannibalized; however, in the interim, they help fund new growth initiatives.
- Lower left: Exit. This type of client relationship is unsupportable and should be renegotiated or stopped as soon as legally and morally possible.
- Lower right: Adjust or Limit. These assignments are strategically well aligned, but they are not profitable and may not be generating additional work. An example is the development of emerging technologies where investment is required to be competitive. These engagements need to be closely monitored. Some activities in this category can be promoted and developed into prime work, while others will need to be cut.
- Upper right: Grow. This is the best quadrant for business to fall into. It is profitable, growing, and strategically well matched, representing a virtuous cycle of learning, growth, and profitability. Ideally, relationships started in the other boxes can be directed here.

Method. Use the Portfolio Analysis matrix to evaluate and optimize client relationships:

- Step 1: Diagnose. Assess all current and prospective customers, applying the two dimensions of the Portfolio Analysis matrix. Place each customer in the appropriate quadrant of the matrix. Use large and small circles to denote the size of client engagements. Color coding the circles or markers can also be used to quickly identify specific types of engagements.
- Step 2: Plan. Create plans for each customer. Some merit additional effort and attention, while other relationships may need to be terminated.
- Step 3: Execute. Apply plans and monitor for changes in status.

⊞

Problems and Solutions
Watts Wacker and Jim Taylor

Wait for the future to happen, and you will have no future.
—Watts Wacker[20]

Watts Wacker is perfectly at home in the future. As a former futurist at SRI and now with his own firm, First Matter, he advises top corporations on how to nurture long-range planning capabilities. In *The Visionary Handbook,* he coaches firms to set up an internal futures council to continually assess issues related to their future development. The council creates a future vision for the company and monitors evolving sets of problems and solutions that may have significant impact on the company in the future.

The Problems and Solutions matrix (Figure 6.18) asks, "How do we apply company resources to the problems and solutions in our future vision?"

The Two Dimensions and Their Extremes. The Problem and Solution matrix explores two key dimensions: Problems and Solutions:

The Problem. Problems range from today's known problems to emerging issues that a future vision reveals. For example, demographic changes can signal future problems that will require attention.

The Solution. Solutions may be known and obvious today or unknown and yet to be discovered. New technologies (such as wireless) or new paradigms (such as mass customization) frequently start out as solutions to unknown problems.

The Four Quadrants. Different action is needed depending on whether Problems and Solutions are known. The four basic options are described as follows:

• Upper left: Listen. If the futures council is paying attention, it will identify ideas that solve problems that are not yet evident. These solutions challenge the firm to make sense of weak signals from the marketplace and recognize possible

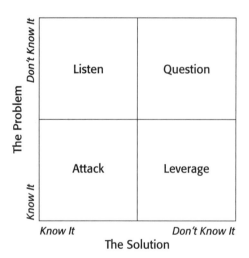

Figure 6.18. Problem and Solution Matrix

future trends. Seek input from thought leaders and mentors whose perceptive contributions can help you re-vision the present and future.

• Lower left: Attack. Sometimes the situation is clear and compelling. You know what's wrong and what you need to do, so take action.

• Lower right: Leverage. The problem is known, but you don't have a solution. In this case, leveraging the knowledge and efforts of partners and friends is suggested to lead more quickly to a solution.

• Upper right: Question. Wacker calls this the fool's box, referring to medieval fools or jesters. Organizations must actively nurture renegades who question and present bold ideas if they are to get beyond the limits of today's problems and solutions. In this manner, one remains open to transcendent solutions to tomorrow's challenges.

Method. The method has three steps:

• Step 1: Form. Establish a futures council within the firm composed of people at different levels.

• Step 2: Assign. Charge the futures council with creating a vision of the future. Include in the vision a list of questions (problems) and answers (solutions) that could have an impact on reaching the company's future vision.

• Step 3: Follow up. On a continuing basis, test the futures council's list of problems and solutions against the matrix, and take appropriate action.

Reference

Wacker, W., Taylor, J., and Means, H. *The Visionary Handbook*. New York: Harper-Collins, 2000.

⊞

Dialectical SWOT Analysis:
Strengths, Weaknesses, Opportunities, and Threats
Inspired by the East Lancashire Training and Enterprise Council

Opportunities are like buses. There is always another one coming.
—Richard Branson[21]

SWOT is the acronym for strengths, weaknesses, opportunities, and threats. In a traditional SWOT analysis, these four categories are investigated independently and fed into the planning process. In dialectical SWOT, we treat Strengths and Weaknesses as internal factors and Opportunities and Threats as external. Traditional SWOT analysis generates a powerful and reasonably comprehensive strategic snapshot. The unique value in this approach comes from juxtaposing information from these two categories, as shown in Figure 6.19. Each quadrant of the matrix represents a unique combination of Internal and External conditions, and each produces a specific recommendation.

The Two Dimensions and Their Extremes. The SWOT matrix explores two key dimensions: External Environment and Internal Environment:

External Environment. Organizational success depends on sensing and responding to shifting conditions in the business environment. At the most basic level, these represent Opportunities and Threats.

Internal Environment. The ability to compete effectively depends on the resources and knowledge available to the organization. We draw on our Strengths and guard against possible exposure created by our Weaknesses.

The Four Quadrants. Dialectical SWOT defines four zones of risk and reward, each demanding a different response. The key to success often lies in being proactive:

• Upper left: Confront. Threat is matched with organizational strength. Businesses face these conditions all the time—new competitors, legislative changes, commoditization of a core offering, and many others. Mobilize to limit and control the looming danger.
• Lower left: Exploit. Opportunity is matched with strength. This is a business's growing edge, where it can capitalize on areas of strategic advantage.

Figure 6.19. SWOT Matrix

The one caution here is to be careful not to ignore other demands. Vital and scarce corporate resources are too easily drawn to exciting and rewarding growth-oriented projects, which can deplete the organization's ability to deal effectively with more mundane and defensive challenges.

• Lower right: Search. Opportunity is matched with weakness. This quadrant represents a conundrum. Opportunities exist that the organization can recognize but is not equipped to tackle. The gap may be financial, scale, location, or any of a number of other factors. Creative options are needed. If you don't act on the opportunity, perhaps a competitor will, with potentially disastrous consequences.

• Upper right: Avoid or Prepare. Threat is matched with Weakness. Some threats are avoidable, and others are not. Confronting competitive Threats with Weakness is not only dangerous but also resource draining. When possible, it is best to avoid such situations. Consider the company about to enter a price war with a much larger and better-financed adversary. Sometimes, however, the threat cannot be sidestepped and must be addressed, whatever the cost.

Method. Follow these steps to conduct a dialectical SWOT analysis:

• Step 1: Generate lists of strengths, weaknesses, opportunities, and threats. Be sure the people involved in completing this task have the necessary knowledge and independence to report in an honest (not fearful or protective) way.

• Step 2: Assess the interactive effect of the internal (Strengths and Weaknesses) and external (Opportunities and Threats) observations. Place the conclusions onto the dialectical SWOT matrix.

Reference

East Lancashire Training and Enterprise Council. [http://www.nvq5.com/].

⊞

Market Tipping
Adapted from Carl Shapiro and Hal Varian

Don't plan to play the high[er] stakes, winner-take-all battle to become the standard unless you can be aggressive in timing, in pricing, and in exploiting relationships with complementary products.
—Carl Shapiro and Hal Varian[22]

It is not unusual for technology markets to be dominated by a single technology standard, and sometimes by a single large firm. The Market Tipping matrix (Figure 6.20), introduced by Carl Shapiro and Hal R. Varian in *Information*

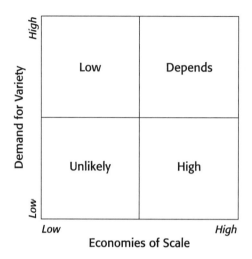

Figure 6.20. Market Tipping Matrix

Rules, examines whether a developing technology market will tip to a single dominant player. It is risky to compete in "tippy" markets, since losers can end up with zero market share.

The Two Dimensions and Their Extremes. The Market Tipping matrix explores two key dimensions: Demand for Variety and Economies of Scale:

Demand for Variety. Demand for Variety ranges from Low, in which one standard prevails (such as the QWERTY keyboard), to High, in which the market supports competing standards (as in data storage technologies). Variety should not be confused with implementing a standard design in a broad fashion. DVD players are implemented in different styles, but to users, compatibility with the existing interfaces and formats is more important than style. When customer demand for variety is low, the dominant player can be dislodged only by vastly superior technology or favorable economics, such as low or no switching costs.

Economies of Scale. Economies of Scale refer to cost advantage as a result of size or volume. They can be demand side or supply side in nature and range from Low to High.

The Four Quadrants. The matrix describes four degrees of likelihood that a market will "tip" to a single supplier:

• Upper left: Low. Products requiring highly specialized electronics or software, from one-of-a-kind medical devices to Saturn rockets, fall into this category. Customer requirements are so specialized that standardized manufacturing is impossible.

• Lower left: Unlikely. Low Demand for Variety and Low Economies of Scale are usually found together when products are introduced and demand has not risen to the point where it triggers positive feedback or provides manufacturing economies of scale. For example, Apple's Newton satisfied a small group of customers but never created a mass market.

• Lower right: High. This is what Shapiro and Varian refer to as a classic "tippy" market. Users want to choose a product that will win in the marketplace. Once they make their collective decision, powerful network effects set in. The CD format, introduced by Sony and Phillips in 1982, took seven years to overcome vinyl and audiocassettes in the market. Once its dominance was established, it moved into other devices. Now, computers, audio players, DVD players, and even some video cameras can read CDs.

• Upper right: Depends. Many technology markets start out in this quadrant, with lots of competing products and firms. But demand for variety diminishes as market needs coalesce and mature. Currently, users of Linux software can choose from a half-dozen popular varieties of the Linux operating system. If all these versions continue to work well together, they may continue to divide the market.

Method. You need to make qualitative judgments about variety and scale to determine the likelihood that a market will tip to a dominant vendor or standard:

• Step 1: Assess demand. Determine customer demand for variety.

• Step 2: Assess tippiness. Determine economies of scale. Will high volumes lead to lower costs in sourcing, manufacturing, transportation, marketing, distribution, and retailing? If these are combined with network effects on the demand side, you are dealing with a market likely to tip.

• Step 3: Determine impact. Describe the impact of this market's tippiness on your proposed offering or plan.

Reference

Shapiro, C., and Varian, H. R. *Information Rules: A Strategic Guide to the Networked Economy.* Boston: Harvard Business School Press, 1999.

STRATEGIC OPTIONS FRAMEWORKS

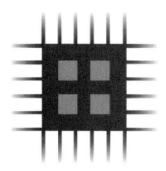

What are our main strategic options? How do we differentiate our offerings? How do we tailor our offerings for different markets?

The core of strategy is design of the value proposition and how it is competitively positioned and delivered. Debate about these points in organizations can be extensive and heated, with many people convinced that they are right and others are not. Ultimately, direction must be set, and unanimity of support and understanding for the strategy can spell the difference between winning execution and lackluster performance.

Strategic Options frameworks offer criteria for generating and prioritizing ideas. Paradoxically, limiting the field of focus spurs the imagination and improves the richness of output. More than the other matrices in this book, these frameworks support collaborative efforts where many views are aired in a noncompetitive atmosphere, and the best ideas can be selected and built on by interdependent members of teams and larger communities.

⊞

Corporate Strategy
H. Igor Ansoff

> Of course much that is new and different has been added, but the rock on which everything has been built was provided by Igor Ansoff.
> —David Hussey[23]

Ansoff's 1965 classic, *Corporate Strategy,* contains one of business's most important and enduring strategic formulations. Before becoming a distinguished academic, writer, and consultant in the mid-1960s, Ansoff progressed through a series of planning positions at the Rand Corporation and Lockheed, ending this phase of his career as vice president and general manager of the Industrial Technology Division at Lockheed Electronics. Experience with diversification planning helped him formulate key issues and tensions that firms face in choosing a growth strategy. The operating problem is akin to determining the best way to milk a cow. The strategic challenge is of a different order: "But if our basic interest is not the cow but in the most milk we can get for our investment, we must make sure that we have the best cow money can buy."[24] In strategic terms, this translates into product-market combinations that are most advantageous to the firm. The Product-Market matrix (sometimes called the Corporate Strategy matrix) defines the options for achieving this (Figure 6.21).

The Two Dimensions and Their Extremes. The Product-Market matrix explores two key dimensions: Product and Market:

Product. Businesses are built around products and services that define their value offering. Most offerings are limited in at least two ways: time, in that their relevance diminishes and redesign or renewal is usually required, and transferability, in that they tend to work best under certain market conditions. Ansoff noted that modifying the core offering is a key strategic choice.

Market. Generally applied as Market options, this dimension distinguishes between customer markets that are well established and known to the firm versus all the rest that are not.

Figure 6.21. Product-Market Matrix

The Four Quadrants. In Ansoff's terms, each of the four possible options defines a core strategic response to a different set of internal and external conditions. Careful assessment leads to better understanding and decision making:

- Upper left: Product Development. Marketers understand the enormous value of a positive customer relationship and the goodwill and trust that go with it. This relationship capital allows a company to make new product offers more effectively and inexpensively to existing customers than to new ones. The advantages of this must be weighed against the possible damage resulting from negative spillover from the new to the existing product experience should it not be entirely satisfactory. When Stihl, the maker of the world's top chain saws began to sell augurs, hedge trimmers, and complementary items such as cut-retardant leg chaps, it was practicing Product Development. Heineken has achieved great success by introducing over eighty brands around the world.
- Lower left: Market Penetration. This is the de facto strategy: change nothing and sell more of the same to existing customers. When a business does not consciously select a growth or diversification strategy, it is doing this. When Stihl sells to the forestry industry, it is in this quadrant, as is Heineken when it supplies beer to European drinkers. This is the preferred strategy when a company's product is performing well and there is room to increase market share.
- Lower right: Market Development. A well-developed product can be introduced into new markets to extend its value. This is ideal when little modification is required and room for growth in the original market is restricted. Products as diverse as food, pharmaceuticals, and automobiles fit this category. When Stihl reached out to recreational users and North American buyers, it was employing a Market Development strategy, as was Heineken when it began exporting its beer outside Europe, with great success.
- Upper right: Diversification. Diversification represents a near total strategic overhaul, simultaneously trading in both Product and Market. It is the most challenging, costly, and risky of the options. New skills and relationships need to be developed. Companies choose this strategy in conjunction with one or more of the others or when they have recognized a crisis. Ideally, there is a gradual migratory path leading from the known to the unknown. It would be easier for Stihl to evolve into a retail hardware supplier, say, than a candy manufacturer or entertainment company. The recent misfortunes of Seagram's Distillers' and Vivendi's (historically a water and utility company) painful transformation into a communications, media, and entertainment company are a reminder of the riskiness of Diversification.

Example: Green Mountain Coffee Roasters. Green Mountain Coffee Roasters (GMCR) began as a house brand at a small café in Waitsfield, Vermont, in 1981.

Brewed from high-quality beans roasted on the premises, the coffee quickly became a favorite of locals and vacationers. Before long, it had expanded far beyond the café walls to become one of the top specialty coffee companies in America, generating annual revenues of $97 million with a growth rate close to 20 percent.[25]

It is hard to think of a more generic item than coffee, the second most highly traded commodity in the world after oil. The $55 billion industry in the United States is dominated by four global companies (Nestlé, Procter & Gamble, Sara Lee, and Kraft) that buy almost 50 percent of the world's coffee. The specialty category of excellent brewed coffee took shape in the 1970s, with several brands and retail chains gaining great popularity. Starbucks has emerged as the category gorilla, growing from a single outlet in 1971 to almost six thousand locations worldwide today.

Green Mountain Coffee Roasters has followed a different path to success, staying clear of the fiercely contested retail outlet market space, which coincidentally would not have fit the company philosophy of matching quality product and experience with ecological and ethical practices.

In Ansoff's terms, GMCR started life as most start-ups do, with an attractive value proposition that the originators were uniquely qualified to deliver (Figure 6.22). Their first expansion efforts took the form of Market Penetration. The popular coffee almost sold itself: visitors bought bags to take home with them and eventually began to order by mail. GMRC sold more of the core

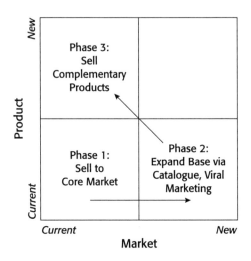

Figure 6.22. Green Mountain Coffee Roasters Strategy

product to existing customers to max out its return on the original business platform.

Success with the core business led to a second strategic phase, Market Development. The demand for high-quality, ethically produced coffee was expanding, and this demographic segment of the population was not opposed to paying a premium to attain what they wanted. With excellent positioning and word-of-mouth viral marketing in their favor, they expanded the customer base through mail order sales, eventually producing an on-line and paper catalogue.

The third strategic phase, Product Development, grew in conjunction with catalogue-based sales, as customers welcomed a range of complementary item offers, from cups to roasters.

Context. The Product-Market matrix is one of the most intuitive and flexible strategic frameworks, applied by planners and decision makers in organizations of all sorts and sizes. The ideal time to use the framework is at the start of the planning cycle or to help in making tough decisions about business focus.

Method. The Product-Market matrix presents a structured approach to investigate and prioritize four basic strategic options for expanding a business. The method typically starts with what is and ends with what is imaginable. Risk increases as strategy moves further from the current situation:

- Step 1: Diagnose. Define the product-service focus for analysis. A company with multiple offerings is advised to consider each separately at first.
- Step 2: Envision. Consider each of the four strategic options, beginning in the lower left quadrant. The prime questions are, "Should the offering stay the same or should it change?" and "Should we focus on current customers or new ones?"
- Step 3: Decide. Assess the attractiveness of each of the four strategic options. In most cases, pursue the easiest path as the top priority.
- Step 4: Design. Build a clear action plan to implement the chosen strategy.

References

Ansoff, I. *Corporate Strategy.* New York: McGraw-Hill, 1965.

Hussey, D., and Ansoff, I. "Continuing Contribution to Strategic Management." *Strategic Change, 8*(7), 375–392.

⊞

Generic Strategy
Adapted from the work of Michael Porter

Competitive advantage grows fundamentally out of the value a firm is able to
create for its buyers.
—Michael Porter[26]

In his epic 1980 book, *Competitive Strategy,* Michael Porter lays out one of the
most complete and coherent foundations in the field of strategy. Each industry
is shaped by a set of competitive forces that determine its nature and profitability in structured and predictable ways. Competition within industries is
natural and inevitable. Firms gain a competitive advantage by creating value for
buyers. Strategy should be intentional, not accidental or optional. Two central
issues shape the work of the business strategist: the attractiveness of the industry and the relative positioning of a firm within an industry.

An industry's attractiveness is largely determined by the interplay between
a set of core competitive factors. Applying what is now known as Porter's Five
Forces model, strategists are directed to a careful consideration of Entry Barriers, Buyer Power, Supplier Power, Threat of Subsitutes, and Rivals to understand
the structural makeup of an industry. For example, concentrated Buyer or Supplier Power limits the range of freedom and negotiating room, while low Barriers to Entry will keep incumbent competitors more vigilant and price sensitive
than ever before. Not all industries are equally attractive, and Porter offers a
rich analytic approach to determining what is going on and where to concentrate investment efforts.

Profitability and long-term sustainability depend on a firm's positioning
within an industry. Even some relatively unprofitable industries, like computers and cable television, reap sizable rewards for certain of the value chain participants. In Porter's modeling of Generic Strategy options (Figure 6.23), he
maintains that firms may possess a myriad of interesting and unique strengths
and weaknesses. However, their competitve advantage is determined by one of
two things: low cost or differentiation. Strengths are relevant to the extent that
they enable or block these two strategies. The context in which this advantage
is pursued can be either broad or focused, creating an additional set of strategic approaches. Companies are advised to avoid straddling more than one
option, since dilution limits their ability to execute their strategy and makes
them vulnerable to others with greater focus and discipline.

Porter has continued to develop his ideas on competition and strategy, first
looking at their application to governments in the *Competitive Advantage of*

Figure 6.23. Generic Strategy Matrix

Nations, and more recently the competitive importance of geographically based clusters like Silicon Valley for computing, Grand Rapids, Michigan, for furniture, and northern Italy for weaving.

The Two Dimensions and Their Extremes. The Generic Strategy matrix explores two key dimensions: Competitive Advantage and Competitive Scope:

Competitive Advantage. Firms must choose between Lower Cost and Differentiation. These are inherently in contradiction to one another, since Differentiation generally requires a higher level of investment.

Competitive Scope. Firms can compete Broadly across an industry, or they can Focus Narrowly on one or several segments.

The Four Quadrants. Porter writes, " 'Being all things to all people' is a recipe for strategic mediocrity and below average performance, because it often means that a firm has no competitive advantage at all."[27]

Firms often gain advantage by adopting one of the generic strategic approaches, and then relinquish it when they attempt to pursue one of the other strategies in tandem. While it may be tempting at times to do this (Porter refers to this as "getting stuck in the middle"), it is rarely advisable or sustainable. Each of the four options in the matrix is a unique response to industry structure and the strengths a company can call on:

• Upper left: Cost Leadership. This is the clearest of the generic strategies. Cost Leadership involves achieving the lowest costs in an industry while maintaining an acceptable level of quality. Typically, only one competitor can win with this strategy. Low costs are attainable in a variety of ways, drawing on the industry structure and the company's strengths. Some of the cost-limiting sources are preferential access to raw materials, better production methods, economies of scale, and more efficient distribution channels. A common low-cost strategy is to offer the no-frills version while ensuring that the most highly weighted aspects of customer value are preserved. It is important to maintain what Porter calls parity in the offer to prevent erosion of customer goodwill due to an unacceptable drop in quality as compared with available alternatives.

- Lower left: Cost Focus. In the Cost Focus strategy, a firm takes advantage of the unique needs of a segment of an industry that is difficult or uneconomical for the Broad Cost supplier to service adequately. Sometimes Broad Cost competitors must overperform to meet the special needs of some segments, where a less costly solution or product would suffice. This occurs in the world of high-tech equipment when manufacturers sell higher-grade devices and components set to a lower performance level. Or there may be custom requirements that lend themselves better to smaller, more tailored low-cost offerings. A group with special dietary needs may be better served by a company that can focus exclusively on them than by generic suppliers. Porter uses the example of a small paper mill's superior ability to execute cost-effective, low-volume runs of high-quality specialty paper.

- Lower right: Differentiation Focus. The Differentiation Focus strategy applies the principle of added value within a small segment of a market rather than across the entire market. Customer needs are sometimes met in an uneven way, with some groups left to adapt a good deal of the offering to meet their requirements. Rural markets may require extra service; an in-depth understanding of a special technology may be worth extra money to customers seeking reliability and risk reduction.

- Upper right: Differentiation. In differentiating, a firm sets out to deliver some unique form of value that customers recognize and appreciate. A differentiation strategy depends on developing or exploiting talents and resources that set the company's offer apart in a way that is both meaningful and difficult to replicate. The reward for successfully differentiating is customer loyalty and the right to charge a premium price. Examples of differentiated offerings are plentiful, from fine wines to high-tech products from Apple and RIM. When you think quality and hard to replace, you have the basis for differentiation.

There are numerous ways firms go about differentiating themselves. They can add features and functionality to a product, improve process effectiveness to the point that it is truly significant, or dramatically enhance service quality, creating a noticeably better experience than their competitors. Unlike Low Cost, a number of competitors can pursue Differentiation strategies simultaneously, each exploiting a different valued attribute of the offering.

Example: Automotive Industry. By the turn of the twentieth century, an assortment of electric-, steam-, and gasoline-powered vehicles were being produced by a large number of mostly small craft operations.[28] Each automobile took several days to build, and product performance was spotty. Use of cars was reserved for the wealthy, who drove primarily for luxury and sport. The industrial revolution had provided the means for manufacturing key automotive ingredients like metal and rubber. It was the application of assembly line thinking to building the car itself that enabled wider access by lowering prices and increasing volume and quality control capabilities.

The Generic Strategy view is that over time, the strongest strategy will win. Companies need to draw on their strengths to respond competitively to the industry context, which is defined by Porter's five forces. The history of the automotive industry is instructive, as illustrated by the strategic approaches of a number of well-known companies (Figure 6.24).

In 1913, the Ford Motor Company introduced the first moving assembly line in the automobile industry and quickly became the largest car company in the world. Buyers wanted a reliable low-cost option and gladly traded uniqueness for the new standard. For almost a decade, Ford dominated the market, setting the pace for suppliers and customers, without any real direct competitors in sight.

In the 1920s, General Motors (GM) read the market forces right, offering attractive features at premium prices to an increasingly affluent public that was becoming more familiar and trusting of automotive technology. Rallying to GM chairman Alfred Sloan's famous *differentiation* dictum, "A car for every purse and purpose," GM went on to become the number one car company.

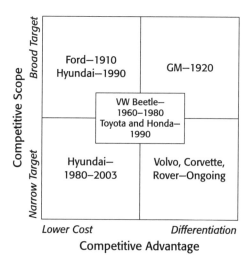

Figure 6.24. Automotive Industry Generic Strategy Matrix

Focused Cost strategies appeal to buyers willing to do some of their own maintenance and put up with a bit of inconvenience. The Russian-made Lada was sold for several years in the West at a remarkably low price; however, the consistently poor quality and after-sales service record finally deterred even most bargain hunters. The Korean Hyundai has aggressively won market share in recent years with a higher-quality low-cost offering.

A number of Focused Differentiation brands have succeeded at the higher end of the price spectrum. Volvo, Rover, Corvette, and others have been able to attract and retain loyal customers for decades by providing a unique driving experience.

Due to the size and complexity of the automobile market, it has regularly been possible for some companies to succeed with the more dangerous stuck-in-the-middle strategy. The VW Beetle did this through the 1960s and 1970s, as have the top-selling Honda Civic and Toyota Tercel more recently.

But even in this large and diversified industry, we see that companies must eventually choose a clear strategy to remain competitive as tastes change and imitators find ways to duplicate successes and remove the uniqueness of an offer.

Context. Porter's Generic Strategy is often used in conjunction with the five-forces diagnosis in devising corporate strategy. The most natural fit for the approach is in very large firms that can realistically pursue the scale of options contained in the model. It is useful for firms of all sizes for taking stock of competitive conditions and plotting the strategies of competitor firms.

Method. Generic Strategy is determined through a careful analysis of competitive forces. The steps describe the process at a high level:

- Step 1: Define. Define the domain of business interest and industry boundaries.
- Step 2: Scan. Complete an analysis of the five forces at play in the industry.
- Step 3: Diagnose. Determine which of the generic strategies is most suitable, given the industry analysis and the unique strengths and weaknesses of the firm.
- Step 4: Plan. Develop a plan to implement the chosen strategy.

References

Porter, M. *Competitive Strategy.* New York: Free Press, 1980.

Porter, M. *Competitive Advantage.* New York: Free Press, 1985.

Porter, M. *Competitive Advantage of Nations.* New York: Free Press, 1988.

Porter, M. *On Competition.* New York: Free Press, 1998.

⊞

E-Business Opportunity Matrix
Andy De and Alex Lowy

Exploitation of e-business involves capturing key changes in value contribution from the physical marketplace to the virtual information space.
—Alex Lowy[29]

Computer devices and networks make it possible for businesses to transform their offerings in two ways (Figure 6.25). First, they can change the Context—the environment in which transactions take place and the experience of consuming a good or service. As the Context moves from physical to virtual, new forms of value, such as greater inventory or twenty-four-hour availability, become possible. Alternatively, they can extend or redefine the Content of a current offering by using computer technology to add information to it. In many instances, it is possible to combine approaches, adding both virtual and informational value. Amazon's on-line transactions enable customers to buy books from any Internet browser twenty-four hours a day, and the Customer Review feature adds an information service to the book-buying experience. Hertz lets customers reserve cars on-line, while its airport kiosks provide maps and tourist information that add value to the car rental environment.

The Two Dimensions and Their Extremes. The E-Business Opportunity matrix explores two key dimensions: Context and Content:

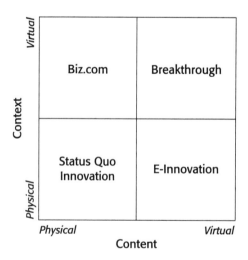

Figure 6.25. E-Business Opportunity Matrix

Context. The environment in which customers transact, consume, or receive support can be located in the Physical or Virtual realm.

Content. The core value of an offering can be Physical (for example, a book) or Virtual (for example, monitoring location or status).

The Four Quadrants. Companies should consider a mix of e-business Context and Content strategies to dramatically improve value propositions:

- Upper left: Biz.com. The Biz.com quadrant maps opportunities made available by simply moving a physical product or service to the Web context. On-line banking enables customers to check accounts and transfer money from any browser.
- Lower left: Status Quo Innovation. This is the starting point for reinvention. Although the focus of the exercise is on technology-enabled transformation, many good ideas involve nondigital innovations—basic improvements to the status quo business.
- Lower right: E-innovation. These add a virtual content dimension to an offering within the existing physical environment. For example, ATM machines revolutionized banking by offering information and transactions twenty-four hours a day at the local branch.
- Upper right: Breakthrough. The most spectacular opportunities answer the question, "How can the Web and related technologies help create totally new competencies, products, or services that can be leveraged across multiple vertical markets?" On-line mapping software changes both the Context and Content of finding directions, adding new value that can be used in transportation, telecommunications, public safety, and other fields.

Method. This tool is best used with groups tasked with identifying new opportunities.[30] A work team of five to eight people is ideal:

- Step 1: Assess. As a group, discuss how you could use computers, networks, and mobility to change product design, manufacturing, distribution and delivery, sales and marketing, transactions, and customer support.
- Step 2: Envision. Ask each individual in the group to write ten e-business ideas that they would like to explore. Write each idea on a single sticky note.
- Step 3: Present. Draw a large version of the E-Business Opportunity matrix on a white board or flip chart. Ask the group to present their ideas, placing each sticky note in the most appropriate matrix quadrant.
- Step 4: Synthesize. Group similar ideas. For example, you may have five ideas related to product delivery that can be combined into a single innovative project. Define and prioritize the idea groupings that make sense as possible e-business projects.

Reference

Tapscott, D., Ticoll, D., and Lowy, A. *Digital Capital: Harnessing the Power of Business Webs.* Boston: Harvard Business School Press, 2000.

⊞

Global Product Planning
Warren Keegan

After the product was launched, the company discovered that the British consume their cake at tea time. The cake they prefer is dry, spongy and suitable for being picked up with the left hand while the right manages a cup of tea.
—Warren Keegan[31]

Geographical expansion presents an attractive way a company can develop its business and reap further rewards from a successful offering. On the surface, it might seem obvious that every successful product in a specific market should be sold around the world. Reality is quite different. Local competitive, cultural, supply chain, and regulatory conditions present challenges. Companies differ in their readiness to sell into a global market and need to think seriously about their commitment to developing the necessary competencies. Warren Keegan has devised a useful framework for considering the major strategic options for pursuing such growth, looking at both the Product itself and the Communications strategy (Figure 6.26).

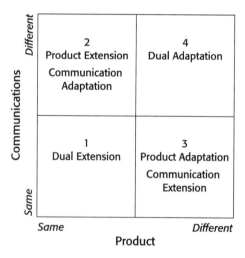

Figure 6.26. Global Product Planning Matrix

The Two Dimensions and Their Extremes. The Global Product Planning matrix explores two key dimensions, Communications and Product:

Communications. This refers to the way an offering is marketed and advertised. The approach may remain the same, or it may be altered to address local needs and tastes.

Product. The offering can remain unchanged, or it can be modified to accommodate the new context.

The Four Quadrants. In geographical expansion, both the Product and the Communications strategy may or may not be altered to reflect local market requirements. Consideration of possible combinations defines four major expansion strategies. Companies can choose one or several of the options for their strategic approach:

• Upper left: Product Extension/Communication Adaptation. This strategy is ideal when the product can be sold as is to meet a different set of needs. Perrier mineral water became popular in Europe for its healthful properties, but succeeded in North America as the chic beverage choice in restaurants and bars in place of a cocktail. The biggest differences in product use can be seen between developed and less developed economies. Bicycles and scooters are primary leisure items in one and primary transportation in the other.

• Lower left: Dual Extension. Under the right conditions, this strategy is the easiest and cheapest to implement. Software and construction tools and materials are examples of Dual Extension. It is easy to make erroneous assumptions or overlook subtle differences that ultimately derail a wholesale extension of both Product and Communications. Something as innocent as soup tells the story. Campbell learned the hard way that diners in the United Kingdom preferred a more bitter-tasting mix than Americans, and Knorr found Americans surprisingly unfriendly to their powdered package variety.

• Lower right: Product Adaptation/Communication Extension. Some products and brands have universal appeal even when the product undergoes varying degrees of modification. Exxon modifies its fuel formula for different geographies and weather conditions, but to the customer, it's still, "Put a tiger in your tank." The breakfast cereal Mueslix tastes completely different in Europe than it does in North America.

• Upper right: Dual Adaptation. In some cases, both the Product and the Communications strategy need to be modified to fit a variety of local conditions. For years, Unilever sold its fabric softener in different-sized bottles and under a variety of brand names in European countries. Hallmark and other greeting card companies modify their design, packaging, and marketing for the European and North American markets due to cultural idiosyncrasies. American cards contain prepared messages, while the European ones leave blank space for personal notes.

Method. The matrix is useful in two contexts: planning the geographical expansion of a single product offering and reviewing a company's portfolio of businesses.

- Step 1: List key product features.
- Step 2: Select target markets.
- Step 3: Ask how well the product would work in these markets: perfectly (Extend), well enough (Adapt), or not at all (consider dropping).
- Step 4: Ask how well marketing promises and basic product functionality would transfer to these markets: directly (Extend), with work (Adapt), or not at all (consider dropping).
- Step 5: Locate the product offer on the Global Product Planning matrix, and build a plan.

Reference

Keegan, W. *Global Marketing Management.* Upper Saddle River, N.J.: Prentice Hall, 1999.

⊞

Generic Network Strategy
Carl Shapiro and Hal Varian

The information age is built on the economics of networks, not the economics of factories.
—Carl Shapiro and Hal R. Varian[32]

A network market is one in which the value of the product to any particular user increases with the number of users. For example, a fax machine becomes more valuable as more fax machines are connected to the network. Each new purchaser is buying the value of being connected to all of the other machines on the network. This creates strong positive feedback that drives adoption, a dynamic common to many high-technology markets.

Varian and Shapiro identify four generic strategies for innovators in network markets. Two crucial elements determine the nature of the network strategy: Migration Strategy and Platform design (Figure 6.27). Migration strategies are either in line with existing technology (evolutionary) or represent a more radical departure (revolutionary). Platform design options range from technical standards that are closed and proprietary to ones that are open and public.

The Two Dimensions and Their Extremes. The Generic Network Strategy matrix explores the two key dimensions of Migration (or Adoption) Strategy and Platform:

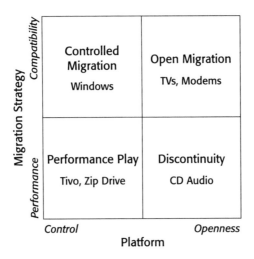

Figure 6.27. Generic Network Strategy Matrix

Migration (or Adoption) Strategy. Migration (or Adoption) Strategy can emphasize Compatibility or Performance. Compatibility is an evolutionary approach in which new products are fully capable of integrating with existing technology. The Performance approach is revolutionary and makes existing hardware and media obsolete.

Platform. A single vendor may control the technical specifications and business opportunities of a platform, or it may be open so that anyone can design and sell products for it. Control generates maximum value for the firm through customer lock-in and licensing opportunities, but Openness may ignite positive feedback more quickly. A mix of Control and Openness is often the optimal approach.

The Four Quadrants. Each quadrant defines a different strategic approach. Businesses need to assess both the competitive environment and the innovation itself in selecting the best option:

• Upper left: Controlled Migration. Controlled Migration is often the least risky strategy because it does not orphan existing technology. For example, when a user upgrades Windows, all existing documents remain usable. The strategic challenge in Controlled Migration is to give current customers sufficient reason to upgrade.
• Lower left: Performance Play. Performance Play offers customers a new product that is not backward compatible and is available from only one manufacturer. Customers fear lock-in, and competitors may offer technology that is

more open, as happened in the case of VHS versus Sony's controlled Beta format. Conversely, such a strategy works well if performance is important enough. Nintendo, Sony, and Microsoft video game players are examples of Performance Play strategies.

• Lower right: Discontinuity. Customers fear buying a new, unproven technology owned by a single vendor. Discontinuity overcomes this by creating an open platform, so that there are plenty of suppliers that can support the product. When all the manufacturers in an industry line up behind a single standard, as happened with CD audio, it becomes much easier to dislodge existing technology.

• Upper right: Open Migration. Open Migration reduces risk for customers by ensuring that new products are backward compatible with existing hardware and software and that many vendors can compete. The television industry, with a nudge from government, has always operated on an Open Migration basis.

Method. One's current market position—strong or weak—and the ability to gain cooperation from other hardware and software firms have a great impact on network strategy:

• Step 1: Assess the market. Does the market in which your product competes exhibit strong network characteristics?

• Step 2: Diagnose strategic fit. Does your product fit neatly into one of the quadrants, or could it conceivably fit one of the other strategies as well?

• Step 3: Envision. Make a list of the potential risks and payoffs of pursuing each of the strategies available to you. Which has the least risk and which the greatest payoff?

• Step 4: Plan. Select the most promising strategic option, and create a plan that reduces foreseeable risks.

Reference

Shapiro, C., and Varian, H. R. *Information Rules.* Boston: Harvard Business School Press, 1999.

MARKETING AND COMMUNICATIONS FRAMEWORKS

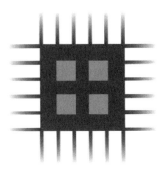

How will we position ourselves in the marketplace? What is our communication plan?

Much as strategy defines core value, marketing determines how it will be presented. In an increasingly competitive, overdeveloped marketplace, decisions about how, when, and to whom become significant determinants of success. A movie is the core value, and almost everything postproduction is marketing. The *Lord of the Rings* movie was split into three audience experiences, each a year apart to build anticipatory excitement and sustain interest and identification with the story and its characters.

The evolution of mass media to targeted communications is permitting increasingly customized marketing plans to be aimed at tightly defined customer segments. Frameworks selected for this section help to model customer characteristics and needs so that messaging decisions are well matched to unique preferences.

⊞

Mass Customization: The Four Approaches
B. Joseph Pine II and James H. Gilmore

Each customer is unique and they all deserve to have exactly what they want at a price they are willing to pay.
—Joseph Pine[33]

For the first half of the twentieth century, the developed economies were defined by mass production. Markets were large and homogeneous; customer segments, where they existed, were defined crudely. Mass manufacturing and mass markets delivered finished goods at reasonable prices to many of the world's citizens. In exchange, some things were lost. In terms of quality, many early manufactured goods were not better than the handmade goods of the craft economy; indeed, they were inferior. In all instances, customers needed to sacrifice choice and customization in order to obtain the benefits of manufacturing economies of scale.

In the 1970s, firms around the world began chipping away at the mass production model, primarily through paying attention to incremental process improvements in design and manufacturing. By the early 1980s, Japanese firms had taken the quality lead in market after market, dominating consumer electronics and toys and eventually taking a large slice of fields such as autos and machine tools. Many of the flexible manufacturing techniques pioneered in this era enabled shorter product runs and quicker production process changes, leading to an explosion in consumer choice in dozens of industries. For example, from 1950 to 2000, the average supermarket went from offering three thousand items to fifty thousand or more.

More recently, this trend has crystallized in the practice of mass customization, characterized by variety, time-based competition, just-in-time production, shortened product life cycles, continuous process reengineering, and customer-centric database marketing. Examples abound, from Burger King's strategy of cooking each burger for a specific customer ("Have it your way!") to the telephone companies that have gone from offering one-size-fits-all residential service to hundreds of flexible (and sometimes confusing) packages aimed at different groups and individuals. Mass consumers, media, and markets are being replaced by diverse populations, targeted media, and markets of one.

In *The Experience Economy,* Pine and Gilmore identify four approaches to mass customization (Figure 6.28). Core to their thesis is the idea that the sacrifices that customers make in purchasing and consuming offerings drive the opportunities for mass customization. In the past, these sacrifices were commonplace and embedded in aphorisms like: "You can have any color as long as it's black," and, "Speed, quality, and price; choose any two." Today, we still have to make trade-offs. No business can offer an infinite choice of styles and materials plus immediate delivery. However, mass customization strategies enable businesses to meet customer needs by strategically removing sacrifices that matter to specific individuals. The Mass Customization matrix offers a powerful tool for analyzing customers' sacrifices, and selecting the mass customization approach that best fits their needs.

The Two Dimensions and Their Extremes. The Mass Customization matrix explores two key dimensions: Product and Representation:

Product. One can offer a standard unchanging product, or customize the product for individual customers.

Representation. Representation can be standard or uniquely structured for each customer. Aspects that can vary include marketing, packaging, delivery, pricing, and support choices.

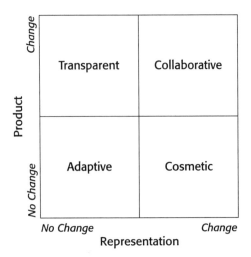

Figure 6.28. Mass Customization Matrix

The Four Quadrants. Four Mass Customization strategic approaches are defined by varying the extent to which Product and Representation are modified:

• Upper left: Transparent. Often, customer needs are predictable or can easily be deduced. Companies as different as Ritz-Carlton and Lands End observe and record customer preferences in order to minimize the sacrifice customers make in repeatedly filling out forms or making their preferences known. In this way, offerings can be customized within a standard package for individual customers.

• Lower left: Adaptive. Adaptive customizers offer a standardized product that customers can adapt to fit personal usage patterns. Adaptability is built into the product so that customers can personalize it after purchase. The Adaptive approach works well when there is a standard offering but so many variations in style and usage that sorting through the alternatives can be difficult. Select Comfort of Minneapolis manufactures and sells the Aero bed. Its unique air chambers enable couples to select different levels of firmness on either side of the bed. Many luxury cars enable drivers to adapt the seat and mirrors to their personal driving style and then recall it with the touch of a single button. The recently introduced Toyota Scion was designed to make it easy for after-market producers to sell customized add-ons to the car, enabling owners to individualize their car's appearance and performance attributes.

• Lower right: Cosmetic. This approach works best when different customer segments use a product the same way but receive personalized value from specialized packaging, marketing appeals, and delivery options. Banks, for example, have experimented widely with checking, savings, and loan offerings that differ primarily in how the product is represented to customers. The underlying service does not change, but the manner of representation and delivery personalizes the experience and adds convenience.

- Upper right: Collaborative. The Collaborative customizer works closely with the customer to determine the value to be created. Drum Workshop, a maker of professional equipment for drummers, lets shoppers try out various colors and styles on-line, save the data, and send the order to the retailer of their choice. When customers are faced with a multitude of confusing options and may have to live with the product for a considerable time, Collaborative customization helps them feel confident in their choices.

Example: Herman Miller. Herman Miller is a leading office furniture producer and progressive employer that has been named the top furniture company by *Fortune* magazine for fifteen of the past sixteen years. The company's roots lie in its groundbreaking designs, many of them in the permanent collections of leading museums such as the New York Museum of Modern Art and the Whitney.

Historically, Herman Miller built high-quality, durable office furniture for large corporations, offering a wide set of options with millions of combinations of color, fabric, and style. Customers typically placed large orders with long lead times. In effect, many of Herman Miller's orders were customized in terms of styling and design. The sacrifice that customers had to make—speed—was tolerable for large, stable companies that could afford to plan their office changes well in advance of when they were needed.

The same, however, was not true for smaller, less established companies, where the costs of customizing smaller orders or meeting demands for speedier delivery were prohibitive. In the late 1980s, Herman Miller embarked on a continuous improvement campaign that drastically reduced inefficiencies and accelerated manufacturing processes. Most important, it developed technologies that enabled customizing on the fly. If a customer wanted a fifty-five-inch desk rather than a standard fifty-inch model, this could be accomplished quickly. Delivery times were cut significantly, sometimes by up to several months. This set the stage for several new mass customization initiatives.

In 1996 the company rolled out Miller SQA ("Simple, Quick, Affordable"), which offered cheaper office solutions through a selection of no-frills furniture. SQA also offered built-to-order products that targeted smaller companies looking for top quality and fast-growing larger companies that needed quick delivery. Both of these groups were more interested in furniture choices that fit their needs and personalized delivery than with details like the choice of fabric. By limiting choice in the SQA lines, Herman Miller was able to satisfy customers who didn't have time to sift through options, and to deliver much more rapidly than before. SQA integrated aspects of Cosmetic, Transparent, and Collaborative customization strategies (Figure 6.29). In 1998, it launched hmstore.com, enabling customers to configure and order office furniture on-line (Collaborative customization). This concept was extended by the development of Herman Miller Red in 2000, a brand with a limited line of furniture exclusively available on-line (Cosmetic customization) and at a single store in New York City. During this same period, Herman Miller was also making its office systems offerings more modular and flexible, enabling customers to quickly change furniture to meet the varying needs of work groups (Adaptive customization).

Companies that have traveled the path that Herman Miller followed understand the paradoxes of mass customization—lower costs can lead to better service; fewer choices can mean greater customer satisfaction—and have profited from using them to reduce customer sacrifice.

Context. The Product-Representation matrix offers a creative and convenient way to customize products, services, and experiences for customer groups.

Method. The steps below provide a high-level blueprint for creating a mass customized approach to meeting customer needs:

• Step 1: Assess sacrifice. What kinds of sacrifices do customers currently make to purchase and use your product or service? Sacrifices include delays, searching and sorting challenges, and lack of personalization. List up to three sacrifices.

• Step 2: Diagnose. Which mass customization option would enable you to overcome these sacrifices? If you have more than one product, place each in the ideal quadrant.

• Step 3: Envision. Imagine ways to streamline the experience so that customers are offered only what they need, and nothing more.

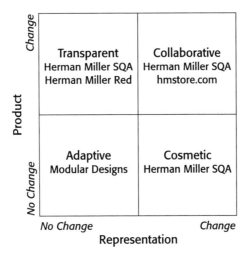

Figure 6.29. Mass Customization Matrix: Herman Miller

• Step 4: Implement. Explore the implications of your mass customization assessment with appropriate staff, and develop solutions.

References

Pine, B. J. II. *Mass Customization.* Boston: Harvard Business Press, 1993.

Pine, B. J. II, and Gilmore, J. H. *The Experience Economy.* Boston: Harvard Business School Press, 1999.

Pine, J., and Pine, J. "The Four Faces of Customization." *Harvard Business Review,* Jan.-Feb. 1997.

⊞

Attentionscape
Thomas H. Davenport and John C. Beck

Companies that succeed in the future will be those expert not in time management, but in attention management.
—Thomas Davenport and John C. Beck[34]

In a world overwhelmed with information, attention becomes our scarcest resource. Davenport and Beck's *The Attention Economy* describes how attention works and can be leveraged as a key asset in a knowledge economy. The Attentionscape tool (Figure 6.30) helps companies measure attention so it can be man-

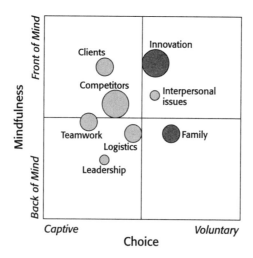

Figure 6.30. Attentionscape Matrix

aged better. This has relevance both within firms, looking at how executives and employees direct their interests, and outside firms, focusing on customers.

The Two Dimensions and Their Extremes. The two dimensions of Mindfulness and Choice define the Attentionscape matrix:

Mindfulness. Attention that is conscious and deliberate is Front of Mind. If it is unconscious and spontaneous, it is Back of Mind.

Choice. Captive attention is thrust on you, as when you are at a movie theater or at work. Attention is Voluntary when you choose to give it, as in watching television.

The Four Quadrants. Through the use of different sizes and shading of shapes, the Attentionscape presents four dimensions of information in a 2 × 2 format. Although this makes the model complex, it rewards careful study. Mindfulness is on the vertical axis, Choice on the horizontal. The third dimension, Aversion versus Attractiveness, is illustrated by the shading of the circles. An issue is considered Aversion based when we are afraid of the consequences of not paying attention to it. Many health and disease issues might fall in this area. Attraction-based attention is given to those things that fascinate and please us. Attractiveness is indicated by the darkness of the circles—the darker the circle, the more attractive the subject is. Amount of attention, the fourth dimension, is communicated by the size of the circles. The framework is illustrated here with a hypothetical survey of executives at a single company:

• Upper left: Front of Mind, Captive. The attention paid to clients, teamwork, and competitors is Captive. In this case, the Attentionscape reveals what may be a problem. As the size and shading of the circles indicate, employees appear to be paying more attention to competitors than to clients.
• Lower left: Back of Mind, Captive. Issues such as leadership and teamwork are not usually given conscious attention by this group. Furthermore, the attention paid to teamwork is mildly aversive. It indicates this is an area where executives have to pay attention but probably don't want to. The company may need to adjust incentives if it wants to improve performance in these areas.
• Lower right: Back of Mind, Voluntary. Some issues are highly attractive but may not be as pressing as captive issues. The danger here is that important, voluntary priorities may not get their share of attention without support and encouragement from the company.
• Upper right: Front of Mind, Voluntary. In this case, innovation is highly attractive and receives voluntary and conscious attention. It may be that innovation is one of the firm's key values and that the need for attention is reinforced by company policy, compensation, and other factors. The attention paid to interpersonal issues may indicate unresolved issues among executives.

Method. The authors have created an Attentionscape software program to score survey respondents' answers to questions about attention. Here is a modified method that you can use to create a personal Attentionscape:

- Step 1: Define. Create a list of items that occupied your attention in the past day. Include both work and home.
- Step 2: Diagnose. Qualify the type of attention that is paid to each item. Determine where it falls between Front of Mind or Back of Mind, Captive or Voluntary, and Aversive or Attractive.
- Step 3: Quantify. Rank the degree and amount of attention each item receives from 1 to 5, with 5 being the highest score.
- Step 4: Score. Place each item on the matrix, using larger circles for items that received the most attention and darker colors for those that are most attractive.
- Step 5: Adjust. Consider the implications of the analysis, and identify desirable changes.

Reference

Davenport, T. H., and Beck, J. C. *The Attention Economy: Understanding the New Currency of Business.* Boston: Harvard Business School Press, 2002.

⊞

Managing Customer Loyalty
Werner Reinartz and V. Kumar

> No company should ever take for granted the idea that managing customers for loyalty is the same as managing them for profits. The only way to strengthen the link between profits and loyalty is to manage both at the same time.
> —Werner Reinartz and V. Kumar[35]

The assumption that loyal customers are good customers is worth questioning. This advice is the result of the authors' study of the relationship between customer loyalty and profits. They investigated three common beliefs about loyal customers: (1) it costs less to serve loyal customers, (2) loyal customers are willing to pay more for bundled services, and (3) loyal customers provide good word-of-mouth marketing—they evangelize.

Reinartz and Kumar found that the link between loyalty and profit was often tenuous at best. In studies of four industries (grocery, mail order sales, brokerage, and corporate service providers), they found that 15 to 20 percent of a company's typical customers fall into the categories of loyal and unprofitable or highly profitable but not loyal. Their conclusion was that companies spend too much money managing relationships and marketing to customers who are not worth the investment. Figure 6.31 graphically illustrates the relationship between these two factors and the four possible outcomes.

The matrix explores two key dimensions: Customer Profitability and Customer Relationship:

Customer Profitability. Individual Customer Profitability depends on the frequency and quality of their purchasing, as well as the costs of selling to and servicing them.

Customer Relationship. Long-term customers are those who make frequent purchases over a period of one or two years.

The Four Quadrants. The matrix helps to identify four types of customers based on their profitability and purchasing patterns:

* Upper left: Butterflies. These are customers who are profitable but disloyal. In some industries, such as brokerage, it is common for large customers to shop around, spreading large deals among several firms. Businesses naturally want to invest time in reselling to profitable customers but not to butterflies, which is a waste of money.
* Lower left: Strangers. Strangers are customers who appear one time and are gone. From a customer relationship management standpoint, the best thing to do is invest as little as possible in strangers.

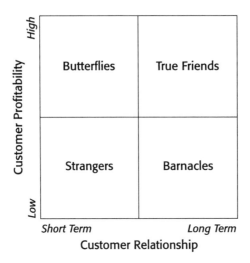

Figure 6.31. Choosing a Loyalty Strategy Matrix

• Lower right: Barnacles. Barnacles are customers who continue to order but do not order enough of the right things frequently enough to be profitable. In a retail or Web environment, these may be customers who shop only during sales; in business, they may be customers who require a lot of attention but purchase only the least profitable offerings. The challenge with Barnacles is figuring out how to get them to buy more, more often, or cut them loose.

• Upper right: True Friends. The best customers are defined as those who buy a lot from you and are repeat customers. In addition, they display attitudinal loyalty: they provide testimonials to your firm, opt in to your e-mail offerings, and identify your business positively on surveys. True friends respond well to gentle treatment. Hard selling and too much attention can turn off even good customers, according to research.

Method. Analysis depends on your ability to measure customer profitability and loyalty. Profitability is driven by many factors, including the costs of informing, transacting, supplying, and servicing customers. Reinhart and Kumar are skeptical of approaches that emphasize recency and total revenue in analyzing customers, because too many Butterflies and Barnacles are included. They have developed a method based on event history modeling that looks at the period of time over which a customer has made purchases and the frequency of those purchases. A simplified version of this method provides a sense of how it might be used:

• Step 1: Define profitability. Establish measures and methods for tracking account profitability.

• Step 2: Assess loyalty. Sample existing customer data in order to come up with a rough formulation of the percentage of your customers who fall into the Butterfly, Barnacle, Stranger, and True Friends categories.

• Step 3: Eliminate unnecessary expense. Determine in a general way how much you spend on unnecessary services for all quadrants. Are you making expensive sales calls on Barnacles that will never generate enough profit to cover the costs? Are you sending gifts to Butterflies whose activity pattern makes it clear they will never return? Are you inundating True Friends with too many catalogue mailings? Generate a list of ways you are expending money and time needlessly.

• Step 4: Plan. Select three customer retention expense areas to investigate further for change or elimination.

Reference

Reinartz, W., and Kumar, V. "The Mismanaging of Customer Loyalty." *Harvard Business Review,* July 2002.

⊞

Likelihood to Buy
Simon Majaro

A strong brand brings reassurance to customers by providing a perception of permanence and quality.
 —Simon Majaro[36]

Companies are wise to invest in establishing solid, trusted, highly recognizable brands. On occasion, the company itself assumes brand-like characteristics, where customers associate positive attributes to any products they introduce. Companies benefiting from this effect include IBM, Procter & Gamble, and Cisco Systems, to name a few. A company that is not well known and trusted faces a tougher marketing challenge, and this should be factored into plans. Simon Majaro frames the branding and competitive marketing task as a mix of company recognition and the uniqueness of the offering (Figure 6.32).

The Two Dimensions and Their Extremes. The Likelihood to Buy matrix explores two key dimensions: Supplying Company reputation and Product uniqueness:

Supplying Company reputation. Supplier companies vary in the extent to which they are well known and trusted.

Figure 6.32. Likelihood to Buy Matrix

Product uniqueness. Products can offer unique features that differentiate them, or they can be common and widely available.

The Four Quadrants. The combination of the two factors contained in the matrix determines the likelihood of customers to buy and the investment that will be needed in marketing and sales:

• Upper left: Known and Unique. This is the most powerful combination of factors, making it easy for customers to decide to buy. Assuming that the product is well designed to meet a need, it is likely to be a hit.
• Lower left: Unknown and Unique. The product is well differentiated, but the customer is left needing to work out whether he or she trusts the supplier. Marketing and sales efforts are needed to bridge the gulf.
• Lower right: Unknown and Me Too. This is the weakest combination of factors, making it highly unlikely that customers will decide to buy. Realizing this early in the process can save a lot of heartache and investment.
• Upper right: Known and Me Too. The supplier is well known and trusted, but there is little to differentiate and recommend the product to buyers. This is not always an insurmountable problem; it depends on such factors as price, the degree of competition, and the amount of risk customers associate with the product experience in question. Once again, investment in marketing and sales is required.

Method. Companies can apply this framework in developing the strategic marketing plan for a product or line of business:

• Step 1: Define. Describe the product, and define the target market.
• Step 2: Diagnose. Locate the product on the Likelihood to Buy matrix.
• Step 3: Evaluate. Assess the implications of step 2 for the product strategy.

Reference

Majaro, S. *The Essence of Marketing.* Upper Saddle River, N.J.: Prentice Hall, 1993.

RISK FRAMEWORKS

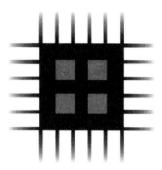

What business risks do we face? How grave are these? How much is the opportunity worth to us? Will we be able to pull it off?

Risk represents the distance between vision and viability. No business decision is more central than the calculation of risk. Risk is never eliminated, but it is mitigated by careful assembly of all the critical elements: a powerful and timely idea, a plan, funding, and the competencies to execute the plan.

Risk is ultimately about making the right trade-offs. Many goals are attainable, but at what cost? The frameworks in this section present a range of ways to determine whether to proceed with a plan.

⊞

Revenue and Profitability
Adapted from Adrian Slywotzky and David Morrison

Profitability is an extraordinarily complex phenomenon. Without a clear understanding of how profit happens and how businesses must be designed to capture it, there will not be any profit.
   —Adrian Slywotzky and David Morrison[37]

Businesses need to be profitable if they are to survive. At its simplest, profit is what returns to owners and shareholders after all expenses have been paid, or total revenues minus total costs. The precise definition and measurement of these factors is a subject of great concern to economists and accountants, sometimes leading to confusion, financial crisis, and even scandal.

Arguably, there is no more basic and central business question: Are we trying to increase sales as is reflected in revenues, or do we want to make a profit? By lowering price and increasing marketing, we can boost sales and the business.

Or we can raise prices, improving our profit margin per unit, and risk a reduction in overall revenues. The resolution of this dynamic tension resides in the goals and assumptions that underlie the business.

Through most of the twentieth century, growth and profitability were treated as synonymous. Companies were encouraged to win market share, culminating in the type of thinking reflected in the now famous GE strategy of withdrawing from markets where it could not be among the top two or three players. The drive to grow at any cost became more intense through the 1990s as companies competed for dominant positions in the Internet economy where network effects added even more advantage to the traditional economies of scale available to larger companies.

In their book *The Profit Zone,* Adrian Slywotzky and David Morrison describe how market share ceased to ensure profitability in the mid-1980s. New technologies, global production and market contexts, and more informed and proactive consumers were altering the nature of competition and profit. Profit was increasingly tied to customer value, which was becoming harder to predict and control. Companies needed to build profitability directly into their business models. Growth and market dominance were no longer sufficient; DEC, GM, Kodak, and a host of other companies saw their profitability erode even as they maintained a number one or two position in their industries.

As profit zones shift, companies need to ask themselves, Where will I be allowed to make a profit? and What unique value do we deliver? Slywotzky and Morrison present twenty-two profit models, drawing on the practices of profitability masters like Andy Grove at Intel, Robert Goizueta at Coke, and Nicolas Hayek at Swatch. These leaders focus simultaneously on the customer and on profit. They constantly ask where the profit zone is today and where it will be tomorrow. Their companies accurately identified the shift out of the product era to a market constructed around customers and profit and modified their businesses to avoid being mired in no-profit zones.

The modeling of Revenue and Profit in Figure 6.33 is our own summary of key ideas, offering a starting point to a fuller consideration of the planned pursuit of profitability.[38] For a detailed exploration of profit modeling, we recommend reading *The Profit Zone.*

The Two Dimensions and Their Extremes. Businesses have two primary measures of financial performance: top-line revenues and bottom-line profits. Application of the terms varies, and there is considerable debate as to the most valid and useful form of measurement and reporting. Purpose, strategy, and law influence whether EBITDA (earnings before interest, taxes, depreciation and amortization), free cash, or retained earnings is the profit measure of choice in a given situation. The financial manipulations and irregularities leading to the

Figure 6.33. Revenue and Profitability Matrix

demise of companies like Enron and Arthur Andersen in 2002 tested the elasticity of permissible practices and definitions, pointing to a need for standards and oversight.

> Revenue. Revenue is the total amount of money paid to a company for products and services delivered to the market. Revenue is reflective of market acceptance and appreciation for what a company offers.
>
> Profit. Profit is the money that a company earns after all costs are paid out. Profit is reflective of the amount of added value created, as well as a measure of discipline and efficiency in operations.

The Four Quadrants. The relationship between Revenues and Profitability can be viewed from three useful perspectives:

• Life cycle. Businesses progress through a predictable series of developmental phases. They begin in the lower left quadrant as start-ups requiring investment and then proceed to a marketing phase (upper left), where sales increase ahead of profit. Following this, depending on conditions and the nature of the business, they advance to either the upper or lower right quadrants as they mature and become profitable. The cycle ends with a return to the left side of the matrix as the business wanes.

• Portfolio. In multibusiness companies, there is a need for offerings at different stages of maturity and profitability. While profitable lines are essential, it is equally important to invest in future capabilities. And some parts of a business may themselves be unprofitable while being essential for the success of other parts of the enterprise. Each quadrant is legitimate, and planners need to consider current and future needs carefully.

• Performance status. The Revenue and Profitability of a business is or is not acceptable. Performance targets should be set at the beginning of a period and monitored.

The Revenue and Profitability matrix describes four primary types of relationship between the two dimensions:

• Upper left: Growth. High revenues do not always equate with profitability, no matter which measure is applied. In the 1990s, AOL and many high-tech firms reported major bottom-line losses while maintaining top-line growth. Price wars led to unsustainable margins over the long run. The old joke of "losing on each item but making it up in volume" is increasingly suspect. For several years, GM reported losing over $100 per car just to maintain market share.

Nevertheless, this can be a legitimate component of a larger integrated competitive strategy. Maintaining a strong market brand in consumer goods often demands living with high-volume sales at low margin. In this way, the product can dominate its category. Consider Coke. When it is purchased in the grocery store, price and margin are low. By maintaining high brand value, the company is able to charge a higher price for alternative channels such as vending machines, raising overall profit.

• Lower left: Investment. Low revenues and profits typify start-up and R&D initiatives. Investment is geared to developing future capability. This is the positive view. It also describes unhealthy businesses unable to gain meaningful sales traction. Any business falling into this quadrant should be there by design, with a plausible plan for adding value within a reasonable time frame.

• Lower right: Boutique. Not all businesses need to grow larger to be successful. This approach is consistent with what Michael Porter calls the focused differentiation strategy.[39] In addition, certain value propositions depend on scarcity (of a skill, material, or experience) for a good amount of their profit. Take as examples clothing design and high-end vacation packages. Boutique profit models often depend on relatively rare resources, creating natural barriers to entry by competitors.

• Upper right: Maturity. The most profitable businesses are able to increase their top and bottom lines, expanding scale while preserving margin. Established brands like Coke and Shell have achieved this, as have global powerhouses like GE and Procter & Gamble. Managing High Revenue–High Profit businesses is a balancing act demanding discipline and agility. As soon as a large profit zone is established, it becomes a target. The biggest danger for these companies is becoming complacent as value migrates away from them. This can happen to entire industry ecosystems, as it has recently with recorded music and long-distance telephony.

Example: Three Paths: General Electric, Apple Computers, and Intel. Three well-known company histories illustrate the explanatory power of the Revenue and Profitability matrix. Each of these companies has faced challenges and achieved success by pursuing profitability in its own way (Figure 6.34):

• General Electric. When Jack Welch took the helm in 1981, GE was a large manufacturing firm with a market value of $13 billion. When he left in 2001, the company was a diversified global solutions provider worth $125.9 billion. Welch inherited leadership of a company in the upper left quadrant: High Revenues and Low Profitability. Through a series of interventions, the company refocused on high-value areas and improved efficiency. First was Welch's "Be No. 1 or No. 2 or Get Out" strategy. Over a two-year period, the company learned to be self-critical about the businesses most worth being in. Second was the Work-Out program, doubling the organization's rate of productivity. With a keen focus on customers and profitability, Welch moved GE into the upper right quadrant.
• Intel. Intel was founded in 1968 to build semiconductor memory products. By the late 1970s, it was a world leader in the manufacture of DRAMS (dynamic

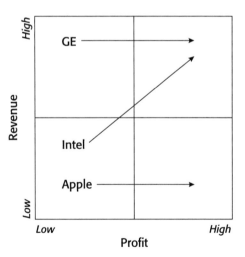

Figure 6.34. Profitability Paths Matrix

random access memory chips), and the market was growing fast. By the mid-1980s, an inflated U.S. dollar and high-quality, low-cost Japanese competition took the profit out of the business, and by 1985 Intel was losing money. This part of the business had slipped from the upper right quadrant to the upper left.

In 1971, Intel had introduced the world's first microprocessor. Intel executives Andy Grove and Gordon Moore made the tough decision to exit from the memory chip business and place all resources behind microprocessors. A pattern of extensive investment in R&D and passionate customer service has taken Intel from the lower left to the upper right quadrant several times. The pattern continues to this day, with 2002 investment in R&D being over $4 billion, representing 15 percent of net revenues. Projected R&D spending in 2004 is $4.8 billion.

• Apple Computers. From its earliest days, Apple has been a leader in user-friendly, innovative design. Created by Steve Wozniak and Steve Jobs in 1976 and inspired by the playful, user-oriented science of Xerox's PARC, the company has released a series of well-loved products, perhaps best epitomized by the Macintosh 128.

Rather than take the Apple operating system and graphical user interface public, Apple chose to restrict use to its own products, and it enjoyed many profitable years (the lower right quadrant). The decision differentiated Apple computers from the more clunky PC types, drawing a devoted following of designers and students. But the decision not to pursue a more open licensing strategy has been questioned by many over the years, as the bulk of the computing world has moved to standardize around the Microsoft and Intel platform.

Context. Modeling of Revenue and Profit is relevant for both steady-state and new business planning. It is useful at the start of business cycles for forecasting capital needs and expectation setting and at the end of cycles to evaluate success. As a portfolio planning aid, the framework is helpful in ensuring there are adequate initiatives in each of the target quadrants.

Method. The focus of this matrix is on profitability, providing a mechanism to make goals and critical factors more explicit. As a result, performance monitoring, intervention, and decision making become easier. Two primary applications are outlined below.

Here are the steps for profitability tracking in a single business:

• Step 1: At the start of a business cycle, forecast target revenue and profitability. Locate this point on the matrix.

• Step 2: Identify several other possible scenarios, comprising different combinations of revenue and profit. Describe factors that might lead to these outcomes. Are there steps that can be taken to prevent the more negative scenarios?

• Step 3: Monitor progress on a quarterly or monthly basis to measure success. Implement corrective actions if results are unacceptable.

These are the steps for portfolio modeling:

• Step 1: Define. Place each of the businesses on the matrix, positioning them in the appropriate quadrant.
• Step 2: Diagnose. Stepping back from the matrix, reflect on the current mix, considering such factors as overall balance, profitability and return on capital, diversity, interdependencies, competency development, and investment in new, future sources of profit.
• Step 3: Envision. Adjust the mix to reflect a strong current and future set of businesses.
• Step 4: Follow up. Monitor to ensure that the businesses perform as planned and continue to represent the values ascribed to them.

Reference

Slywotzky, A., and Morrison, D. *The Profit Zone: How Strategic Business Design Will Lead You to Tomorrow's Profit.* New York: Times Business, 1997.

⊞

BCG: Product Portfolio Matrix
Bruce Hendersen

The framework is simple on the surface, but has a lot of hidden depth. It's when you get into the depth that you discover both its power and flexibility.
—Simon Trussler[40]

Mention "2 × 2 matrix" to someone in a business context, and more often than not, that person will think of the BCG Grid. The names of the four quadrants—Dogs, Stars, Problem Children, and Cash Cows—have become standard popular terms and a convenient shorthand in strategic discussions. What has made the framework so powerful and enduring is its amazing breadth; not only is it a method for structuring strategic priority-setting discussions, it also represents a business typology, making it possible for planners to think about a portfolio of holdings from an investment perspective.

BCG founder Bruce Hendersen created the Product Portfolio matrix (Figure 6.35) in the early 1970s to assist conglomerate organizations to analyze the relative worth of their different business units, subsidiaries, and products. Not only did it help to establish BCG as a leader in the strategy consulting domain, it

Figure 6.35. BCG Product Portfolio Matrix

played an important role in defining and legitimizing strategy as a management discipline practiced by professionals and consultants.

The Two Dimensions and Their Extremes. The framework combines quantitative and intuitive features to produce an accurate and consensual picture of the investment worthiness of different business holdings. Each business unit is assessed with respect to its market (Market Growth) and then compared to the other business units owned by the conglomerate firm (Relative Market Share). Relative Market Share and Market Growth form the basis for analysis:

Market Growth. Market Growth serves as a proxy for cash requirement. A market that is expanding rapidly requires more investment to maintain a competitive position.

Relative Market Share. Relative Market Share is a proxy for cost competitiveness and is derived from an essential BCG concept, the Experience Curve, which calculates the costs of production as a function of learning and size. Relative Market Share is determined by dividing the percentage of market held by a firm by the percentage held by its largest competitor.

The Four Quadrants. The portfolio approach brings rationality to the business investment process. Business units and markets proceed through a predictable cycle of maturation, which needs to be factored into decision making:

• Upper left: Stars. These are the high fliers—businesses with a high relative market share in a growing market. However, they still require investment to maintain market share, so they might not be as profitable as Cash Cows. They might even need more investment than they return in profit (resulting in a short-term net loss). But these will be tomorrow's Cash Cows providing market share is maintained.

• Lower left: Cash Cows. The darling of the aging executive and owner alike, these businesses have high market share in a market with low growth. Maintaining current operations becomes the main cash requirements for this mature business. Like a great wine or cheese, it has cellared sufficiently and is ready to be harvested for profits as cash flow remains positive.

• Lower right: Dogs. Dogs are businesses with low market share in low-growth markets. The market may or may not be in decline. Despite the temptation to divest, dogs can have significant advantages, depending on market conditions. For example, the market might be positioned to grow, redefining potential worth. Or the business might be cash flow positive and capable of being restructured to maintain positive cash flow for a significant length of time. The business might also have significant strategic or brand importance, meriting retention to fend off competitors as a "guard dog."

• Upper right: Question Marks (or Problem Children). These businesses compete in high-growth markets, but they have a relatively low market share and may need significant investment to improve their position. Consultants tend to like clients who own a few of these (and the pockets to pay fees), as careful analysis is needed to determine if it is best to invest more, sell the business, or reposition to focus on a specific market niche (among other options).

Example: Dow versus Monsanto. "In the 1960s and early 1970s," write George Stalk and Thomas Hout, "a classic portfolio battle was waged by Dow Chemical against Monsanto. In this battle, Dow actively managed its portfolio for advantage, and Monsanto did not."[41]

Firms that reinvest based on profitability alone risk overspending on mature business lines while under-funding those in early stages of growth. It was not uncommon in the 1960s, however, for large multi-business companies to approach the market with a profit center orientation that did exactly this. Companies like GE and Westinghouse were leading practitioners of the strategy, promoting business unit accountability and rewarding financial results with independence and growth capital. During this period, Dow approached the market with the portfolio strategy reflected by the BCG Grid, while rival Monsanto pursued the prevailing profit center approach (Figure 6.36).

Monsanto began the period with the stronger portfolio. Seven of its businesses were facing growth in demand greater than 20 percent, as compared with Dow, which had only two businesses in this position. Following a course of reinvesting based principally on proven success and profitability, Monsanto overlooked emerging trends and opportunities. Of fourteen businesses growing at

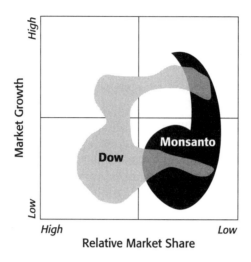

Figure 6.36. Dow versus Monsanto Matrix

an annual rate of 15 percent or greater, it expanded only three of those businesses faster than demand. It lost ground to competitors in eleven of fourteen growing areas. Dow, in contrast, pursued strategic growth in the portfolio-based manner, investing boldly according to plan. Of the twenty-three growing businesses in its portfolio, twenty of them were expanding faster than demand. Confident in its business direction, Dow borrowed to grow, secure in the belief that well-planned debt constituted less risk than underinvestment. Dow's debt-to-equity ratio stood at 1.1:1 as compared with the much smaller 0.46:1 ratio at Monsanto.

Through this period, Dow's business grew steadily, while Monsanto's stagnated. In portfolio management terms, Monsanto overspent on nongrowth businesses and failed to invest in launching a robust set of new Stars for future profitability. It wasn't until 1981 and the efforts of CEO Dick Mahoney that Monsanto tackled its portfolio imbalances, leading the company back to a path of strategic growth and more respectable returns on equity.

Context. The BCG matrix is used for analysis and to support strategic decision making. Because of the need for data-based calculations to map the locations of each business onto the 2 × 2 grid, it is seldom used during workshops for brainstorming new ideas and concepts. This is a persuasive tool that can be used to gain group consensus around the findings of an analysis.

Method. The following steps provide a high-level blueprint for conducting Product-Portfolio analysis:

- Step 1: Set the scope. Determine the unit of analysis by deciding whether business units, subsidiaries, product categories, or products are to be analyzed.
- Step 2: Define the portfolio. Collect the list of businesses held by the company in question for the agreed-upon units of analysis.
- Step 3: Calculate revenues. For each business within the list, gather the following pieces of information:

Sales (revenue) numbers for the current year and for the past several years (two years minimum).

For every competitor being analyzed, calculate sales (revenue) numbers for the current year and for the past several years (two years minimum).

- Step 4: Calculate Market Growth and Relative Market Share. Find or calculate the Market Growth rates for each business being analyzed: This year's industry revenues – Last year's industry revenues/Last year's industry revenues × 100 percent. Calculate the Relative Market Share by dividing the firm's (or business unit's) market share (revenues may be compared) by that of its largest rival.
- Step 5: Complete the grid. Plot each item on the grid based on the calculated values for Market Share and Market Growth, and analyze the results.

References

Stalk, G. Jr., and Hout, T. M. *Competing Against Time.* New York: Free Press, 1990.

Stern, C. W., and Stalk, G. Jr. *Perspectives on Strategy.* New York: Wiley, 1998.

⊞

Impact-Uncertainty Matrix
Adapted by William Ralston

The quest for certainty blocks the search for meaning. Uncertainty is the very condition to impel man to unfold his powers.
—Erich Fromm[42]

For the past thirty years, the Impact-Uncertainty matrix (Figure 6.37) has been one of SRI Consulting Business Intelligence's (SRIC-BI) most widely used and effective tools for analyzing the external environment. It is applied in scenario planning, strategy management, issues scanning, and technology planning. The tool's key benefit is that it focuses management's attention on the most important external issues that drive future threats and opportunities.

An Impact-Uncertainty exercise begins by focusing on corporate decisions that may be greatly affected by changes in the external environment. These external

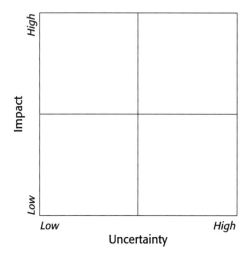

Figure 6.37. Impact-Uncertainty Matrix

forces can include a wide range of shifts and trends in areas such as industry demand and supply, demographics, the natural environment, social attitudes, business practices, and technological innovation. Specific external forces or drivers are identified that could influence the decisions in question. The potential impact of each issue on future threats and opportunities for the organization is assessed, and then the uncertainty of future outcomes for the issue is described.

The Two Dimensions and Their Extremes. The Impact-Uncertainty matrix explores two key dimensions: Impact and Uncertainty:

Impact. External factors range from high to low in their likely impact on the success of a decision.

Uncertainty. External factors vary to the extent that their occurrence and outcome are predictable, ranging from high to low.

The Four Quadrants. The Impact-Uncertainty matrix quickly sorts factors according to their relative priority:

• Upper left: High Impact, Low Uncertainty. Sometimes trends warn you of things that will happen with a high degree of certainty. Demographic changes, for example, can have a huge impact on strategic decisions, and companies can plan for them years in advance. Identifying these highly probable, high-impact factors is basic to planning, and the impact of items in this quadrant must be factored into current plans.

• Lower left: Low Impact, Low Uncertainty. External factors that fall into this quadrant are relatively unimportant. We know what their outcomes will be, and their impact is minimal. These items should receive a low level of attention.

• Lower right: High Uncertainty, Low Impact. Things that fall into this quadrant are not worth too much executive focus; they tend to be long term and relatively unimportant to the decisions at hand. Over time, these peripheral issues should be monitored because they could move into other quadrants.

• Upper right: High Impact, High Uncertainty. Our greatest concern is with the forces and decisions that fall into the high impact–high uncertainty category. These are the forces for which you should delay decisions as much as possible in order to get better future information. These are also the issues that will form the basis for full-blown scenario analysis.

Example: Petrochemical Industry. Representatives from three oil and petrochemical companies and three consulting firms were brought together by SRIC-BI consultants to identify and discuss issues that affect the future of the world's energy business.[43] High-level results of the discussion on global warming are displayed in Figure 6.38.

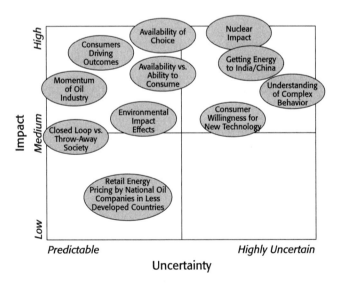

Figure 6.38. World Energy Business Issues Matrix

Subsequent discussion by the participants highlighted a series of key inter-locking issues to monitor in the future, including these:

- Taxes: Governments are torn between their desire to preserve oil-based tax revenue and the need to respond to public pressures on environmental and supply issues. Government policy will drive investment in new technologies.

- Technology: Uncertainty around climate change and taxes creates uncertainty regarding alternative energy investments and where future competitors will come from.

- Temperature: The timing and goals of government policy and investments will modify as perceptions of temperature change evolves. Potential new technologies could greatly extend the use of fossil fuels or have just the opposite effect, allowing competing or new sources of energy to eliminate the need for oil altogether.

Context. Impact and Uncertainty are relevant to any strategy development, technology planning, or issues management exercise. This framework is ideal for determining which issues to pay attention to and identifying strategic actions.

Method. The following process is suggested for assessing the values of the issues and placing them on the matrix:

- Step 1: Focus. Select an important strategic decision to examine.
- Step 2: Scan. Identify the full set of external issues and forces that could have an impact on the decision's success.
- Step 3: Assess the impact. Estimate the future impact of each issue on the decision's success or failure.
- Step 4: Assess likelihood. Decide what the degree of uncertainty is or how well future outcomes can be predicted. (It's important to make the step 3 and step 4 assessments in this order.)
- Step 5: Score. Based on assessments in steps 3 and 4, place the issues on the matrix. Direct most attention to the items on the top half of the matrix. The High Impact, Low Uncertainty issues are considered predetermined, and decisions must work under the expected outcomes. The High Impact, High Uncertainty issues represent the forces that will drive future threats and opportunities for the organization.

Reference

SRI Consulting Business Intelligence. [http://www.sric-bi.com].

⊞

Entrance and Exit Strategies
Robert Hayes and Steven Wheelwright

All the world's a stage,
And all the men and women merely players.
They have their exits and their entrances.
—William Shakespeare[44]

Often in life, victory belongs not to those who are best at the game, but rather to those who know when to play and when to walk away. Baseball coaches face this classic dilemma many times over with pitchers. Should a fading hurler be pulled even if he is only three strikes away from the end of the game? Should a defensive player be put in the field in the late innings of a big game in order to protect a lead? The coach needs to make these choices based primarily on the abilities of the players, but sometimes other factors are more important, like the match of pitcher to batter or the momentary need for a shake-up. A gambler walks into a casino and has a choice: play an empty table or a hot one. When she is up several thousand dollars, is it time to walk away or play another hand? Making money on the stock market is as much about selling at the right time as it is choosing sound investments.

The Entrance and Exit Strategies framework (Figure 6.39) helps managers confront entrance and exit options in a planned and informed way. It quickly

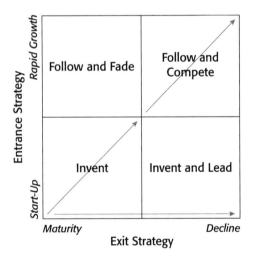

Figure 6.39. Entrance and Exit Strategies Matrix

reveals the capabilities and culture of the organization in relation to the competitive landscape of an industry and helps to identify hurdles the strategy must overcome.

The Two Dimensions and Their Extremes. The Entrance and Exit Strategies matrix explores two key dimensions: Entrance Strategy and Exit Strategy:[45]

> Entrance Strategy. One can join a market in either the Start-Up phase, when demand is primarily from early adopters, or during the later Rapid Growth phase, after initial risk is removed.

> Exit Strategy. Ultimately, the choice is whether to leave the game when the market is maturing and attracting big competitors, or at some later date. Each departure point has its unique benefits and requirements.

The Four Quadrants. Companies need to choose a strategy that complements their natural strengths and avoid adopting a strategy better suited to a different sort of competitor:

- Upper left: Follow and Fade. These firms attempt to jump in and control the industry but are beaten by the competition and forced to leave early. In most cases, they fail to recover their investment.
- Lower left: Invent. These are visionaries who enter markets early, striving to prove the value of their offerings and establish customer demand. With their goal achieved and profit margins narrowing with the entrance of major players, these companies exit to develop their next idea. Venture-oriented private firms often fall into this quadrant.
- Lower right: Invent and Lead. These innovators hope to establish and dominate a niche throughout an entire product life cycle. To succeed, they need to restructure business processes and develop operating competencies such as commodity production and selling. The redirection is often difficult; these companies struggle to maintain their entrepreneurial cultures and ability to invent.
- Upper right: Follow and Compete. These large firms have capital and the desire to extend their brand into the given product category or industry. They wait until the product stabilizes and the market is predictable, and then they bring a quality offering to market at a highly competitive price. With core competencies in production, advertising, and customer service, they aim to own the market.

Method. Follow these steps to conduct a high-level Entrance and Exit Strategy analysis:

- Step 1: Define. Identify the market you are considering entering.
- Step 2: Assess. Determine your entrance and exit approach and those of all competitors you expect to face over a two- to five-year period. Place them on the matrix.
- Step 3: Design. Integrate the impact of competing entrance and exit strategies into your strategic and financial plans. Create a high-level mitigation plan for those who will compete directly in your quadrant.

Reference

Hayes, R. H., and Wheelwright, S. C. "The Dynamics of Process-Product Life-Cycles." *Harvard Business Review,* Mar.-Apr. 1979, pp. 127–136.

CHAPTER SEVEN

Organizational Frameworks

Structure Frameworks
Good to Great Matrix of Creative Discipline
Employee Motivation
Alliance Drivers
Team Types

Leadership and Culture Frameworks
Situational Leadership
*The Four Power Players
   in Knowledge Organizations*
T-Group Leadership

Learning and Change Frameworks
SECI

Human Capital
Differentiation and Integration
Means and Ends
The Change Grid
Learning and Change
Similarities and Differences

Process Frameworks
The Four Realms of Experience
Make versus Buy
Four Square Model
Product and Supply Chain Architecture
Telematics Framework
The Virtue Matrix

The prime organizational challenge has shifted from efficiency to agility (Figure 7.1). It's not that efficient operations are no longer important; they simply are not enough, and businesses are building structures and processes that ensure rapid sense-and-response ability.

To maintain pace with dynamic external environments, firms are flattening their vertical structures, empowering front-line staff, and forming external partnerships that provide access to necessary but noncore capabilities. With each move in this direction, some formal power is forfeited. Control is being replaced with knowledge as firms tap the resources of three critical constituencies: em-

The Archetypal Organizational Dilemma

Core Question: How can our organization be more effective?

Key Issues: Design and management of structure, jobs, and processes

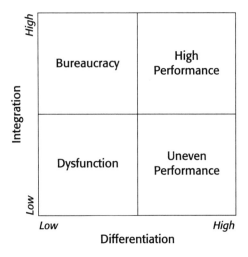

Figure 7.1. The Archetypal Organizational Dilemma

ployees, strategic partners, and customers. Business leadership today consists of directing and aligning the efforts, creativity, and goodwill of numerous disparate parties without the luxury of formal authority to set goals and enforce compliance.

A BRIEF HISTORY OF ORGANIZATIONAL THEORY

The modern business organization was born during the industrial revolution in the processing and manufacturing industries of England, Europe, and the United States. Masses of people migrated from rural farming communities to work in the new factories, using processes that were tightly defined and left little room for creativity or initiative.

Built to leverage the power of machine technology, early organizational models were mechanistic and rational, the primary goal being to maintain efficient and reliable operations. It was all about the machine and the assembly line, finding economies of scale through technical design and efficient management.

The human relations school of organizational management grew in reaction to the impersonal and often exploitative aspects of the scientific approach. Supported by parallel developments in individual and social psychology, proponents focused on human potential, feelings, and job designs that led to work that was fulfilling as well as efficient. Work innovations like GE's Hawthorne experiment, MacGregor's Theory X and Y, and Frederick Herzberg's Job Enrichment demonstrated that happy, engaged workers were more productive: treat someone like a gear, and the person will think like one; treat her with respect, and she will seize the opportunity to perform responsibly and professionally.

In dialectical terms, a tension had set up between the two philosophies, which eventually gave rise to integrative approaches drawing on the best of both schools of thought. Socio-technical systems, like the original form of the corporation, first appeared in England, in the coal mines shortly after World War II. A blend of the two approaches, it captured the interest of two types of companies: those where social problems engendered by the technical-rational approach were creating motivational or labor problems, and progressive companies with visionary and adventurous leaders interested in establishing ideal, high-performance working conditions. Two well-known examples were GM's Saturn plants and Shell's redesign of its chemical processing facilities.

As in the case of strategy, traditional approaches to achieving organizational effectiveness are being challenged by the forces of complexity (faster, more dynamic contexts make agility a necessary core competency), technology (digital technologies enable better, cheaper work production, and communications make technology a core competency), and globalization (redefinition of the location of workers and available markets sets wider boundaries for firms).

The result of these factors is a reconceptualization of the firm, work, and day-to-day operating challenges. The contemporary self-organizing, complexity-managing, risk-mitigating, constantly learning business organization is different. Prime skills now include sensing the environment; recognizing and resolving dilemmas; creating and sharing knowledge; retaining, motivating, and training talented employees; and partnering with suppliers and customers.

A 2 × 2 VIEW OF ORGANIZATION DEVELOPMENT

This chapter explores a rich assortment of organizational frameworks in the following four categories:

- Structure: The way we design jobs and business processes either helps or hinders effectiveness. These frameworks assist us to define and structure work in ways that improve performance.

- Leadership and culture: Organizations are communities bound by shared values and rules. Some of these are formal; many are implicit.

Leadership is provided by a variety of individuals, some drawing on formal authority and others calling on their ability to influence through expertise, seniority, or relationships.

- Learning and change: Managing change may well be the new norm, however it remains a challenging and often painful process. Learning is viewed as a key enabler of healthy and successful change processes.

- Process: Systems can be greatly improved by applying a process design orientation. We do this by treating each process step and transaction as modular components that may or may not be ideal or even necessary. Working with prescribed tools and principles, existing sequences can be upgraded and whole new steps created.

STRUCTURE FRAMEWORKS

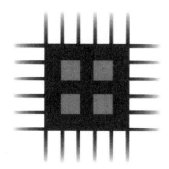

How do we organize work and people?

Organization design is meant to facilitate productivity through engineering individual and collaborative efforts. It would be hard enough to do this right if we all agreed on goals and design principles and if technologies and conditions didn't constantly change.

We sometimes overlook structural problems because structure is difficult to design and painful to change. At other times, we mistakenly turn to structure to fix interpersonal, process, or competitive problems. The frameworks in this chapter offer a variety of ways to approach the design of work and organizations sensitively, carefully, and creatively.

⊞

Good to Great Matrix of Creative Discipline
Jim Collins

> The question of "Why greatness" is almost a nonsense question. If you're engaged in work that you love and care about, for whatever reason, then the question needs no answer.
> —Jim Collins[1]

The Good to Great matrix (Figure 7.2) comes from the book of the same name by Jim Collins of Stanford University. Collins examined the financial performance of 1,435 Fortune 500 companies over three decades to find those capable of lifting their financial performance above the market and above the averages for their industry. His intent was to identify the special qualities that enabled organizations to ascend from sustained good performance to sustained great performance.

Figure 7.2. Good to Great Matrix

Collins's methodology included exhaustive secondary research, long-term financial analysis, and extensive interviews with company executives. One of his key findings was that good to great companies were successful on two cultural dimensions: Discipline (the ability to set goals and enforce accountability) and Entrepreneurialism (a culture of freedom, innovation, and risk taking). The tension between creativity and innovation, on the one hand, and discipline and financial control, on the other, is well known to CEOs. Synthesizing the two forces over the long term is surprisingly rare: only 11 of 1,435 companies were able to make it through Collins's research filter and qualify as good to great.

Most successful start-ups do not go on to become great companies. As a business becomes successful, it grows in complexity. In time, the characteristic easygoing informality of the start-up becomes a liability rather than an asset. Many firms flounder when it becomes necessary to impose tighter discipline on the organization. As professional managers replace the entrepreneurs who started the firm, the culture undergoes changes. If left unchecked, it becomes increasingly hierarchical, internally focused, and ultimately a place where creative innovators no longer want to be.

The Two Dimensions and Their Extremes. The Good to Great matrix explores two key dimensions: Culture of Discipline and Entrepreneurial Ethic:

Culture of Discipline. Firms with a Culture of Discipline excel at setting and achieving business goals. They institute mechanisms for planning, measuring, and changing course as needed, and have trained managers to use them.

Entrepreneurial Ethic. Entrepreneurial Ethic means that a firm has maintained a start-up kind of enthusiasm for customers and products. These organizations encourage innovative thinking and reward action over analysis.

The Four Quadrants. Firms may start out as Entrepreneurial ventures; however, Discipline is eventually needed to sustain operational effectiveness. Collins describes four outcomes of the trade-offs between these two factors:

• Upper left: Hierarchical Organization. The hierarchical firm is effective at setting goals and managing to meet objectives. However, it has become focused on the wrong attribute at the core of the organization. In the Good to Great view of the world, discipline is a means to enabling more innovation and creativity, not an end in itself. In Hierarchical Organizations, leaders overvalue order and control, and drive innovative rule breakers out of the firm.

• Lower left: Bureaucratic Organization. In the Bureaucratic Organization, goals are set but not met. Accountability is diffuse. Failure may not be rewarded, but it is tolerated. Many firms develop this type of culture at some point in their life cycle. For a recent example, consider the national telephone companies prior to privatization.

• Lower right: Start-Up Organization. In the start-up phase, firms depend almost solely on innovation for success. Entrepreneurial activity is rewarded, and risk takers who succeed become stars. The few start-ups that become great firms build on their innovations to create methods for repeating that success and nurturing freedom in the firm.

• Upper right: Greatness Organization. Great organizations build a culture of freedom and innovation, and then introduce enough discipline to ensure cooperation without creating unnecessary bureaucracy. Their cultures are inclusive and forgiving—employees have no fear of bringing bad, but realistic news to executives—and open to innovation.

Example: Kroger and A&P. In 1950, A&P was the world's largest retailer, and Kroger was a midsized competitor.[2] Around 1970, Kroger research determined that market demand was shifting. Customers wanted superstores: well-lit, clean outlets with lots of services and much wider selection than traditional grocery stores. Through the 1970s, Kroger remade the company in response to changing customer demand (Figure 7.3).

Up to that point, both A&P and Kroger tended to have older, smaller stores in slow-growing parts of the country. Kroger rebuilt itself from the ground up,

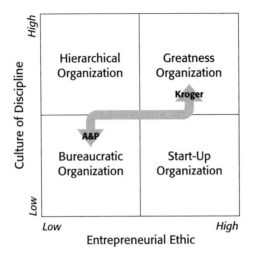

Figure 7.3. A&P versus Kroger Matrix

store by store, going so far as to pull out of regions where its new superstores were unlikely to succeed.

In contrast, A&P stayed mired in the past. The CEO conducted himself as if he were the caretaker representative of the founders, often wondering, "What would Mr. Hartford [the founder of A&P] do?" in response to strategic questions. Attempts to change the existing supermarket model were regularly shot down, and promising new store experiments were nixed. It is no wonder that customers increasingly overlooked its stores. As sales fell, the company engaged in ruinous price wars, which sucked up profits that could have been used to improve stores, as competitors were doing. Over three decades, the once-great Atlantic & Pacific Company fell apart, as Kroger's stock outperformed it eighty times over. In 1999, Kroger became the nation's largest grocery chain.

Context. The Good to Great matrix invites sobering comparisons between a firm and its competitors on two vital dimensions. And, it poses a question: Is your firm settling for merely being good when it could be great?

Method. Follow the steps below to conduct a high-level analysis of your organization's adequacy regarding discipline and entrepreneurialism:

• Step 1: Assess the culture of discipline. Rank yourself and three competitors (from highest to lowest) in terms of discipline. How consistent are the firms at hitting their financial performance targets? Are employees focused on internal politics or on listening to the market and customers? Are processes in place to manage and track performance properly?

- Step 2: Assess entrepreneurialism. Rank yourself and competitors in terms of entrepreneurialism. Ask the following questions: Are new ideas encouraged? Is failure tolerated within the culture as long as people take responsibility for their actions? Is the organization making strategic moves that indicate a keen sense of how the industry is changing and evolving? Is it an innovation leader within its field?
  - Step 3: Determine your current state. Using what you have learned, place your firm and competitors on the matrix.
  - Step 4: Create an improvement plan. Consider implications of the current state, and identify areas needing improvement.

Reference

Collins, J. *Good to Great.* New York: HarperBusiness, 2001.

⊞

Employee Motivation
Inspired by Frederick Herzberg

If only a small percentage of the time and money that is now devoted to hygiene, however, were given to job enrichment efforts, the return in human satisfaction and economic gain would be one of the largest dividends that industry and society have reaped through their efforts at better personnel management.
—Frederick Herzberg[3]

If we remove the dissatisfaction from a job, we do not necessarily end up with a motivated employee.[4] Job satisfaction and dissatisfaction are not opposites; rather, they describe two different, and critical, aspects of work. Fulfilling, motivating work derives from the design of the work itself—Motivators—while dissatisfaction results from poor work conditions—Hygiene (Figure 7.4). Better lighting, for example, removes a problem but does not make a job more interesting or meaningful. This was the insight that Frederick Herzberg introduced in his 1966 book, *Work and Nature of Man,* and classic 1968 *Harvard Business Review* article, "One More Time: How Do You Motivate Employees?" Too often, efforts to motivate concentrate on Hygiene factors. Applying Herzberg's framework gave birth to the job enrichment movement of the 1970s and continues to influence current approaches to job design and high performance.

The Two Dimensions and Their Extremes. The Motivating Employees matrix explores two key dimensions: Motivators and Hygiene:

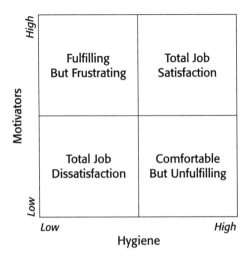

Figure 7.4. Motivating Employees Matrix

Motivators. These are factors that are intrinsic to the job, such as achievement, recognition, the work itself, responsibility, growth, and advancement.

Hygiene. These are factors that are extrinsic to the job, such as company policy, administration, supervision, interpersonal relationships, working conditions, status, salary, and security.

The Four Quadrants. The effective design of work recognizes the need to address both Motivator and Hygiene factors. Inattention to either one places a drag on overall job satisfaction and organizational performance effectiveness:

• Upper left: Fulfilling But Frustrating. The work itself is interesting and worth doing; however, environmental conditions get in the way. People would do great work if only the barriers were removed.

• Lower left: Total Job Dissatisfaction. Both the job and working conditions are poor. Performance effectiveness is low and motivation is highly unlikely without serious efforts at improvement.

• Lower right: Comfortable But Unfulfilling. Working conditions are excellent, but the work lacks sufficient challenge or opportunity to achieve something meaningful. Employees could do great work if they wanted to, but they won't because they are not motivated.

• Upper right: Total Job Satisfaction. The ideal situation exists when both Hygiene and Motivator factors are addressed. Employees feel good about the working environment, there are no unnecessary barriers to performance, and the work is highly motivating.

Method. Herzberg proposes a ten-step process for applying these ideas for job enrichment. The core of the approach is contained in three steps:

- Step 1: Identify the target job.
- Step 2: Conduct a Hygiene audit. Ask, "What is frustrating about this job?" Address key issues.
- Step 3: Conduct a Motivator brainstorm session. Ask, "What would make the job a richer and more meaningful experience?" Consider the core Motivator factors: achievement, recognition, the work itself, responsibility, and growth or advancement.

References

Herzberg, F. *Work and Nature of Man.* New York: World Publishing Company, 1966.

Herzberg, F. "One More Time: How Do You Motivate Employees?" *Harvard Business Review,* Sept.–Oct. 1987, pp. 53–62.

Herzberg, F., Mausner, B., and Snyderman, B. B. *The Motivation to Work.* New Brunswick, N.J.: Transaction Publishers, 1993.

⊞

Alliance Drivers
John Harbison and Peter Pekar Jr.

The companies that are most successful with alliances have learned the importance of embedding the capability to create alliances in the corporate structure.
—John Harbison and Peter Pekar Jr.[5]

The Alliance Drivers matrix (Figure 7.5) is based on long-term research into more than five hundred major firms and six thousand strategic alliances. In their book *Smart Alliances,* Harbison and Pekar document how alliances have grown in importance as drivers of corporate revenue growth and as a source of strategic advantage. (They defined strategic alliances as partnerships among relatively equal firms that involve long-term commitments with shared resources, funding or equity.)

The research demonstrates that two factors, Globalization pressures and Capability Gaps, have played a major role in determining the need for corporate alliances in recent years. The degree to which these drivers are present varies greatly by industry. In some sectors, firms must establish a worldwide presence if they are to stay competitive. In others, the need to continually update and

Figure 7.5. Alliance Drivers Matrix

acquire new capabilities drives alliances. Although there is little direct tension between Globalization and Capability Gaps, the dialectical conflict is implicit and important. Alliances are inherently risky and involve complex issues of dependency and control.

The Two Dimensions and Their Extremes. The Alliance Drivers matrix explores two key dimensions: Globalization and Capability Gap:

Globalization. Globalization refers to the pressure to establish an international presence and succeed in foreign markets. Industries with high levels of global consolidation (autos, telecommunications) fit this definition.

Capability Gap. Capability gaps arise when companies lack the skills, knowledge, or scale to meet fast-changing market demands. Increasingly, firms are turning to partners to fill those gaps.

The Four Quadrants. The degree to which Globalization and Capability Gap drive the need for an alliance defines four strategic approaches:

• Upper left: Channel Access. Some foreign markets require a large retail and wholesale distribution network in order to compete effectively. In such cases, firms need to seek local partners with a significant footprint in their home territory.

• Lower left: Pooled Resources. In industries such as steel, paper, and utilities, products have high weight-to-value ratio, creating transportation difficulties or other barriers that insulate firms against foreign competition. Companies in these businesses should ally in order to reduce risk and exploit economies of scale.

• Lower right: Critical Mass. In industries such as health care and entertainment, firms find themselves facing new market demands as industry boundaries blur. They should consider partnering with firms outside their traditional business domain to build a critical mass of skills and audience. Such was the case with Microsoft and NBC, which coinvested to create MSNBC.

• Upper right: Global Leadership. Firms in industries characterized by rapid technological innovation, like computers, telecom, and electronics, should seek partners that can fill in capability gaps that provide an immediate technological edge. The Sony-Ericsson partnership to produce mobile phones is one such alliance.

Method. Harbison and Pekar include a robust alliance planning method and a detailed matrix for analyzing alliance needs and opportunities. We suggest the following exercise as a way to initiate a review process:

• Step 1: Scan. Make a list of recent or planned strategic alliances at your firm.

• Step 2: Assess. List the technologies, capabilities, access to markets, and other assets you hope to acquire through strategic alliances. Check whether the drivers in Table 7.1 are present.

• Step 3: Diagnose. Using the information you've gathered, plot your strategic alliances on the matrix. Consider the implications of the matrix. Are alliances addressing the globalization forces and capability gaps you face?

Reference

Harbison, J. R., and Pekar, P. Jr. *Smart Alliances.* San Francisco: Jossey-Bass, 1998.

Table 7.1. Aligning Drivers with Strategy

Driver	Quadrant
Risk sharing	Left quadrants
Geographic access	Upper quadrants
Economies of scale	Left quadrants
Market or channel access	Left quadrants
Technology access	Right quadrants
Funding	Right quadrants
Skills leverage	Right quadrants

⊞

Team Types
Kimball Fisher

Teams should be set up to elicit not the compliance of the workforce, but its commitment.
  —T. Harris and C. Daniels[6]

Collaboration is increasingly important in the knowledge era. Team effectiveness is a prime forum for collaboration and thus an important driver of high performance. Yet we tend to approach the vast assortment of work teams in the same way, rather than recognizing structural and contextual differences. Kimball Fisher has written extensively on the subject of teams and has helped many organizations to improve their team practices. The effort begins with getting clear about business and organizational requirements and the type of teams that are needed. Teams differ in their Duration and Scope. Each of the four team types resulting from this model has unique performance properties and development needs (Figure 7.6).

The Two Dimensions and Their Extremes. The Team Types matrix explores two key dimensions: Duration and Scope:

Duration. Teams are created to tackle a short-term need, or they are ongoing.

Scope. Teams perform within a single, defined area, or they are tasked with outputs that touch multiple operations.

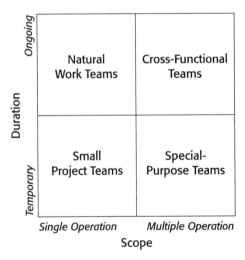

Figure 7.6. Team Types Matrix

The Four Quadrants. Team structure needs to align with task requirements and organizational values:

• Upper left: Natural Work Teams. The most common types of teams are those formed around business functions and processes in organization, like the radiology department in a hospital or the R&D group in a midsized software company. These teams have ongoing responsibilities to deliver defined outputs.

• Lower left: Small Project Teams. Temporary teams are created within business units to solve a specific problem or assist in the design of new methods. Examples include resolving equipment problems and scheduling vacations.

• Lower right: Special-Purpose Teams. When a short-term task cuts across a larger portion of the organization, an interfunctional team is required. Participants bring technical knowledge as well as the ability to represent the interests of their colleagues.

• Upper right: Cross-Functional Teams. Communication and coordination across organizational boundaries are often achieved with cross-functional teams. These typically meet on a regular basis to review systemwide issues and provide representative input. Examples are safety, training, and quality improvement.

Method. Team form should be guided by task function and organizational culture:

• Step 1: Diagnose. Determine if a team is required by considering such issues as interdependence, need for communication, and ability to influence.

• Step 2: Envision. If there is a need for a team, identify which of the four types is required.

• Step 3: Design. Recruit team members, orient them, and operate with clear expectations, role, authorities, and processes.

References

The Fisher Group. [http://www.thefishergroup.com/].

Mohrman, S. A., Cohen, S. G., and Mohrman, A. M. Jr. *Designing Team-Based Organizations: New Forms for Knowledge Work.* San Francisco: Jossey-Bass, 1995.

LEADERSHIP AND CULTURE FRAMEWORKS

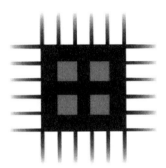

What leadership and culture are needed? How do we diagnose the current state, and how do we improve it?

Most observers agree that culture and leadership are key factors in attaining organizational health and productivity. Defining these qualities and the methods for strengthening them, however, is a more elusive undertaking. Fortunately, we have numerous examples of excellence in both areas to draw on. The frameworks in this section tend to reflect best practices, emphasizing balance and adjustment to situational requirements.

Situational Leadership
Paul Hersey and Ken Blanchard

> The leader needs to match their leadership behaviors to the performance level of the individual or group. This is really a follower-driven model, not a leader-driven model.
> —Paul Hersey[7]

> This helps people figure out if organizational leadership needs to be more like Genghis Khan or Mr. Rogers; we find that pretty important!
> —Anonymous

After spending years trying to prove otherwise, the preeminent leadership researcher Ralph Stogdill concluded in 1948, "A person does not become a leader by virtue of the possession of some combination of traits."[8] This acknowledgment gave rise to a procession of multifactored, contingency-based leadership models. The best-known and most widely used of these is Situational Leadership, formulated in 1969 by Paul Hersey and Ken Blanchard (Figure 7.7).

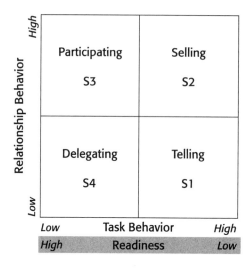

Figure 7.7. Situational Leadership Matrix

Situational Leadership maintains that leader effectiveness depends on matching style with task requirements and follower maturity level. The model focuses on behavior rather than attitude.

The Two Dimensions and Their Extremes. The Situational Leadership matrix explores two key dimensions: Relationship Behavior and Task Behavior:

Relationship Behavior. Relationship behavior refers to the extent to which leaders are concerned with the socioemotional needs of staff, encourage progress, and actively listen.

Task Behavior. Task behavior refers to the extent to which leaders initiate, define, plan, and organize work.

The Four Quadrants. The Situational Leadership model allows leaders to quickly map followers' task-specific performance into four readiness levels, each demanding a different leadership style. It can also be used by external parties such as recruitment firms and human resource departments to identify hiring priorities when filling management vacancies. The action required of the leader defines each quadrant as a uniquely different leadership style.

What sets this model apart is its recognition of differences among those who are to be led. Staff exhibit varying degrees of readiness, and this determines which of the four leadership styles will be most appropriate. If followers are unwilling or unable to take responsibility, the Telling style of leadership is most appropriate. If they are fully capable of doing the work and willing to accept responsibility for the task, the Delegating style of leadership is the best fit:

• Upper left: Participating. Followers are able but unwilling to be responsible. Participating and development are needed to coach and reassure the person whose motivation and focus are flagging.
• Lower left: Delegating. Followers are willing and able to take responsibility. The leader recognizes their ability by showing trust and maintains a less active role and relationship with them. Delegating works for both parties, increasing scope for development and job satisfaction for the employee, while freeing the leader to focus on other tasks.
• Lower right: Telling. Followers are unable and unwilling to take responsibility. A strong, directive leadership style is needed. Intimidating or overwhelming tasks are two examples where a Telling approach is recommended.
• Upper right: Selling. Followers are unable but willing to take responsibility. Task direction is coupled with socioemotional support and rationale for why work needs to be completed in a particular way.

Example: U.S. Army. The U.S. Army recruited approximately 79,500 young men and women in 2002, creating a standing force of 475,000 soldiers. Recruits enter untrained and unskilled, and over a period of several years they progress from this state of relative ignorance to readiness for the two basic situations the army must face: war and peace. These different contexts present a challenging set of demands, calling on sensitivity, awareness, and leadership competencies at the highest level.

The years following the Vietnam War and the Persian Gulf Conflict were extended periods of peace. During these eras, retention and development of talent depended on offering meaningful growth and interesting assignments without the looming threat and the experience of waging war.

Conflicts in Yugoslavia and the Middle East have once again forced a return to the primary war role and capability. But turning on a dime from peace to war is not easy.

Situational Leadership helps to determine the appropriate leadership style for different contexts and to define the leadership competencies most required by army officers (Figure 7.8). In peacetime, recruits move quickly from the Telling style of being led to the Selling mode, where a primary goal is to retain the motivation and loyalty of troops in the face of minimal external danger and demand. In the case of high-potential officers, the Participative style is needed to tailor development opportunities to the individual.

In wartime, it is essential that soldiers can operate in the Telling mode, where command and control direction is often mandatory. There isn't much time for

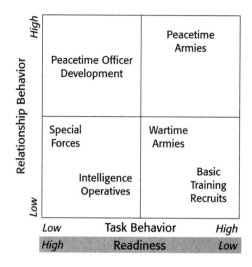

Figure 7.8. War and Peace Leadership Matrix

Selling, except when will is flagging and troops need inspiration; think of Churchill in the most trying periods of World War II and, more recently, Norman Schwarzkopf in Desert Storm. For certain high-risk missions, total Delegation is necessary as teams operate independently.

Context. Situational Leadership is used by managers to plan how to approach a given subordinate and by executives and human resource specialists when determining how to hire managers and leaders for a team.

Method. An early version of the Situational Leadership questionnaire was published in the May 1976 issue of *Training and Development Journal.* Twelve multiple-choice questions help to identify one's preferred leadership style and the level of staff readiness. The object of the exercise is to match leadership style with the unique needs of each staff member.

Since that time, Hersey has continued to update the original work and published new versions of diagnostic survey tools. At its most basic, here is how to apply the Situational Leadership framework:

• Step 1: Assess. Assess the readiness of each member of a work group for specific tasks. Readiness refers to the Ability to complete the required task assignment and Willingness. Assessment can be done with the help of a Situational Leadership survey tool or by carefully and systematically appraising the readiness of each individual.

- Step 2: Evaluate. Locate all the workers on the grid to reflect their relative Readiness.
- Step 3: Assess. Assess the manager's style of leadership. The first step in being able to vary your leadership approach is gaining awareness of what you are currently doing to succeed. The manager may be generalizing this method across all staff and situations, meeting with the greatest success where his or her natural talents and inclinations are well suited to the situational needs.
- Step 4: Design. Review each of the staff relationships, and construct a plan to address situational needs. Recognize that some cases may place role pressures on the leader or even the larger work system. Performing a variety of leadership functions depends on several things: awareness of staff needs and one's preferred style, agreement by both parties to play reciprocal roles in a respectful and sincere way, and competency on the part of the leader to provide different forms of leadership. Leadership coaching and training may be required to help the manager successfully behave differently.
- Step 5: Review. Before implementing leadership plans, it is important to step back to regard the larger leadership and organizational landscape you have created. A solution at one level can create organizational or work design problems elsewhere. For example, a manager can support a wide span of control if most work is delegated to mature professionals who operate independently. If the leadership solution involves lots of coaching, a new level of supervision may be required to relieve the time burden being placed on the manager.

Reference

Hersey, P. *The Situational Leader.* New York: Warner Books, 1992.

⊞

The Four Power Players in Knowledge Organizations
Karl-Erik Sveiby

Many putative "leaders" fondly imagine they are running their organizations when all they are doing is allowing them to run themselves. They do not understand the power play at work and are measuring the wrong things.
—Karl-Erik Sveiby[9]

Formal roles and processes often take a back seat as organizations become increasingly dependent on knowledge.[10] Resentments and misunderstandings can easily occur in such environments, as individuals perform their tasks with only limited awareness of their impact on the firm and those in other positions. Karl-Erik Sveiby, one of the founders of the Knowledge Management movement, argues for higher awareness and conscious management of the interchange between the four fundamental roles that tend to arise in such contexts. Both Professional (content) and Organizational (process) Competencies are necessary and in the right balance (Figure 7.9).

The Two Dimensions and Their Extremes. The Four Power Players matrix explores two key dimensions: Professional Competence and Organizational Competence:

Professional Competence. This refers to the content of the business, the company's core value proposition.

Organizational Competence. This consists of administrative, communications, and related maintenance functions.

The Four Quadrants. The dimensions represent the two knowledge traditions that can be found in most organizations. These traditions must find a way to coexist constructively and respectfully:

• Upper left: The Professional. Knowledge businesses as typified by the consulting firm are built around this role. Customers demand their expertise. They represent the essential value of the business in the marketplace. Professionals thrive on solving thorny problems. They dislike routine and solving problems the same way over and over. This tendency creates tension with the administration and those trying to increase productivity: the managers. Professionals

Figure 7.9. Four Power Players Matrix

often appear to be self-absorbed and thoughtless about administrative needs. Operating with a different sense of urgency and purpose, they are however capable of higher levels of consideration and collaboration when informed and appropriately motivated.

• Lower left: The Support Staff. Success in professional firms often depends on freeing up front-line staff from administrative and detail work. Support staff play the crucial role of handling the many tasks that are not dependent on professional expertise but are nonetheless critical. There is a tendency for these people to fall out of the communication loop and resent others, principally the professionals, who often display little sensitivity to organizational rules and needs.

• Lower right: The Manager. Managers have designated authority to make sure work is coordinated and completed in a sustainable and acceptable way. They are responsible primarily for the organizational priorities of the firm, making it possible for others to be creative and client centered. Managers work through other people, in contrast to professionals, who work with other people. Managers therefore often find themselves at loggerheads with the professionals.

• Upper right: The Leader. Leadership provides direction and passion that defines and drives the business. In knowledge-based firms, leadership does not always come from formally designated leader roles, and it can be more difficult to assert. Nonetheless, it is essential. A prime task of formal leadership is to provide professionals with the conditions to exercise their creativity for the benefit of customers. Because of the enormous and often conflicting demands, some successful companies split this role. For example, one person may be in charge of professionals, while someone else is responsible for marketing and administration. Leadership in a newspaper, for example, is divided between the editor and the publisher.

Method. The framework is useful for diagnosing and clarifying individual roles and organizational balance. Problems arise when roles are missing or are not being well executed:

• Step 1: Assess the need for the four primary functions (more, less, or okay as is)?
• Step 2: Identify who is in each role.
• Step 3: Assess the effectiveness of each function.
• Step 4: Assess the health of the relationship between the roles.
• Step 5: Make adjustments to improve within the four functions or between the functions.

Reference

Sveiby, K.-E. *The New Organizational Wealth: Managing and Measuring Knowledge-Based Assets.* San Francisco: Berrett-Koehler, 1997.

⊞

T-Group Leadership
Richard Nelson-Jones

Plotting the way that a leader works on a simple two-dimensional continuum
like the following (Didactic ↔ Facilitative) is an unsatisfactory way to look at
group leadership style.
—Richard Nelson-Jones[11]

Training groups are settings where participants improve life skills of a primarily social and leadership nature.[12] Effective leadership of such groups calls for
a balance of intellectual content—didactic instruction—and participatory self-
discovery—facilitation (Figure 7.10). Leaders need to develop both of these skills
and learn when each is most appropriate.

The Two Dimensions and Their Extremes. The T-Group Leadership matrix
explores two key dimensions: Didactic and Facilitative:

Didactic. This is a content-oriented, telling orientation. The teacher is the
expert who imparts a predefined body of knowledge to students.

Facilitative. This is an experiential, helping orientation based in observation, process, and sharing of responsibility. The agenda is generated in a
here-and-now manner, and the way solutions are achieved is often more
important than the solution itself.

Figure 7.10. T-Group Leadership Matrix

The Four Quadrants. Leaders need to match their role with what is required in the situation. In any training group, a certain amount of tension between the didactic and facilitative emphasis is inevitable:

• Upper left: Content Leadership. Content leadership employs a traditional teacher-student approach. The teacher is in control and responsible for defining and imparting knowledge. This approach is appropriate for phases of learning and under certain circumstances, such as large classes.
• Lower left: Leadership Abdication. Leaders who are too invisible add little, frustrating the group and wasting time that could be spent productively. Leaders need to take responsibility for their role and contributions.
• Lower right: Process Leadership. Process leaders focus on the moment, with the group interaction setting the agenda. This approach is most useful when working with small, intact work teams where the goal is performance effectiveness.
• Upper right: Balanced Leadership. Learning needs change dynamically in training groups. At one moment, the priority is making sense of an incident, calling on high facilitiative skills; at the next moment, it is acquiring a deeper understanding of a concept like trust or interpersonal conflict, calling on didactic mastery. Excellent training group leaders have developed both competencies.

Method. Leaders increase their effectiveness by matching their approach to situational requirements:

• Step 1: Diagnose. Consider the learning needs and capabilities of team members.
• Step 2: Design. Prepare experiential design and materials in accordance with needs.
• Step 3: Deliver. Deliver the training, monitoring success and adjusting as necessary.

Reference

Nelson-Jones, R. *Group Leadership.* Thomson Learning, 2003.

LEARNING AND CHANGE FRAMEWORKS

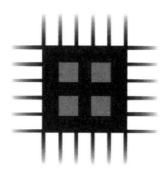

What new competencies are needed? What change is required? How do we manage the change?

The old saying, "If it ain't broke, don't fix it," has been replaced with the metaphor of "perpetual whitewater." At times, it really does appear that the only constant left is change. Adjusting to this state of affairs, organizations are building more flexible roles and structures and designing business processes that deliver just-in-time value to minimize waste and excess inventory.

Learning is a key enabler of change. In some businesses, training and development is a fully integrated function, preparing staff well in advance of change initiatives. Too often, though, it is an afterthought, competing with other tasks for scarce time and attention.

Frameworks in this section address the two topics of learning and change as an integrated whole, underscoring their interdependency.

⊞

SECI
Ikujiro Nonaka and Hirotaka Takeuchi

In an economy where the only certainty is uncertainty, the one sure source of lasting competitive advantage is knowledge.
—Ikujiro Nonaka and Hirotaka Takeuchi[13]

The notion of tacit knowledge in the SECI model (named for the four forms of knowledge conversion identified in the matrix: Socialization, Externalization, Combination, and Internalization) is based on the work of philosopher Michael Polanyi, who in 1966 classified knowledge into two categories: tacit and explicit. For Polanyi, knowledge that could be expressed and stored in words and numbers represented a small portion of human knowledge. The greater part represented hunches, intuition, values, images, beliefs, principles, and mental models of the world that enable us to work and socialize effectively. In 1995, Ikujiro Nonaka and Hirotaka Takeuchi published the SECI model (Figure 7.11) to help people understand how tacit and explicit knowledge interact within organizations and how the management of those interactions, which they called knowledge conversions, could be a source of competitive advantage. Their subsequent publications expanded on this model, and their insights have had a profound effect on how corporations now think about knowledge assets and knowledge management.[14]

Corporations have been receptive to this message, and for good reason. Over the past fifty years, the balance of value within firms has shifted from physical assets to intangible knowledge assets. When combined with the impact of increasing global competition, this has forced a fundamental change in organizational structure, from vertical, hierarchically integrated firms to ones that are increasingly horizontal, flat, and modular.

In the traditional model, work was conceived at the top of the hierarchy and executed at the bottom. Information flowed quickly down and not so quickly back and forth and up the chain of command. It is increasingly clear now that the knowledge that management seeks to control is created and leveraged daily by personnel throughout the organization, including unskilled, manual, and clerical workers.

In order to get their jobs done, workers continually create new knowledge. When they hit roadblocks, they invent solutions: they figure out how to operate equipment more efficiently, work around technology problems and design

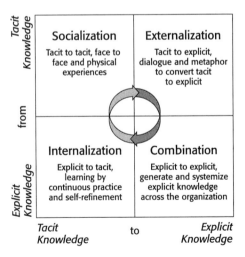

Figure 7.11. SECI Matrix

flaws, solve customer issues, and coax productivity out of informal organizational networks. Nonaka and Takeuchi's SECI matrix provides a systematic way of viewing the life cycle of knowledge development and transfer among workers within the firm.

The Two Dimensions and Their Extremes. The SECI matrix explores two key dimensions: Tacit Knowledge and Explicit Knowledge:

Tacit Knowledge. Tacit knowledge is highly personal and difficult to share. How do you communicate physical skills like becoming a master glass blower or learning how a second baseman makes a double play? How does a mother sense the needs of her child before they are expressed? And how does your most skilled computer technician diagnose problems in seconds that might take others hours? As Larry Prusak, executive director of IBM's Institute for Knowledge Management, says, "Knowledge is sticky, staying close to individuals and contexts."[15] Most of these kinds of knowledge don't translate quickly through books and computers. They are embedded in us as a result of our life experiences and the skills we practice on the job.

Nonaka and Takeuchi define two aspects of Tacit Knowledge: the cognitive and the technical. In the cognitive dimensions are the beliefs, ideals, and views of the world that are so deeply ingrained in us that we are frequently unaware of them. By shaping the way we see ourselves and the world around us, the cognitive dimension provides a foundation for all our interactions. The technical dimension refers to skills and know-how and personal ability to get our jobs done that have been set in place through long experience and practice.

Explicit Knowledge. Explicit Knowledge consists of knowledge that we communicate in formal language. It is discrete and can be captured and transmitted digitally. It can be encoded in a wide range of forms, such as books, manuals, and electronic databases.

The Four Quadrants. Each type of knowledge can be converted. When viewed as a learning process, the SECI matrix takes the form of a spiral. The four stages of knowledge conversion describe how organizations create, manage, and transfer knowledge. In the upper left, the process starts with Tacit "sympathized" Knowledge, hard-won worker skills that must be shared and socialized to become Explicit "conceptual" Knowledge (upper right). Once converted to Explicit Knowledge, it can be combined and integrated into explicit forms that can be shared throughout the organization. As workers reinternalize what they learn, it becomes Organizational Knowledge (lower left), part of the shared knowledge of the firm. Ultimately, newly trained workers begin to practice their skills on the job, slowly turning Explicit into new Tacit Knowledge over time (upper left):

- Upper left: Socialization (Tacit to Tacit). Socialization involves capturing knowledge through physical proximity and direct interaction with people. It is a Tacit-to-Tacit exchange. For example, people who work with mentors learn by observing, children watching their parents learn through imitation, and students watching an artist or craftsman at work learn by practicing what they have seen done by others. When we share physical space, activities, and experiences, we find numerous ways to learn from one another.
- Lower left: Internalization (Explicit to Tacit). Internalization refers to the conversion of Explicit Knowledge into the organization's Tacit Knowledge. In this stage, workers learn by doing and by training, turning the organization's wisdom into skill and knowledge of their own. They internalize the knowledge and increasingly rely on their own skills and judgment.
- Lower right: Combination (Explicit to Explicit). Combination is the conversion of Explicit Knowledge to new Explicit Knowledge. There are three main elements: combination, dissemination, and processing. First, Explicit Knowledge is captured and combined with other knowledge to create deeper, more complex levels of understanding. For example, a strategist who purchases an outside research report and integrates it into a strategy document she is writing is creating new Explicit Knowledge from two prior sets of explicit information. In the dissemination phase, the organization attempts to disperse the new knowledge through internal publications, meetings, and other processes. Finally, in the processing stage, new knowledge is edited internally into strategies, plans, and reports that make it easier to share and apply within the organization.
- Upper right: Externalization (Tacit to Explicit). Externalization is the stage of Tacit-to-Explicit information conversion. Articulating Tacit Knowledge in forms that others can understand—words, concepts, instructions, figurative language, and pictures—externalizes it. In practice, this often occurs though dialogue with others (work groups) and creative techniques such as hypothesis development using metaphors and analogies.

Example: Communities of Practice at Xerox. Many firms today face the complex challenge of maximizing the long-term value of Tacit Knowledge. Operational knowledge, as in processes such as check cashing and auto assembly, can be codified, reengineered, and taught to others. But how do you transfer craft skills and insights? For example, if you wanted to become a master consultant, the best way to do that would be to work with one. In fact, this is exactly the approach taken by firms such as McKinsey, which believe that young recruits must spend lots of time with top consultants in order to learn the client management and creative conceptual skills that lead to success in their business.

Companies such as Buckman Laboratories, Xerox, and Johnson & Johnson are among the leaders in the emerging field of knowledge management. At these companies, a great deal of effort goes into supporting communities of practice:

groups of people who share similar goals and interests and employ common tools and language in performing their work. The problems they experience are common, and they work together to learn and create solutions. In reality, a community of practice may be a far-flung virtual group of programmers or an in-house marketing team drawn from many disciplines. The output of communities of practice is knowledge as well as social capital—norms of trust, reciprocity, and citizen participation. As workers come together in an organic fashion to solve problems, they improve the overall efficiency of the organization. As the technology for global cooperation has improved, firms are finding it easier to foster collaboration that serves customers and empowers employees to take the lead in creating and converting new kinds of knowledge.

John Seely Brown, chief scientist of Xerox, relates the story of how communities of practice were developed among the company's repair technicians beginning in the early 1990s. When he was asked to design knowledge systems for technicians, he began by asking anthropologists to study the activities of the people in the field. He wanted to know how they learned and shared information. The main finding was that when a problem was encountered, a technician would call another technician and tell him the "story" of the machine (Figure 7.12). They would then share story "fragments" about other repair experiences, weaving a narrative together until they arrived at a solution for how to fix the machine. Storytelling continued when technicians got together for coffee and doughnuts in the morning before going into the field, serving as an informal method through which best practices were shared.[16]

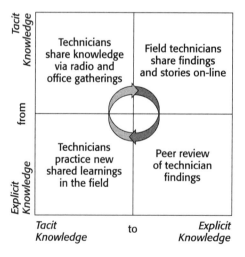

Figure 7.12. Xerox Repair Technicians SECI Matrix

To leverage this knowledge further, Brown created a community of practice by providing field technicians with two-way radios. These were always on, so the reps remained connected to their own instantaneous community of experts. Although this helped individual technicians improve their work in the field, it did nothing to improve the learning of technicians across the rest of the firm.

Brown was challenged to create a system that tapped the minds of the community of practice, not just the mind of one expert technician. In response, he and his team deployed a system they called Eureka, which enabled technical reps to share their stories over the Web. Periodically, specialists would validate the stories. In this way, individuals with specific knowledge became known to the whole community, and answers to very specific questions became available globally as soon as they were discovered. Brown estimates that learning increased 300 percent and saved Xerox up to $100 million per year.

Context. The SECI matrix is useful for raising awareness of how knowledge is managed in an organization. This awareness can be factored into the design of knowledge-sharing strategies and systems to improve knowledge creation, storage, and exchange practices. Each of the quadrants represents a diagnostic category and improvement opportunity to explore.

Method. Try the method that follows to examine an area of practice in your organization:

- Step 1: Define. Identify an aspect of organizational performance where there is a knowledge issue or gap.
- Steps 2–5: Diagnose. Examine and improve by tracing the handling of knowledge in this area through the knowledge life cycle by following the four phases of the SECI:

Upper left: Who has the knowledge? How is it shared or socialized?

Upper right: What mechanisms exist to make the knowledge explicit in the firm? Who is responsible for that?

Lower right: How is knowledge about this aspect of organizational performance synthesized with knowledge from other sources outside the firm? Where and how does that happen?

Lower left: What processes are in place to train and support further internalization of this new knowledge?

- Step 6: Envision the payoff. Answer the question: How would the improvement in knowledge capture and transfer lead to higher levels of performance within the firm? Cost reductions? Time savings? Quality improvements?

References

Brown, J. S., and Duguid, P. "Organizational Learning and Communities-of-Practice: Toward a Unified View of Working, Learning, and Innovation." *Organization Science*, 1991, *2*(1), 40–57.

Nonaka, I., and H. Takeuchi, H. *The Knowledge-Creating Company: How Japanese Companies Create the Dynamics of Innovation.* New York: Oxford University Press, 1995.

Nonaka, I., and Toyama, R. "A Firm as a Dialectical Being: Towards a Dynamic Theory of a Firm." *Industrial and Corporate Change*, 2002, *11*, 995–1009.

⊞

Human Capital
Tom Stewart

Random hiring of Ph.D.'s won't cut it. What are you going to do with them? Human capital needs its customer and structural siblings to make a difference.
—Tom Stewart[17]

Thomas Stewart, executive editor of the *Harvard Business Review,* is one of the pioneers of the Knowledge Management movement and the author of two of its most important books, *Intellectual Capital* (1997), and *The Wealth of Knowledge* (2001). Intellectual capital, comprising human, structural, and customer components, is the new driver of competitiveness. The year 1991 was pivotal: worldwide investment in intangible information technologies (such as computers, telephones, and personal digital assistants) overtook money spent on machines (farm machinery, factories, metal, and plastics, for example) involved in the production of tangible products. As the "weight of value" continues to decline, it becomes increasingly important to create meaningful ways to define, identify, develop, manage, and measure these intangible assets.

Stewart makes the argument for strategic management of three primary forms of intellectual capital: human, structural, and customer. In the domain of human capital, certain types of knowledge assets hold much higher value to firms than others. By focusing on two criteria, Difficult to Replace versus Important to Customer, businesses can determine the relative importance and difficulty of the replacement of its business functions and the competencies they depend on. The Human Capital framework (Figure 7.13) offers a clear and useful method for organizations to assess operations and determine the best treatment of divisions and positions throughout the company.

The Two Dimensions and Their Extremes. The Human Capital matrix explores two key dimensions: Difficult to Replace and Important to Customer:

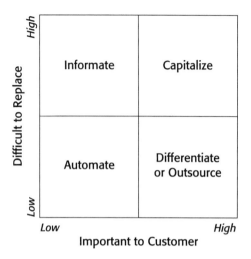

Figure 7.13. Human Capital Matrix

Difficult to Replace. Some skill sets are more difficult to replace than others. Jobs based on scarce competencies (such as cardiac surgery) or unique knowledge about the business (such as auditing and communications) are higher in this regard than those consisting of repetitive, procedural work (for example, assembly line worker, cleaning staff). This dimension is primarily indicative of the importance of a role within the organization as opposed to representing a customer perspective.

Important to Customer. Certain competencies in the firm are more directly tied to customer value creation than others. Those aspects of value that attract and reinforce customer loyalty are central to a firm's identity and competitiveness.

The Four Quadrants. "A company's human capital," writes Stewart, "is in the upper-right quadrant, embodied in the people whose talent and experience create the products and services that are the reason customers come to it and not to a competitor. That's an asset. The rest—the other three quadrants—is merely labor cost."[18]

By considering Human Capital in the same way we treat other corporate assets, firms can make better strategic choices about organizational structure, recruiting, and training. Difficult to Replace and Important to Customer are two defining characteristics of all the roles and employees in an organization. Applying this framework demands a degree of analytic dispassion, favoring the needs of the business over those of individuals. As Stewart points out, it doesn't really matter if your employees are all brilliant or extremely hard working if they are producing nonessential results. The Human Capital framework places the focus on organization design and strategic deployment of staff, increasing the value of their output. As the framework indicates, the goal is to upgrade the value of the firm's Human Capital by directing it either up and to the right or out of the organization through options such as outsourcing or automation:

- Upper left: Informate. Businesses rely on the contributions of staff functions that are complex, nuanced, and take time to learn. Although it is difficult to replace these individuals, their work is often underleveraged and invisible to customers. Customers don't really care about internal audit, billing, or complex factory process work unless they are done wrong. The strategic interest in this quadrant is to derive additional benefit from a functional activity. Informating a task means enriching it with added-value education or service. This is what GE did a few years ago when it redefined and augmented its internal audit process, changing it from mere numbers checking to a consultative service providing useful feedback and best practices advice. Another example is the move to equip call center staff with better customer intelligence tools, allowing them to target and deliver personalized value to callers based on their characteristics and likely needs.
- Lower left: Automate. Many businesses find themselves somewhat dependent on low-complexity, semiskilled workers. Although the success of the business may indeed depend on the contributions of these employees, the individuals hired to do the work are interchangeable and easy to find. McDonald's and most of its competitors have designed their outlets with this in mind. The most basic repetitive work is automated out of the process. The remaining tasks, like food preparation and order taking, are routinized so that low-salary staff can be quickly trained and deployed as required. McDonald's, for example, is able to function smoothly in spite of annual turnover rates ranging geographically from 50 to 300 percent.
- Lower right: Differentiate or Outsource. Some work is extremely high in value yet not identified directly with specific individuals. Consider the cover design of a book or quick technical support provided to users of a piece of computer hardware or software. Although these services are vital to the success of a business, they can be found fairly easily. Firms can consider two actions to increase the value of this category. The first is Outsourcing such a service, which can be economical while permitting the company to focus its energies on other more essential and differentiating activities. Firms can afford to be world class in specialized areas like logistics and product assembly by moving the function to a trusted strategic partner like UPS or Solectron.

Differentiating occurs when a set of generic capabilities is organized and packaged as an integrated offering at a higher level of perceived value. A clear example is the migration of computer hardware and software companies to the consulting and information technology systems solutions business.

- Upper right: Capitalize. The upper right quadrant is the target zone where companies should concentrate their Human Capital. These are the prime innovators, leaders, and service providers working at jobs that differentiate the firm and delight customers. They span roles like research chemist, top sales representatives, and movie stars. As the percentage of a firm represented by this category increases, its competitiveness and relative value rise.

Example: The Metamorphosis of the Automotive Industry. Early in the twentieth century, the Ford Motor Company became the dominant global automobile manufacturer when it introduced its famous moving assembly line. A rope would pull the vehicle along, making it possible for fifty employees to remain in fixed positions and add their defined contribution in a controlled and efficient manner. The time it took to build one Model T dropped from twelve hours to one and a half, and the cost fell from $850 to $250.

With this amount of improvement, the vertically integrated business firm model became standard in the industry. Ford's Rouge River manufacturing plant was famous for the depth of its value chain, ranging from rubber plantations in South America for tires to glass manufacturing facilities. While General Motors offered a wider set of product selections than its main competitor did, it followed a similar business architecture and vertical culture. When GM president Charles Wilson was being considered for the position of secretary of defense for the United States in 1953, he was asked if he thought his position with GM might cause some conflict of interest. He replied, "I cannot conceive of any because for years I thought what was good for our country was good for GM and vice versa."[19]

The tightly integrated philosophy and business structure that made this response possible continued to dominate the industry well into the second half of the century. Improved communications and collaboration technologies eventually transformed this. Today, all the major auto companies are global; they are sourcing, manufacturing, and selling around the world. A well-established system of suppliers and the movement toward standardized parts and communications has resulted in a much more open and horizontal industry model.

The automotive industry took on a whole new shape as production technologies and communications systems improved (Figure 7.14). Companies and whole subindustry groups formed to offload portions of value creation at attractive prices and terms.

Repetitive manual work and mindless reminders and tracking functions have been automated out of the human part of the system. Most modern auto plants make extensive use of robotics and smart quality process control technology.

Internet-based problem-solving systems make the best company experts' knowledge available to customers, informing talent that was previously hidden

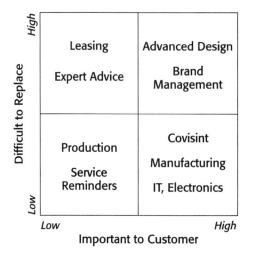

Figure 7.14. Automotive Industry Matrix

inside the organization. Other services, like leasing and sales information, have undergone a similar change.

Probably the greatest amount of change has occurred in the work falling in the lower right quadrant. Outsourcing and strategic partnering now account for a significant share of the automotive value chain. The creation of Covisint in 2000 by GM, Ford, and Daimler Chrysler as a common electronic trading environment has accelerated the growth of partnering within the industry. Daimler Chrysler estimates that close to 70 percent of its suppliers are now on-line via Covisint and applying a common quality management tool called Powerplay.com. EDS, at one time owned by GM, still provides the vast majority of its information technology services.

Increasingly, the role played by the automotive company itself is of a knowledge-intensive and strategic nature. Customer relationship management and positioning and caring for the brand are core assets carefully comanaged with the dedicated dealer networks. Design and marketing of the vehicles is central to differentiation, as is business and pricing strategy. As in other manufacturing industries, increasing amounts of production are treated as a commodity service that can be outsourced, leaving the company free to concentrate on planning and coordinating the inputs of low-cost specialist partners and suppliers.

Contexts. The framework is useful for firms engaged in strategic improvement exercises or when they are considering outsourcing functions.

Method. A Human Capital review and design process helps a company to understand and improve its deployment of talent. Each of the steps here can be

completed in a variety of ways, depending on who does the work and how extensive the redesign needs to be. For example, in step 2, a single person can deliver
a high-level set of recommendations, or one work group can be established for
each of the four quadrants to conduct a fuller set of reviews and proposals:

- Step 1: Analyze work. Analyze work done within the organization, placing all functions and roles in question into one of the four quadrants.
- Step 2: Identify improvement opportunities. Explore opportunities to
improve the deployment of Human Capital within each of the three suboptimal
quadrants. For example, how can work falling into the upper left quadrant be
informated, or that in the lower left be automated?
- Step 3: Create improvement plans. Prepare a set of recommendations and
plans for Human Capital improvements, and prioritize these for desirability and
feasibility.
- Step 4: Enhance key assets. Consider how the human capital in the upper
right quadrant can be enhanced as well as protected.

References

Stewart, T. *Intellectual Capital: The New Wealth of Organizations.* New York: Currency,
    1997.
Stewart, T. *The Wealth of Knowledge.* New York: Currency, 2001.

⊞

Differentiation and Integration
Jamshid Gharajedaghi

> Development of an organization is a purposeful transformation toward higher
> levels of integration and differentiation at the same time.
>   —Jamshid Gharajedaghi[20]

Systems thinkers see organizational and cultural development as a balancing
act between the proliferation of new ideas, entities, and behaviors and the effective integration and management of these things. The corollary is simple: as the
rate of change and differentiation increases, the need for integration rises in kind
(Figure 7.15).

Healthy organizations and societies encourage individual initiative and development, while ensuring coordination of efforts and sharing of knowledge. Social
systems of all varieties are in a constant process of change, slight or extreme.
In times of greater turbulence, both positive and negative, more change is called
for. Recall the economic and political upheaval in the former Soviet Union or
the rush of creative competition in Silicon Valley during the 1990s. When the

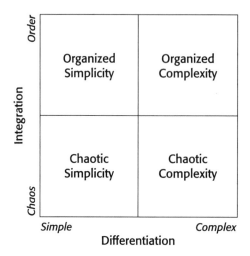

Figure 7.15. Differentiation and Integration Matrix

rate of change outstrips a system's ability to integrate it, the effect can be over-whelming and destructive, leading to failure and dysfunctionality. When both forces are working together, progress can be exhilarating, as occurred in Europe during the Rennaisance and in the operation of excellent companies like Dell and GE.

The Two Dimensions and Their Extremes. The matrix explores two key dimensions: Differentiation and Integration:

Differentiation. Differentiation is the pursuit of new and diverse directions for growth and development. This is essentially artistic in nature, leading toward greater complexity and autonomy for the parts of a system.

Integration. Integration efforts establish order and stability by creating meaningful trade-offs and links between diverse system elements. The orientation is more scientific, emphasizing rationality, instrumentality, and conformity.

The Four Quadrants. With the introduction of energy and intention, systems evolve from simple to complex and from chaos to order. This process, called negentropy, is a prime feature of living systems and assumes a reasonable amount of balance between creative (Differentiation) and synthesizing (Integration) forces. The not uncommon tendency to emphasize one or the other in isolation creates extreme environments in ways that are self-reinforcing. In the worst of cases, the system must approach complete destruction before a reversal of direction can be initiated:

- Upper left: Organized Simplicity. This state dominates when forces for control and order prevail at the cost of new ideas and approaches. A form of stability is attained, but it tends to be rigid and authoritarian. Although efficiencies are often realized, energy is lost, and long-term viability is jeopardized.
- Lower left: Chaotic Simplicity. This quadrant describes a relatively simple condition with low levels of organization. This might be the case during a period of low demand or, conversely, a system that is at a point of giving up efforts to cope effectively.
- Lower right: Chaotic Complexity. Chaotic Complexity prevails when innovation and experimentation are pursued without restraint and accountability. Diversity can overload the system, depleting it of resources and focus. Duplication of efforts, errors, and conflicts are real dangers.
- Upper right: Organized Complexity. Healthy progress through experimentation, learning, and integration is achieved by moving concurrently toward higher levels of complexity and order. Innovations are supported in ways that contribute to overall system improvement; knowledge is shared, and self-correction is ongoing.

Example: Health Care Cost Crisis: Butterworth. A viable and affordable health care system is arguably a cornerstone of a successful society and a fair measure of its performance. An aging population in the United States is placing increasing demands on an already fragile and overburdened health care infrastructure. As Gharajedaghi observes, "The present health care system has its origin in sickness care."[21] People expect access to adequate care in a reasonable time frame at a price they can afford.

A series of payment and service delivery options have been spawned, including fee for service, health maintenance organizations (HMOs), independent (self-insured) companies, Medicare (for those over age sixty-five), and Medicaid (for those lacking means). Although these are helpful measures, the combined effect of these approaches has been an escalation in patients' expectations, with little countervailing pressure to limit demand.

Butterworth Health Systems is an HMO operating in the Grand Rapids, Michigan, area. Recognizing the symptoms of an accelerating gap between patient expectations and the affordability of care, a search for new alternatives based on an understanding of needs and limits was initiated. The four quadrants in Figure 7.16 describe the evolution of responses that Butterworth and other HMOs have attempted.[22]

The lower left quadrant, Streaming, describes the early years of operation. In this phase of its existence, the facility served a defined segment of the population. The lower right quadrant, Overwhelming Reactive, describes unsuccessful efforts to creatively accommodate a multitude of expectations and payment mechanisms. It was clear that order needed to be achieved to maintain system viability, pushing the organization to the upper left quadrant, Enforced Compliance.

Figure 7.16. Butterworth Health Systems Matrix

Added pressures on the system led to efforts to Enforced Compliance as a way to control and manage demand. The system was becoming at once increasingly bureaucratic and mechanistic, while remaining incapable of meeting expectations with the existing resources and funding arrangements. Gharajedaghi writes, "HMOs have been forced to use a bureaucratic system and a mechanistic mode of operation to manage the most emotional and sensitive behavior of a human system of health care."[23]

Option 4, Preventive Proactivity, came about through a design exercise in 1996 led by INTERACT (a Pennsylvania-based consultancy where Jamshid Gharajedaghi is managing partner and CEO). The distancing of patient need from payment responsibility was driving expectations beyond the service ability of the company within funding levels set by payment bodies like insurance companies and governments. By promoting health and illness prevention, Butterworth was able to reduce the volume of higher-cost acute care demand from patients. The solution (in reality more complex than this description) helped to transcend the stuck place where all options appeared to be unworkable by appealing to a more primary aspect of self-interest of the system beneficiaries, the patients.

Context. Differentiation and Integration is part of a design approach that offers a powerful and intuitive method for social system redesign. It is effective as a timely and nonthreatening intervention to prevent excessive chaotic or bureaucratic buildup. Due to its structure, it scales easily from serving as a convenient context for reflecting on a situation to a more structured and systematic program approach.

Method. The systems approach to organizational improvement models the whole and all its parts in dynamic relationship. A systems intervention is sensitive to balancing degrees of Differentiation and Integration, proceeding in a series of iterations toward a more desirable state that is feasible and supported. INTERACT's approach has the following characteristics:

- Problem definition and solution building are distinct and separate processes.
- Stakeholder buy-in is important.
- Design occurs at three interdependent system levels: structure (inputs, means, causes), function (outputs, ends, efforts), and process (know-how, sequence of activities).

The output of an intervention is a new architecture that enables desired performance and benefits and resolves or eliminates defined problems.[24] Guided by an understanding of systems principles, an intervention follows a three-phase sequence:

- Step 1: Understand the context.
- Step 2: Define the problem.
- Step 3: Design the solution.

Reference

Gharajedaghi, J. *Systems Thinking: Managing Chaos and Complexity.* Boston: Butterworth-Heinemann, 1999.

⊞

Means and Ends
Russell Ackoff

> Put another way, one cannot impose cooperation on another without a fight, or at least so it seems.
> —Adapted from Russell Ackoff[25]

Conflict is inherent in living systems and is not always a problem needing to be solved. Healthy, adaptive systems effectively harness the knowledge and energy of diverse parties. Russell Ackoff first modeled the dynamics of Means and Ends (Figure 7.17) in his 1972 book, *On Purposeful Systems.* Interdependent parties are motivated by the Ends they pursue, with conflicts resulting where Ends are or appear to be incompatible with those of others. The Means whereby Ends are achieved may also be more or less compatible with those of other interested

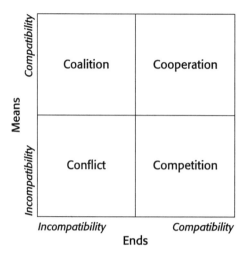

Figure 7.17. Means and Ends Matrix

parties. By addressing these issues, negative conflict can be better understood and reframed into more constructive forms of relationship.

The Two Dimensions and Their Extremes. The matrix explores two key dimensions: Means and Ends:

Means. These are the methods we employ to achieve desired outcomes.

Ends. These are the goals and objectives that we value.

The Four Quadrants. Problem solving and design occur in a series of iterative waves, calling on four sets of activity, each with an associated skill set:

• Upper left: Coalition. Coalitions are formed by competitors to address common, usually short-term problems or adversaries. We find these arrangements in wars, industry, and interpersonal dynamics. A truce is called to focus on the shared threat, after which the parties may well return to conflict.

• Lower left: Conflict. Parties that disagree about both Ends and Means are stuck in Conflict. These situations can become increasingly polarized, resulting in zero-sum, win-lose outcomes. Communication and reframing help improve conflicts. In *On Purposeful Systems*, Ackoff suggests three ways to address Conflict: solve, resolve, and dissolve.

• Lower right: Competition. In Competition, lower-level conflicts provide a useful context for realization of the interests of different parties. Companies within an industry compete against each other for customers yet share the need to educate the public about their collective value proposition. Healthy Competition often creates the most positive conditions for growth and mutual success.

• Upper right: Cooperation. Parties Cooperate when both Ends and Means are compatible. In Cooperation, it is assumed that each party contributes positively to the success of the other.

Method. The framework is useful in transforming unhealthy Conflict situations through dialogue, awareness, and reframing:

• Step 1: Identify the Ends and Means of the parties involved.
• Step 2: Identify the quadrant that best describes the situation.
• Step 3: Creatively investigate the possibility of redefining the Means or Ends of either or both parties to improve the relationship and likelihood of a positive outcome.

References

Ackoff, R. L. *On Purposeful Systems.* Seaside, Calif.: Intersystems Publishers, 1972.

Ackoff, R. L. *The Art of Problem Solving.* New York: Wiley, 1978.

Gharajedaghi, J. *Systems Thinking: Managing Chaos and Complexity.* Boston: Butterworth-Heinemann 1999.

⊞

The Change Grid
Elizabeth Kübler-Ross

> It is not the strongest of the species that survives, nor the most intelligent, but rather the one most responsive to change.
> —Charles Darwin[26]

As individuals and as members of groups within organizations, we all experience losses and need to cope with change. Elizabeth Kübler-Ross provided the basic model for understanding and dealing with such change in her seminal 1965 book, *On Death and Dying.* Drawing on interviews with terminally ill patients, she identified a series of five common stages of grieving and adaptation: denial, anger, depression, negotiation, and acceptance. These insights are applied in the Change Grid model (Figure 7.18) by various change management experts.[27]

The Two Dimensions and Their Extremes. The Change Grid explores two key dimensions: Focus and Time:

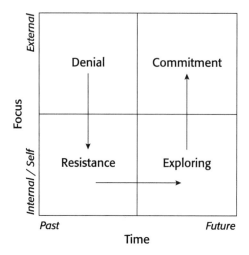

Figure 7.18. Change Grid

Focus. Attention is placed primarily on the External world of relationships, events, and things or on the Internal world of feelings and ideas.

Time. Attention is directed primarily to Past events or Future possibilities.

The Four Quadrants. Adjusting to change as we move from Denial to Commitment takes time. The severity of the change and individual differences affect how quickly one will move through the cycle and return to normal balance. Resiliency is improved by focus, positive outlook, flexibility, organization, and proactivity:

• Upper left: Denial. Our first reaction to negative news is disbelief and rejection. It may simply be too much to absorb. Recognition makes it somehow more real. Virginia Satir, author of *Conjoint Family Therapy*, describes this as a disruption of the status quo, which is uncomfortable and threatening. Anger is often expressed at this stage.

• Lower left: Resistance. We go through a period of experiencing the loss more fully, feeling hopeless and powerless. Often this causes feelings of depression as we resist moving on to building new hopes and plans.

• Lower right: Exploring. With the passage of time, we begin to think about the future again, exploring options for what can be. As William Bridges, author of *Transitions: Making Sense of Life's Changes*, has pointed out, we need to let go of the past and deal with endings before we are ready to start building a new future.

• Upper right: Commitment. Commitment can occur only when grieving is complete and we emerge once again to participate more fully in the external world. This phase is both exciting and somewhat scary, making it wise to proceed incrementally and build in social support.

Method. The framework is useful for planning the introduction of change in human systems. It is also helpful for understanding and coping with the experience of change and adjustment:

• Step 1: Diagnose. What stage are we at now?
• Step 2: Understand. In the early phases, people need support and space to experience their fears and loss.
• Step 3: Provide challenging support. At the appropriate moment, friendly challenge is often important as people prepare to experiment and explore somewhat risky thoughts and changes.
• Step 4: Provide recognition. As people establish plans and invest in new activities, they need encouragement and recognition.

References

Kübler-Ross, E. *On Death and Dying.* New York: Scribner, 1997.

Satir, V. *Conjoint Family Therapy.* Science and Behaviour Books, 1983.

Bridges, W. *Transitions: Making Sense of Life's Changes.* New York: Perseus, 1980.

⊞

Learning and Change
Hubert Saint-Onge

Learning must equal or exceed the level of change in a system for change to succeed.
—Hubert Saint-Onge[28]

An explosion in technology-driven organizational transformation has made change the new constant. The redesign of strategy, structures, and processes is only the first step in implementing change. Staff, partners, and customers must adapt to new approaches, methods, cultural norms, and equipment. This requires learning and practice. In many instances, unlearning is also necessary, as people must let go of habitual patterns and dependencies. Leaders need to anticipate the learning requirements when introducing change, and ensure that systems and support are adequate to ensure success (Figure 7.19).

Figure 7.19. Learning and Change Matrix

The Two Dimensions and Their Extremes. The Learning and Change matrix explores two key dimensions: Learning and Change:

Learning. This is the development of understanding and skills that enable new behavior and processes.

Change. This is the amount and rate of shifting in the organization that creates a demand for adjustment. Factors affecting change include competition, technology, structure, and process innovation.

The Four Quadrants. Change implies Learning. The ability to implement changes is restricted by the amount of learning you can generate. Each quadrant paints a different balance point with predictable consequences:

• Upper left: Restlessness. When Learning outpaces Change, people become frustrated. They have invested time and effort to gain additional knowledge and skill, but they are not given the opportunity to put them to use. Organizations with this profile often lack strategic intent and the sense of purpose needed to provide meaning and urgency.

• Lower left: Functional. There are few markets left where it is business as usual year after year. Change can be postponed but not avoided. By the time Change needs are recognized, the gap may be too large to bridge. Organizations in this quadrant are usually in some form of denial, representing a crisis waiting to happen.

• Lower right: Mayhem. Chaos results when Change outstrips Learning. Sadly, this is an all-too-frequent organizational scenario. Adjustment needs and skill gaps are underestimated, and leaders naively hope that a plan and good intentions will carry the day. Learning takes time and commitment and needs to be included as part of the overall Change design.

• Upper right: Target Zone. High levels of Learning and Change are characteristic of organizations with momentum and direction. These are often organizations in dynamic markets that are making the necessary adjustments and investing in future capabilities. The result is strategic preparedness and the ability to execute on plans.

Method. The framework is useful when considering changes to business strategy or operations. It quickly raises a helpful set of questions about the degree and nature of Change and Learning needed and the balance between these two processes:

• Step 1: Conduct a Change audit. Determine the amount of Change needed and planned. Is it sufficient and well thought out?
• Step 2: Conduct a Learning audit. Review existing plans and commitments for Learning. Are they adequate?
• Step 3: Conduct a Learning and Change assessment. Locate the current situation on the Learning and Change matrix.
• Step 4: Engage in preparedness planning. Make necessary adjustments to increase the likelihood of success of Change initiatives.

Reference

Saint-Onge, H., and Wallace, D. *Leveraging Communities of Practice for Strategic Advantage.* Boston: Butterworth-Heinemann, 2002.

⊞

Similarities and Differences
Jamshid Gharajedaghi

> Interactive methodology deliberately separates the process of defining a problem from the process of designing a solution.
> —Jamshid Gharajedaghi[29]

The systems approach to organizational improvement consists of an iterative series of design and application cycles. In parallel with the changing phases of activity, a range of different orientations and skill sets is required to ensure that proper problem definition, design, and implementation occur. The four contributor types described here (Figure 7.20) are usually found in different process participants; however, flexible individuals are capable of adapting style to multiple requirements when necessary.

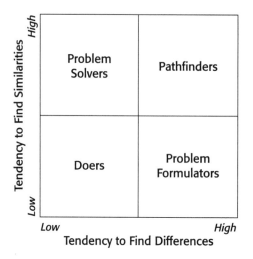

Figure 7.20. Similarities and Differences Matrix

The Two Dimensions and Their Extremes. The Similarities and Differences matrix explores two key dimensions: Tendency to Find Similarities and Tendency to Find Differences:

> Tendency to Find Similarities. This is a natural leaning toward integrating diverse elements, drawing on an ability to recognize similarities between seemingly unrelated matters. This is essentially a scientific orientation.

> Tendency to Find Differences. This is the ability to see differences between apparently similar objects. It is an artistic orientation involved in creating structures, methods, and boundaries.

The Four Quadrants. Problem solving and design occur in a series of waves, calling on four sets of activity:

• Upper left: Problem Solvers. Problem Solvers are integrative thinkers who find the commonality needed among issues and participants to achieve successful solutions.

• Lower left: Doers. Doers are the practically minded practitioners who will carry out the visionaries' plans. They are pragmatic and pay attention to details, schedules, and reality constraints.

• Lower right: Problem Formulators. Problem Formulators help to explore and expand on the situation, raising important questions leading to a well-defined and useful definition of the problem.

• Upper right: Pathfinders. These are the leaders who are capable of seeing the big picture and putting situations into their proper perspective. They are holistic thinkers driven by a clear sense of purpose.

Method. Follow the steps below to deploy different kinds of individuals optimally in solving business problems and implementing solutions:

• Step 1: Establish the problem-solving context, engaging the Pathfinders.
• Step 2: Define the problem, engaging the Problem Formulators.
• Step 3: Pursue an effective solution, engaging the Problem Solvers.
• Step 4: Effectively implement the solution, engaging the Doers.

References

Gharajedaghi, J. *Systems Thinking: Managing Chaos and Complexity.* Boston: Butterworth-Heinemann, 1999.

Gorden, G., and others. "A Contingency Model: The Design of Problem Solving Research Program." *Milbank Memorial Fund Quarterly,* 1974, *52*(2), 185–220.

PROCESS FRAMEWORKS

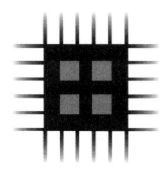

What processes are needed? How are they designed?

Process design is both a discipline and a perspective. As a discipline, it represents an approach and set of tools for mapping the steps in a value creation sequence. A talented and well-trained operations research specialist can identify inefficiencies in most systems and suggest process improvements that will save time and money. As a perspective, it converts social and business processes into sets of definable and measurable transactions, any of which can be adjusted or removed.

⊞

The Four Realms of Experience
B. Joseph Pine II and James H. Gilmore

> While commodities are fungible, goods tangible, and services intangible, experiences are memorable.
> —B. Joseph Pine II and James H. Gilmore[30]

Why do a few dozen coffee beans cost roughly three dollars a cup at Starbucks, a dollar at a diner, ten cents if you buy a large can in the supermarket, and one penny if you purchase them from a grower in Colombia? It's the experience. Certainly Starbucks tries very hard to make sure its product is high in quality and to provide great service, but those reasons don't adequately explain why customers happily pay their prices. They're also buying a great coffee-consuming experience. In their book *The Experience Economy,* Pine and Gilmore delineate how experiences have become a fundamentally new type of offering in the marketplace, taking their place alongside traditional commodities, products, and services.

The history of economic development traces the evolution of value into higher, less tangible forms. In agricultural societies, value resided in the ownership of land. People toiled long hours to produce their own goods, food, and clothing from raw materials. During the industrial revolution, manufacturing defined economic value, and ownership of the means of production became the source of personal wealth. In the 1960s to 1980s, services emerged as the new engine of economic value. Far fewer people were employed in farming, raw material production, or manufacturing. Service businesses such as restaurants, retail, transportation, leisure, financial services, and health care now drove economic growth.

At each stage in this progression, the dominant output from the previous era is commoditized as the basic value and feature set become more readily available and harder to differentiate. In industry after industry today, the traditional product or service has become the platform for an owning or consuming experience that is pleasurable, memorable, and highly valued. Examples include experiential restaurants such as the Hard Rock Café, casinos such as New York, New York in Las Vegas, car brands such as Saturn and BMW, and Barnes and Noble bookstores. These businesses still deliver products and services to customers. However, their value extends well beyond the core offering to include customized, fulfilling, and memorable experiences. In Starbucks' terms, the coffee bean is the commodity, the can of coffee in the grocery store is a product, the cup of coffee at the diner is a service, and an orange and white chocolate frappucino at Starbucks, paid for with a Starbucks debit card and served up by a Starbucks barista with Louis Armstrong singing "What a Wonderful World" in the background, is the experience.

Experience is not the mere addition of entertainment value to a product or service. It means deeply engaging the customer in ways that are uniquely meaningful. Whereas raw materials, products, and services are all transactions that occur outside the buyer, experiences occur within the customer. When businesses talk of "delighting customers," they are describing a sensation they want customers to experience. The business payoff occurs when customers are willing to pay a premium for a product or service because of the experience associated with it. Figure 7.21 maps the different forms of customer experience.

The Two Dimensions and Their Extremes. The Four Realms of Experience matrix explores two key dimensions: Environmental Relationship and Guest Participation:

Environmental Relationship. Environmental Relationship describes the degree to which the guest unites with the experience. If the experience goes "into" the guest, as when watching TV, then the relationship is

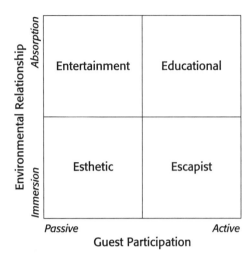

Figure 7.21. Four Realms of Experience Matrix

Absorptive. The experience is being brought into the mind. If the guest physically or virtually goes into the experience, as is the case with playing a video game, the relationship is Immersive.

Guest Participation. Guest Participation ranges from Passive to Active. Symphony or theater attendees are passive participants; they don't influence the performance. By comparison, skiers pay to be entertained and are active participants in their own entertainment.

The Four Quadrants. Consumers increasingly expect rich and engaging experiences to accompany their purchase of goods and services. In many cases, the experience itself is the thing being purchased. The Four Realms framework describes the various basic forms of experience:

• Upper left: Entertainment. Passive and Absorptive experiences, such as hearing a story told around a campfire, are as ancient as civilization itself. These types of experiences still make up the bulk of the entertainment industry today. But increasingly, technology and affluence are opening up the opportunity to include other types of experiences.

• Lower left: Esthetic. Esthetic experiences provide us with a deep, appreciative sense of the real, whether it is visiting a planetarium or a restaurant such as Rainforest Café where guests dine among tropical birds, waterfalls, thunder, and lightning. These businesses don't merely imitate the real world; they seek to provide an authentic experience of what it is like to be out under a nighttime sky or trekking through a tropical rain forest. They want guests to sense and feel deeply.

• Lower right: Escapist. Escapist entertainments completely immerse the guest in the experience. Early examples include motion-ride simulators, games such as paintball, resort casinos, and on-line chatrooms.

• Upper right: Educational. Unlike entertainment, learning and training require the active participation of students. Their minds or bodies must be engaged for learning to take place. Traditional education focused on the teacher as giver and the student as receiver. But that model is being supplanted in many instances by more user-centered, technology-enabled learning activities. Computer edutainment is merely the latest effort to tap into the inherently fun aspects of active learning. At for-profit learning centers and children's museums around the country, education is dispensed interactively as children try their hands at various exercises, games, and technologies in upbeat, information-rich environments.

The four realms of experience are not mutually exclusive. Indeed, employing several together is a recipe for creating more interesting and complete experiences. Cruise lines offer active, immersive sports as part of an escapist experience, Elderhostel offers education at the core of an esthetic vacation, and Land Rover educates customers on wilderness driving techniques with esthetic and escapist off-road expeditions.

Example: Experiential Retail. Many North American consumers have lots of money and not enough time, and they already own too much stuff. For them, the traditional mall is no longer the shopping mecca it once was. Its artificial environments and themed stores seem unnecessary and dated. The Galleria in Sherman Oaks, California, was a highly popular shopping destination in the 1970s and 1980s, but by the early 1990s, changing consumer tastes and a poor economy were taking their toll. The company that owned the property tore it down and replaced the enclosed mall with an open-air "downtown" that was the antithesis of mall artifice (Figure 7.22). Public plazas, street musicians, open-air cafés, trees, and fountains create a place for people to dine, stroll, and connect with one another. The amount of space devoted to food has increased (no time to cook!), and the space given to retail has shrunk (too much stuff!) as giant department stores, all selling essentially the same goods, are replaced by boutiques offering customized items and personalized experience. This trend is being repeated in dozens of shopping venues across the country. Rather than promise great product selection or bargains, the new "downtowns" offer experiences.

Another example is from the small town of Atchison, Kansas (population eleven thousand), where Mary Carol Garrity has designed one of the nation's

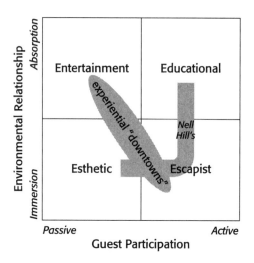

Figure 7.22. Mapping Retail Experiences Matrix

most experiential retail stores. Called Nell Hill's, it offers home furnishings for upscale, discerning customers. People regularly drive two to three hours from Omaha, Kansas City, Topeka, and other towns to shop at Nell Hill's despite the inconvenience.

Why would anyone drive so far to visit a furniture store? For the experience. "If they are going to drive all the way from out of town to get here, then I'm going to make sure they're happy and see something they haven't seen before," says Garrity. Every eight weeks, the store is completely overhauled with new merchandise and displays of furnishings, antiques, paintings, and accessories. Garrity views the staff as "resources," there to help customers develop and achieve an interior design vision. It's common for customers to bring photographs of rooms in their home so Nell Hill's team can advise them on all aspects of design. Customers return again and again not merely to shop but to learn, to see great design, and to imagine. By staging a great experience with esthetic and educational elements and surprising "guests" with new things on each visit, Nell Hill's has transcended the limits of location to establish rewarding relationships with its clientele.

Context. The framework offers a method for envisioning how experiential components might enrich and extend an offering by adding a mix of Entertaining, Escapist, Esthetic, and Educational elements. The authors provide four sets of questions to help you start thinking in this direction.

Method. Consider the following questions, and place your answers in the appropriate quadrants:[31]

- Step 1: Consider Esthetic features. Esthetics make your guests want to come in and spend time with your product or service. What can be done to make your environment more inviting and comfortable for guests?
- Step 2: Consider Escapist features. Escapist elements draw your guests further into your experience. What could you offer to encourage them to become active participants in the experience?
- Step 3: Consider Educational features. Education is active. What do you want your guests to learn from the experience? What information and skill acquisition opportunities attract them?
- Step 4: Consider Entertainment features. Entertainment holds your attention with humor, drama, and surprise. What amusing or narrative elements can you add that would encourage your guests to stay? How can you make their experience more fun?

Reference

Pine, B. J. II, and Gilmore, J. H. *The Experience Economy.* Boston: Harvard Business School Press, 1999.

⊞

Make versus Buy
Charles H. Fine

Supply chain design is the process of choosing which capabilities in the chain a given firm will try to control and which it will outsource.
—Charles H. Fine[32]

Make-versus-buy decisions are a key dilemma for modern manufacturers. Keeping all production activities in-house typically requires too much time, space, money, and management attention to be an effective strategy. Firms often lack the internal capability to make certain components of a product, or they discover that outside suppliers offer superior pricing or quality. This is particularly true when the components in question are standardized or available from a large number of suppliers. The key forces that drive firms to outsource the production of components or entire products are a lack of capability, lack of competitiveness, and need for quality.

Companies should also retain some activities within the boundaries of the firm, particularly those that have to do with important competitive knowledge and customer visibility. In the book *Clockspeed,* Charles H. Fine presents a Make-versus-Buy decision matrix that boils this decision down to two key considerations: Dependency (on suppliers) and the relative modularity of the components (Supply Items) that go into the product (Figure 7.23).

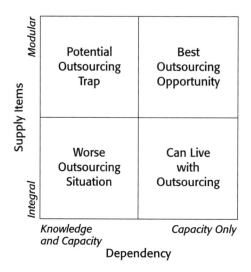

Figure 7.23. Make versus Buy Matrix

The Two Dimensions and Their Extremes. The Make versus Buy matrix explores two key dimensions: Supply Items and Dependency:

Supply Items. Supply Items are the components that go into a finished good. A supply item is Modular if is not indispensable to the overall performance of the product and can be produced at an acceptable cost and level of quality by other firms. For automobiles, Modular products include such items as door handles and light bulbs. Integral products, by contrast, are those in which elements are specifically designed to work with other pieces. Integral products in automobiles might include interiors and drivetrain components. Engine parts from a Chevrolet V-8 won't work in a Toyota 4-cylinder motor. Products in which many components are Modular and interchangeable, such as personal computers, have a Modular product architecture. Products in which most of the components are specifically designed to work with all of the other components to achieve performance goals, such as racing motorcycles, are said to have an Integral product architecture.

Dependency. One can be dependent on suppliers for Production Capacity or for Knowledge *and* Capacity. In the case of Capacity, the firm knows how to make the product but saves money or time through outsourcing. Knowledge refers to specialized abilities in design, manufacturing, or integration of components. In the case of Knowledge Dependence, the firm lacks the skill to design or make the product.

The Four Quadrants. The Make versus Buy matrix helps to evaluate opportunities and costs of outsourcing in a structured and systematic way:

- Upper left: Potential Outsourcing Trap. Being dependent on partners for Knowledge and Capacity is dangerous in situations where suppliers can obtain the same modular parts available to the manufacturer. This happened to IBM with the personal computer, and the result was loss of a market that IBM created.
- Lower left: Worse Outsourcing Situation. In this case, the product is Integral to performance, but the company has little understanding of its design or manufacture. Generally, companies should avoid this level of supplier dependency.
- Lower right: Can Live with Outsourcing. In this situation, the components are ones that are Integral to performance but may be outsourced. Ideally, the component can be obtained from several sources so that the company is not locked into a single supplier. If it is a component that does not offer a specific competitive advantage by itself, then outsourcing may save time and resources. Toyota, for example, outsources some of its manufacture of transmissions even though it clearly has the knowledge and resources to perform this function in-house.
- Upper right: Best Outsourcing Opportunity. The best manufacturing components to outsource are those that do not offer any competitive advantage by themselves. Ideally, these are non-Integral items that are available from multiple sources. Outsourcing in this instance enables the company to devote more resources to other areas of competitive advantage.

Method. The object is to determine where the best outsourcing opportunities lie and where the current supply strategy may be vulnerable:

- Step 1: Analyze supply products and services. Separate key components of production into two groups: Modular and Integral.
- Step 2: Assess dependencies. Examine the items you currently outsource. For each one, ask if you are dependent on the supplier for Capacity or for Knowledge and Capacity. Place each item in the proper quadrant of the matrix.
- Step 3: Draw conclusions about your current outsourcing decisions. Which components that you now manufacture represent good outsourcing opportunities? Which components that you outsource now represent supplier dependency risks?

Reference

Fine, C. H. *Clockspeed: Winning Industry Control in an Age of Temporary Advantage.* Boston: Perseus Books, 1998.

⊞

Four Square Model
Bob Johansen

[Groupware] is a co-evolving human-tool system.
—Douglas Engelbart[33]

Two facts are clear in today's economy. First, the ability to create and manage knowledge is any organization's main source of competitive advantage. Second, almost all value is created collaboratively; very few of us are individual actors on the economic stage. The Four Square Model (Figure 7.24) is a taxonomy of collaboration and communication technologies that inspires us to deeper thinking about the tools that support collaborative value creation.[34]

The term *groupware* typically describes multiuser software that enables computer-supported cooperative work. In his Four Square Model, Bob Johansen, president of the Institute for the Future in Menlo Park, California, takes an expansive view of groupware as the set of physical, technological, and cultural tools that help collections of individuals become high-performing teams. This includes not only software but also the design of work spaces and the overall company culture and approach to teamwork. The model has proven helpful in considering the design of other computer-enabled communication activities, such as long-distance learning.

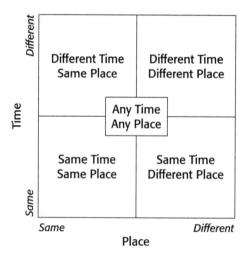

Figure 7.24. Four Square Model

The Two Dimensions and Their Extremes. Time and Space are two basic dimensions all teams must work around:

Time. Individuals may occupy the Same or Different points in time.

Space. Individuals may share the Same physical space or be in Different locations.

The Four Quadrants. Some taxonomic matrices include a fifth cell that is a hybrid of the other four types. In this case, the Anytime Anyplace option is a superset that integrates collaborative knowledge and communication approaches from the four main quadrants:

• Upper left: Different Time, Same Place. People are collaborating in the same spaces in the office but at different times during the day. Examples are team meeting rooms and bulletin and message boards.

• Lower left: Same Time, Same Place. This includes traditional face-to-face meetings using tools such as conference rooms, white boards, and video equipment, as well as what might be called informal groupware—unscheduled communications that take place in hallways and common areas.

• Lower right: Same Time, Different Place. Electronic meetings using presentation technologies such as shared presentations, conference calls, and videoconferences fall into this category. It also includes impromptu communications technologies such as instant messaging.

• Upper right: Different Time, Different Place. Asynchronous communications such as e-mail, voice mail, shared calendaring, and scheduling enable different time and place collaboration. These create new opportunities for collaboration, speeding decision cycles and organizational responsiveness.

• Center: Any Time, Any Place. Firms need to shorten the time between identifying and meeting customer needs. Many corporations are beginning to support staff and customers around the world on a 24–7 basis to do this. Computer technologies are key to coordinating and integrating all four modes of groupware. Organizational cultures that empower teams are equally important.

Method. The Four Square Model suggests methods for evaluating and improving groupware fitness. As a test, try the following exercises:

• Step 1: Describe. In each quadrant, write up to three examples of the kind of groupware your department uses. Include reference to office layouts or corporate cultural practices as well as technologies.

• Step 2: Assess. To what degree are each of the four groupware options being well or poorly deployed?

• Step 3: Improve. What opportunities exist to support more effective collaboration?

Reference

Johansen, R., Charles, J., Mittman, R., and Saffo, P. *Groupware: Computer Support for Business Teams.* New York: Free Press, 1988.

⊞

Product and Supply Chain Architecture
Adapted from Charles H. Fine

> All competitive advantage is temporary. . . . The shorter the industry clock-speed, the shorter the half-life of competitive advantage.
> —Charles H. Fine[35]

Clockspeed refers to the rate at which companies and industries evolve. An industry's clockspeed is somewhat analogous to an organism's metabolism. Inspired by the way biologists study fast-reproducing fruit flies in order to understand genetics better, Charles Fine studied high-clockspeed industries to learn how products and processes mutate and competitive advantage evolves over time. His findings are presented in the book *Clockspeed.*

Fine's research focused mainly on three dimensions of clockspeed: process, product, and organization. Fast process clockspeeds are found in industries such as medicine and semiconductors, where new manufacturing processes are introduced as frequently as every eighteen to twenty-four months. Product quality is highly dependent on a firm's ability to master and implement expensive new production processes quickly. By contrast, slower process clockspeeds are found in areas such as automotive manufacturing, where a particular engine-building process may stay in place for decades.

Fast product clockspeeds are common to fields such as entertainment, publishing, and on-line media, where the product literally can change daily. Contrast this with aircraft manufacturing, where designs that are three decades old continue to be built. Organizational clockspeeds reflect the overall pace of change and decision making in organizations. Clockspeeds typically speed up as one gets closer to the customer. Manufacturing plans must be made years in advance. Decisions in retail are made daily, weekly, and monthly. Fine calls this "clockspeed amplification" (Figure 7.25).

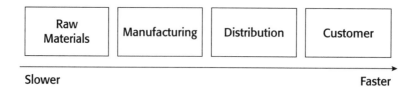

Figure 7.25. Clockspeed Amplification

The notion of clockspeeds can be applied to more than product and process architectures. One can think of one's distribution channel or customer base as having clockspeeds as well. The film industry has witnessed major changes in distribution channels over the past three decades; small local theaters were eclipsed by regional megaplexes; the broadcast networks were augmented by cable, satellite, and now the Internet; and new storage technologies created a retail distribution network for movies that never existed before videotape. Each change eroded a previous competitive advantage and created new winners and losers. The distribution of film seems to operate on a clockspeed of major changes once every decade or two.

Through his study of fruit flies, as well as large firms in automotive, high-tech, and other fields, Fine developed rules of industrial evolution. Both products and supply chains evolve over time, cycling between periods of vertical integration and horizontal modularization. However, unlike natural organisms, businesses evolve intentionally. Managers must choose which competitive threats to meet, which new knowledge and capabilities to add to their organization, and which to forgo. The double helix models how industries oscillate between these two states (Figure 7.26).

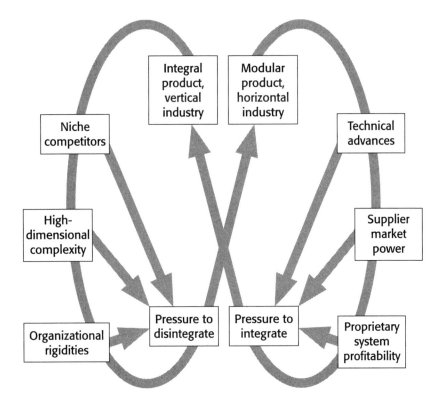

Figure 7.26. The Double Helix

During periods of high integration, industries tend toward a few dominant firms with vertically integrated supply chains. The product architectures are integral, meaning the components are not interchangeable with products from other competitors. Think of the early computer industry. Most products were integral (DEC's software wouldn't run on IBM computers, for example), and the companies were vertically integrated. IBM and each of its competitors made the bulk of their own products and components: chips, computers, operating systems, applications, storage.

On a highly integral product like a military aircraft, every part and system has been designed to perform a specific task. By comparison, today's PC circuit board is built with mostly off-the-shelf modular components.

Many industries start out in the horizontal-modular mode and switch to vertical-integral as the product category matures. In the automotive field, there were hundreds of producers in the late 1800s. Few companies made complete engines and drivetrains, and it was common for many builders to buy these components from other manufacturers. But innovations in design, manufacture, and financing led to rapid consolidation. By the 1920s, it was clear that vertically integrated firms would rule the industry. Today, Fine suggests, the industry may be at the beginning of a new horizontal-modular stage.

This cycle is repeated again and again, pushed along by industry clockspeeds. Once an industry is vertically integrated, pressure to disintegrate builds as niche players create increasing competition, and the organizational rigidity associated with long market dominance sets in. At that point, an industry switches to a horizontal-modular structure. Modular product architectures with standardized interfaces enable many competitors to supply components. This leads rapidly to product commoditization and further horizontalization.

Once an industry is fully horizontal and modular, pressures for reintegration begin to build. New technical advances give power to companies that control crucial supply chain components. Since even major subsystems are decomposable into commodity components, suppliers begin to exert power by bundling, snatching profits from other levels of the supply chain. Enormous profits earned by the larger players are reinvested to fund consolidation. Forces for reintegration are in evidence today in many areas of computer hardware and software, as well as telecommunications.

Fine urges business leaders to think in terms of designing capability chains—managing the competencies underlying all of the organizations in a supply chain. In this way, executives can create the flexibility and skills needed to exploit one temporary competitive advantage after another.

The Two Dimensions and Their Extremes. The Product and Supply Chain Architecture matrix (Figure 7.27) explores two key dimensions: Product Architecture and Supply Chain Architecture:

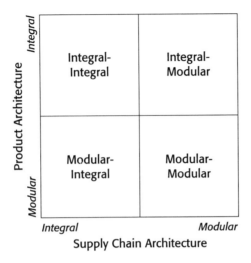

Figure 7.27. Product and Supply Chain Architecture Matrix

Product Architecture. Product architectures may be Modular or Integral. Integral product architectures, typified by autos, racing motorcycles, and medical equipment, are those in which each component contributes directly and specifically to overall performance. Parts and interfaces tend to be proprietary. Modular product architectures use standard interfaces and can employ off-the-shelf components for much of assembly. Personal computers, clothing, and many other products employ modular architectures.

Supply Chain Architecture. Integral supply chains require vertical integration within a primary firm or tight coupling of several firms in order to meet demanding, proprietary design specifications. Modular supply chain architectures are horizontal, with many competing firms specializing in aspects of the overall product.

The Four Quadrants. Integral Product architectures and Integral Supply Chain architectures are a natural fit, as are Modular-Modular combinations. Mixed Product and Supply Chain architectures are less frequent but still occur:

• Upper left: Integral-Integral. Products and components are specifically designed to work with the each other to enhance overall performance. In businesses such as automotive, medical equipment, and furniture, products follow Integral architecture. Toyota has been the premier manufacturer in automobiles for two decades. It tightly controls the manufacture of integral components, out-sourcing only when products become commoditized, and then sparingly.

- Lower left: Modular-Integral. Mixed Product and Supply architectures are less likely than matched ones for a good reason. If your Product is highly Integral, there is less likely to be a vigorous market of suppliers. However, as one moves closer to customers, the need for Integral Supply Architectures increases, sometimes forcing an Integral Supply Architecture on products that are modular. The Zara clothing chain responds to trends quickly by making many of its clothes at its factory in Spain, enabling it to deliver new styles in days rather than months. Most of the apparel industry in North America and Europe out-sources manufacturing, frequently to overseas firms.

- Lower right: Modular-Modular. Apparel, telephones, and personal comput-ers are products with modular architectures and modular supply chains. How-ever, hybrid architectures abound. The automotive business is highly vertical but has always had a strong Modular aspect in its after-market business, where thou-sands of suppliers vie to deliver parts with relatively standardized interfaces such as lights, tires, wheels, and spoilers. Dell's Modular supply chain relies partly on suppliers situated very close to its Texas assembly plants, mimicking some of the communications advantages of a tightly coupled, vertical, integral architecture.

- Upper right: Integral-Modular. Fine suggests that integral products with modular supply architectures are rare. When BMW started building cars in the United States, it found that its suppliers were not used to the tight integration and rapid design iterations that it practiced in Germany. It had to alter its pro-cesses, creating a more modular supply chain in the United States.

Example: Schwinn Bicycle Company. The transition from horizontal to verti-cal to horizontal product and supply architectures has occurred many times in many industries (Figure 7.28). In the mid-nineteenth century, bicycles were hand-built by small craft shops in Europe and the United States. Hundreds, if not thousands, of firms supplied parts to bike builders. In the early twentieth century, the industry started to consolidate. By World War II, Schwinn, the dom-inant firm, began making more and more of its own components, completing the vertical integration of the industry. Schwinn dominated until the 1970s, when mountain bikers and long-distance cyclists began making their own per-formance parts. As dozens of small firms pushed the envelope of bicycle per-formance, Schwinn began falling behind in product innovation. The company completely missed the significance of new trends in biking that would end the vertical-integral structure of the market. Today, the industry is highly modular, with a wide variety of parts suppliers and a fragmented retail market. The Schwinn company, which once dominated 70 percent of the North American market, rode into bankruptcy in 1992.

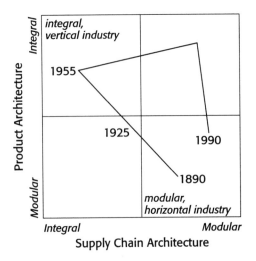

Figure 7.28. Bicycle Industry Evolution Matrix

Context. Products, processes, and capabilities should be designed in concert to optimize customer responsiveness and agility throughout the capability chain. Product and Supply Chain Architectures need to be analyzed within the context of the clockspeed and double helix concepts.

Method. Follow the steps below to conduct a high-level analysis of Product and Supply Chain architecture compatibility:

- Step 1: Assess Product Architecture. Is your product designed with a modular or integral architecture? How does it compare to similar products in your industry?
- Step 2: Assess Supply Chain Architecture. Is your Supply Chain Architecture modular or integral? Is it more or less modular or integral than competitors?
- Step 3: Consider design implications. Is the trend within your industry toward more Integral products and architectures or toward more Modularity? Review the implications of your Product and Supply Chain Architectures in the light of industry trends.

Reference

Fine, C. H. *Clockspeed: Winning Industry Control in an Age of Temporary Advantage.* Boston: Perseus Books, 1998.

⊞

Telematics Framework
Bill Buxton

Visible design is a failure. The only good computer is an invisible computer.
—Bill Buxton[36]

As the former chief scientist for Alias Software and SGI and a computer sciences professor at the University of Toronto, Bill Buxton has devoted much of his life to solving thorny problems related to human-computer interaction. Over the years, he has published extensively on interface design, collaboration, and the social impacts of ubiquitous computing. His Telematics matrix (Figure 7.29) is a usage-based taxonomy of human-to-human and human-to-machine communications. The software industry has devoted most of its effort to overt foreground communications, tasks such as document creation and e-mail, and ignored the deeper and equally important background processing that accounts for the majority of communications. By examining communication activities in this way, the framework provides a new strategic context for making research and design decisions.

Buxton calls himself an inveterate taxonomist. His Telematics matrix has a virtue that he says is common to all great models: it reveals with "surprising obviousness" what we feel we've known all along.[37]

The Two Dimensions and Their Extremes. The Telematics matrix explores two key dimensions: Object of Communication and Ground of Communication:

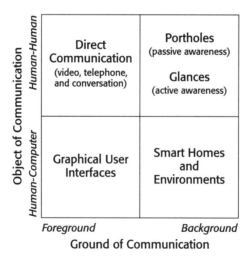

Figure 7.29. Telematics Matrix

Object of Communication. Human-Human Communication includes all the direct, indirect, formal, and informal methods we use to share and glean information from one another. Human-Computer Communication includes the kind of document creation work we do at the computer, as well as entertainment.

Ground of Communication. Foreground Communication is that in which we consciously engage. In the Background are all communications that occur without our direct attention. Examples include news that a coworker overhears from an adjoining workstation or the awareness of a parent who is watching TV but keeping one ear tuned to the children's room.

The Four Quadrants. The Telematics framework helps us to identify and improve four different classes of communication:

• Upper left: Direct Communication. Most computer and communications technology extends our reach and removes the barrier of distance in human-to-human communications. This category includes conscious, front-of-mind activities such as dialogue or attending a lecture.

• Lower left: Graphical User Interfaces. Text or graphical user interfaces are the traditional interface design for personal computers, games, and other communications machines. Many software products today directly facilitate this type of communications.

• Lower right: Smart Homes and Environments. Smart houses and network-connected medical monitoring devices are two examples of environmental communications technology. Designing machines so that they respond to our state and not just our conscious input is an enormous challenge.

• Upper right: Portholes and Glances. Humans are great at simultaneous background processing. We can listen to the radio, cook dinner, and coo at the baby all at the same time. Computers are slow by comparison, often needing to focus on foreground tasks to make headway. This type of computing is largely ignored by today's software, but that will change in the future.

For several years, researchers at Xerox have been experimenting with software for background human-to-human communications. Group awareness tools called Portholes and Glances provide useful real-time information and cues about the availability of colleagues to members of physically distributed work groups.[38] Portholes consist of small, still images of team members in a corner of one's computer screen. Images are refreshed every five minutes. Glances are more active, providing users with an electronic analogue of strolling down a hallway and glancing into other people's offices.

Method. The ideas in the Telematics matrix require us to rethink how software addresses human communications. The framework is helpful in the context of improving collaboration or customer experience. Try this experiment:

- Step 1: Diagnose. List up to three types of communications activities that occur inside your business today for each quadrant of the matrix.
- Step 2: Envision. Could collaboration be enhanced by software that more closely resembled natural human communications? Pay special attention to the two styles of background communications.
- Step 3: Plan. Select the best opportunities to improve communication, and discuss the related software requirements.

Reference

Buxton, W. "Integrating the Periphery and Context: A New Model of Telematics." In *Proceedings of Graphics Interface.* San Francisco: Morgan Kaufmann, 1995.

⊞

The Virtue Matrix
Adapted from the Aspen Institute and Roger Martin

Executives who wish to make their organizations better corporate citizens face significant obstacles.
—Roger Martin[39]

Social responsibility is defined as the obligation of management to engage in activities that improve social welfare and the interests of organizations. Corporate social responsibility (CSR) activities typically include compliance with laws and regulations, innovative employee benefits, handling of ethical issues, and charitable projects that may add to social as well as corporate value.

Most corporations and executives would like their corporations to be good citizens; however, they face structural obstacles to implementing initiatives. Companies that spend on activities that rivals forgo risk undermining their competitive position (see "The Prisoner's Dilemma" in Chapter Eight). By cooperating too closely with government, they may inadvertently invite more government oversight, limiting strategic options. If they pay too much in employee salaries and benefits, they may end up driving jobs to competitors or countries with lower wages and fewer employee protections.

The Virtue matrix (Figure 7.30) was developed at the Aspen Institute in Colorado as part of its Initiative for Social Innovation Through Business.[40] It both explains the drivers of CSR and the dilemmas that arise when firms undertake socially responsible behavior. We have adapted the model to fit the format of this book.

The Two Dimensions and Their Extremes. The Virtue matrix explores two dimensions: Degree of Normalization and Corporate Social Responsibility Behavior:

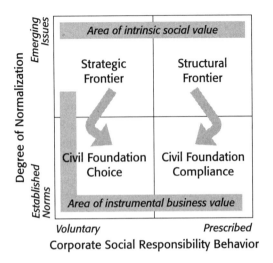

Figure 7.30. Virtue Matrix

Degree of Normalization. Socially responsible behavior can be predicated on widely accepted norms, such as providing health benefits or a safe working environment, or it can represent emerging concerns for which there are no defined norms. Examples of emerging issues include more transparent corporate reporting and support for nontraditional family arrangements. An example where there are no set norms is the issue of how companies handle corruption and bribery in developing countries.

Corporate Social Responsibility Behavior. CSR behavior may be mostly Voluntary, or it may be Prescribed to the extent that it is mandated, defined, or limited by structural, legal, or regulatory barriers.

The Four Quadrants. Tension in this framework resides not only between the two axes but also between the upper and lower halves of the matrix. The lower half is called the Civil Foundation of CSR, which comprises common practices, such as providing employee benefits, and mandated behaviors, such as laws to protect workers. The upper half is the Frontier, where innovations in social responsibility occur. The line between the Civil Foundation and the Frontier is a fluid boundary, changing in response to economic conditions, social norms, and government regulation. In developed societies, for example, the scope of Civil Foundation has moved steadily upward as corporations and governments have become responsible for providing an array of basic social benefits. Countering this, many critics contend that the globalization of work creates pressure pushing the Civil Foundation threshold downward, as economic activities migrate to countries with lower wages and fewer environmental protections.

CSR adds intrinsic value when it benefits employees, customers, and the public at large. It may also enhance corporate performance, as in the case of the Body Shop, which turned socially responsible practices into its main marketing message. Its promise is that when you buy products at the Body Shop, you are helping the environment and the economies of developing nations. CSR adds instrumental value when it clearly benefits shareholders.

- Upper left: Strategic Frontier. These are innovations in social responsibility—new categories of socially responsible behavior that arise due to changing social needs. Providing benefits to domestic partners of homosexual employees is an example of an activity in the Strategic Frontier. It is not yet a social norm in North America but is becoming more widespread. Its main benefit is intrinsic, extending coverage to loved ones in a way that suggests fairness to all employees. A growing number of companies have decided that the benefits of such actions outweigh the costs. As more companies adopt the practice, it becomes a recruiting and retention tool that generates goodwill and over time may migrate downward to the Civil Foundation.
- Lower left: Civil Foundation/Choice. Most socially responsible actions are undertaken by corporations because the benefits outweigh the costs. Activities that are widely practiced become the norm. Examples include support for local charities, which engenders goodwill in the community.
- Lower right: Civil Foundation/Compliance. Compliance includes all of the mandatory regulations and laws that govern socially responsible behavior. Shareholder interests as well as social interests are served when companies abide by laws governing such issues as worker safety, financial reporting, and sexual harassment. Although a single company might gain temporary advantage through occasional noncompliance, as when environmental regulations are skirted, such behavior usually carries enormous costs for shareholders if it comes to the light.
- Upper right: Structural Frontier. Some activities clearly benefit society more than shareholders. For example, if a firm decided to install equipment that exceeded required environmental standards, it might create a higher cost basis than competitors, with no offsetting revenue gain. Since CEOs report to shareholders, there are structural barriers to engaging in this type of intrinsically valuable behavior. In one celebrated case, Aaron Feuerstein of Malden Mills in Lowell, Massachusetts, paid his workers for months after a fire destroyed his textile factory, even though he had no legal obligation to do so. Then he rebuilt the factory in the same location rather than moving abroad, as most financial advisers suggested. However, Feuerstein controlled a closely held corporation. Few public CEOs could afford to be so generous. Feuerstein's efforts came to naught as the firm eventually went bankrupt. It has since been revived, with Feuerstein owning a tiny minority of stock.

Issues in the Structural Frontier typically become norms only if and when behavior is made mandatory through laws or regulations. For example, countries ratifying the Kyoto Protocol on environmental standards will likely trigger mandates for new corporate behavior.

Context. The Virtue matrix provokes us to think more deeply about what should and does generate socially responsible conduct. It is useful for improving discussion and clarity of CSR issues, and for finding better ways to integrate shareholder and social benefits.

Method. Follow the steps below to conduct a high-level analysis of your organization's social responsibility agenda:

- Step 1: Diagnose. Make a list of the main areas of socially responsible activities within the firm, and place them in the appropriate quadrants of the matrix. Include such areas as employee benefits, environmental protection, government-mandated reporting, and charitable activities.
- Step 2: Envision. Identify any new or proposed CSR activities that the firm is contemplating. Place these on the matrix using a different color.
- Step 3: Examine implications. Consider implications for your business of the following two questions. How would undertaking proposed CSR activities ultimately benefit the firm? Are the main drivers of CSR coming from the Strategic or Structural Frontier?

Reference

Martin, R. "The Virtue Matrix: Calculating the Return on Social Responsibility." *Harvard Business Review*, 2002, *80*(3), 68–75.

CHAPTER EIGHT

Individual Frameworks

**Personal Awareness
and Style Frameworks**
Johari Window
Myers-Briggs Type Indicator
Learning Styles Inventory
I'm OK, You're OK:
  The Four Life Positions
Conflict Mode

Professional Effectiveness Frameworks
Social Styles
Getting It Right
Leadership Coaching
Career Transitioning

Decision-Making Frameworks
Prisoner's Dilemma
Urgency and Importance
Influence and Concern

The business importance of individuals is growing as work becomes increasingly knowledge based. Although organizations and markets still determine how work is organized, individuals are the key limiting or success factor more than ever before. This is equally true on the production side of the equation, where design, innovation, and service have become the provinces of critical differentiation, and the consumption side, where active buyers filter an ever-increasing amount of information to communicate preferences and make choices.

The widespread use of computers and communications tools is enhancing the effectiveness of individual workers as it blurs the distinction between roles. Productive work can be done anywhere at anytime, in a factory, an office, or, in many cases, one's kitchen, driving new independence and personal flexibility. In some important ways, we have cycled back to a preindustrial state of affairs, as increas-

The Archetypal Individual Dilemma

Core Question: How can I increase my personal effectiveness?

Key Issue: Fit—matching personal attributes like style, strengths, and interests with context and demand

Figure 8.1. The Archetypal Individual Dilemma

ing numbers of us choose to work outside large, formal businesses, performing a variety of critical value-adding tasks along the way. The new information generalist has arrived, challenged to juggle, optimize, and find personal meaning in a world of limitless variety.

The central experience of individuals today is one of being inundated with options and information. The remarkable improvements brought about by information technology are accompanied by a need to shape and manage the information and opportunities in our lives. Figure 8.1 depicts the archetypal dilemma of effectiveness (contributions made) versus attaining personal satisfaction (needs met). Human potential experts like Frederick Herzberg, Steven Covey, and Michael Macoby tell us that we perform best when work is meaningful and challenging. Throughout most of the history of human work, we have been driven by necessity and the need for physical well-being and survival. For some keen observers, the postindustrial era represents a marked shift away from the fight to survive to a crisis of making choices and finding meaning.

HISTORY OF INDIVIDUAL WORK: THE DANCE BETWEEN SPECIALIZATION AND GENERALIZATION

The history of work can be understood as the story of leverage and control. Sometimes these two forces are aligned. Through most of history, this has not been the case.

Leverage is the ratio of output to input. Knowledge, technology, and organization have contributed to ever-increasing degrees of human leverage. For a crude example, consider the productivity of someone digging with a shovel versus one operating a forklift. Even after the hourly cost of renting and operating the forklift has been calculated, productivity gain measures in the range of several orders of magnitude.

Control describes two things: the freedom to set work goals, methods, and standards, and the amount of value that returns to the worker. In the abstract, most of us would agree these are desirable, especially when applied to ourselves. Indeed, as Western society has flourished since the end of World War II, living standards (value returning to the worker) have risen due to improvements in the factors of production and the widespread adoption of a political system that values market economics and entrepreneurship (freedom to set goals and methods).

A quick walk through the history of human work sets the stage for understanding the needs of the modern worker: what's common through the ages, what's new, and what it means (Table 8.1).

The hunter-gatherer era lasted until eight thousand years ago. Early humans were nomadic, following their food sources in a struggle to survive. We are left with the romanticized image of a primitive, tribal existence, where the basic requirements for life needed to be earned daily. The work was highly special-

Table 8.1. Evolution of Human Work

Era	Leverage	Control	Role	Challenge/ Success Factor
Hunter-gatherer	Low	High activity, high reward	Specialist	How? Physical strength
Agrarian	Medium	High activity, medium reward	Generalist	What? Strength and planning
Industrial	High	Low activity, low reward	Specialist	When? Dignity
Information	High	High activity, high reward	Generalist	Why? Choice and meaning

ized, and although leverage was low, control was high. Hunter-gatherers could work when and where they chose.

The agrarian age lasted approximately ninety-seven hundred years, beginning roughly around 8000 B.C. (dates denoting the duration of eras overlap). The invention of plows and domestication of animals around 7000 B.C. signaled the beginning of work as we know it today. A farmer could extend her reach and yield beyond direct personal effort; stored knowledge grew and began to play a larger role. In comparison with the hunter-gatherers, greater leverage was achieved, and control became a reasonable expectation for many. Still, farming in the early years remained an arduous and risky undertaking, with many bad years to match the few easier, idyllic ones. As leverage grew in the later years with the introduction of better equipment, methods, and science, control dwindled. Farms grew larger, and operating costs and power issues led to concentration of ownership in fewer hands. We rate the agrarian work experience as medium in leverage, with varying degrees of control that diminished over the period.

The industrial age, lasting from the mid-1700s to the middle of the twentieth century, transformed the nature of work once again. Machine technology advanced in power and scale, creating previously unimaginable levels of work efficiency. Labor productivity in the British textile industry increased by 120 times between 1770 and 1812.[1] According to business historian Alfred Chandler, by 1880, fully 80 percent of British workers involved in the production of goods worked in mechanized factories.[2] With the assembly line as the model, the human worker became an extension of the machine and relegated to tasks that were subordinate, programmed, and highly repetitive. Work was once again specialized and low in control.

The information age began in the mid-1960s with the convergence of computing, telecommunications, and media, effecting the most recent great shift in human work. As the industrial period saw a dramatic redistribution of labor away from farming—from over 70 percent in the United States in 1800 to only 1.6 percent today—the information revolution has led people out of factories and traditional professions into a growing array of knowledge-based careers. In large corporations, jobs in innovation, process design, and customer service are replacing the more mechanical and maintenance-oriented jobs of the industrial model organization.

Life in the information era is more complex, but arguably a great improvement over earlier forms. Inexpensive and ubiquitous information systems level the competitive field in ways previously unimaginable. Hierarchy now competes with quality within firms, as best ideas can and often do come from anywhere. As a colleague, Betty Sproule of Hewlett Packard, observed, "Insight is not distributed hierarchically." The brain has replaced the machine as the dominant organizational metaphor. Independent workers and small firms connect with others electronically and operate as well-integrated, intelligent nodes of business networks without needing to be owned by them. Knowledge is creating the possibility of aligning leverage and control for the common worker, who for the first time since the early agrarian period can afford the prime competitive resource: knowledge itself.

THE INDIVIDUAL IN A 2 × 2 CONTEXT

Individual frameworks fall into three categories:

- Personal awareness and style. Some of the best developed and tested 2 × 2 frameworks have been created to enhance personal understanding about style, preferences and how others perceive us. Based on well-established research and modeling from the fields of personality and social psychology, there is a wealth of instrumentation and interpretative support available.

- Professional effectiveness. A significant number of performance and awareness models address work experience directly. Leadership, interpersonal and team orientation, career management, and social style fall into this category.

- Decision making. Personal effectiveness depends on clarity and the ability to act. Frameworks in this section structure decision making in intuitively straightforward and useful ways.

PERSONAL AWARENESS AND STYLE FRAMEWORKS

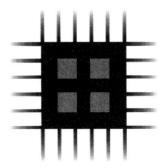

What are my unique strengths, interests, orientation, and values? How can I be more effective in my life?

Understanding and managing oneself is a core competency that touches every aspect of personal effectiveness. We are all somewhat different in style and preferences. As we learn more about our own makeup, we are able to make better sense of experiences and wiser personal decisions. Like petals of a flower, each framework reveals another aspect of our nature. An important part of the personal journey is deciding which of these aspects to explore.

This section contains many of the oldest and best-tested frameworks available. The Johari Window provides a powerful lens into how others perceive us, the Myers-Briggs Type Indicator is probably the most widely applied personality model, and the Learning Styles Inventory is the entry point for understanding how we prefer to learn.

⊞

Johari Window
Joseph Luft and Harry Ingham

Oh would some Power the giftie give us
To see ourselves as others see us!
It would from many a blunder free us,
and foolish notion.
   —Robert Burns[3]

The The Johari Window (Figure 8.2) was developed by psychologists Joseph Luft and Harry Ingham at the University of California and was first presented to a group at the Western Training Laboratory in 1955. Since then, it has been incorporated into hundreds of educational and awareness-training curricula and

Figure 8.2. Johari Window

has been adapted to address unique industry, topic, and community interests. Based on principles of feedback and learning, individuals and groups use the framework to increase levels of openness and self-understanding. It assumes that more self-knowledge is preferable, as is more openness. The framework is used to sensitize one to both of these areas and to expand them.

The Two Dimensions and Their Extremes. The Johari Window is structured in the reflexive form, looking at the same subject matter, oneself, from two perspectives:

> Others' Knowledge: Known to Others versus Not Known to Others. As you participate in activities with others in the world, they learn about you and form impressions based on what you communicate and reveal, as well as from their observations of you.

> Self-Knowledge: Known to Self versus Not Known to Self. There are things about ourselves that we know and understand fully and accurately. You may be funny or a good singer and know these to be true about you. Equally, for most of us, there are qualities about which we are not aware. You may have a good singing voice and truly not realize it. The x-axis divides self-knowledge into these two categories.

The Four Quadrants. Through the exchange of feedback, we are capable of expanding our self-knowledge and modifying behaviors that may annoy others and undermine our success in the world. A 2001 study by Development Dimensions International of five thousand professionals found that an amazing 69 percent of leaders behave in ways that actively derail their careers.[4] Interestingly, 16 percent of leaders were described as unknown to their colleagues. It's hard to trust someone you don't really know. Working to alter your Johari Window helps to change this.

Unlike most other 2 × 2 frameworks, the quadrants are not fixed and equal in size. Think of them as panes in a window, with some more transparent than others. The lines separating the boxes are like shades that can be pulled more or less open. When an aspect of oneself is revealed and shared through the feedback process, one has an opportunity to expand the window of self-understanding. By choosing to share more with others, we are better understood and seen as more authentic. The ideal Johari configuration is uneven, with the public, shared zone larger than the rest:

- Upper left: Open (the Public Arena). This is the self that is well known to both you and others. People tend to trust others who are open to sharing their thoughts candidly and receiving feedback. These people tend to learn more from their experiences and are more effective leaders and influencers. Self-disclosure, however, can feel risky and requires confidence and comfort with oneself. Feedback can also be a scary proposition and is most effective when one seeks it out and when the conditions are sufficiently psychologically safe.

- Lower left: Hidden (the Facade). This box includes things we know or believe but choose not to share with others. We may have a hidden agenda or feel embarrassed about an experience. Often the decision to hide is made automatically, without consciously thinking through the possible consequences. The trouble with hiding behind a facade is that it consumes a lot of energy to hide what is true. And others sense they are not seeing the whole picture when actions and motivations don't line up, eroding trust. Things often turn worse when the reality is revealed. Remember that two recent U.S. presidents, Richard Nixon and Bill Clinton, tried to suppress facts, only to have them blow up in their faces.[5]

- Lower right: Unknown. Within each of us reside talents, opinions, fears, and motivations that are unknown to our self and others. Some of this material lies in our subconscious, surfacing in reaction to triggering events. Blind spots can be dangerous, and it is preferable to be familiar with these parts of ourselves. There are various ways to accomplish this, all of which involve becoming more self-reflective. The Unknown category is problematic when it is permitted to grow and dominate.

- Upper right: Blind. There are aspects about us that others see more clearly than we do. Friends, bosses, and our kids all hold valuable knowledge that can help to complete our sense of who we are. This box represents a major learning opportunity waiting to be tapped. Openness and encouragement of others are needed. People are uncomfortable with giving feedback they worry may be hurtful or that is unwanted. By working with the Johari Window, we can slowly reverse the self-protective mechanisms that keep the light out.

Example: When Being Right Isn't Enough. Geoffrey had worked hard to earn the job and reputation he now enjoyed. He had joined the company as a young engineering graduate twelve years ago. Progressing from analyst to designer and then shift team leader over a seven-year period had felt natural and easy. Somewhere around that time, his advancement stopped, and try as he did, nothing seemed to help his cause. He believed he was effective and respected, perhaps even a little feared, for his laser-like analytic prowess. His performance reviews were consistently positive, if a little vague. He had heard that company management liked it when staff signed up for effectiveness training provided by the in-house professional development group. Geoffrey registered, not expecting much but hopeful this might at least send a message he was serious about his career. If things didn't improve soon, he would start to consider outside opportunities.

Prior to arriving at the session, all attendees were asked to complete a two-page Johari Window questionnaire (Figure 8.3). The session began with reviewing the results. Then the group of twenty participants engaged in a simulation exercise involving building some equipment together using plastic blocks. Geoffrey did this, feeling pretty good about how it went until the group ignored one of his suggestions about halfway through the game. He had been right, and if only they had followed his suggestion, the team would have performed more successfully.

The next thing they did was to fill in the same Johari Window rating form for each other (Figure 8.4) that they had completed prior to the course for themselves. The feedback to Geoffrey was clear and devastating. It didn't matter that Geoffrey had been right about the solution. The group saw him as closed and manipulative. Not only did his team members not appreciate his suggestions, they actively resented him.

Disappointed with the feedback, Geoffrey was asked if the views of the other participants surprised him. He thought about that for a moment. Then the facilitator asked him what had motivated his behavior. Finally, she asked what insights he had about the other members of his team. What could he share with them that would help them to be more effective team members in future? He realized that aside from their rejection of his idea, he had not really observed anything of note. This was stunning to him. He prized himself on his ability to observe and analyze, and here he had noticed nothing worth telling.

He shared all these thoughts, feeling at first anger, then embarrassment, and finally relief. By the end of the day, he knew he was beginning to understand why he was not being considered for promotion in the company. More important, he was beginning to see how guarded and blind his ambition had made

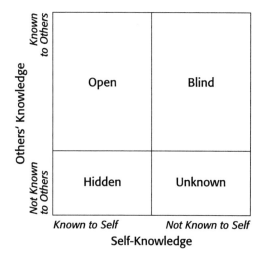

Figure 8.3. Geoffrey's Self-Assessment

Figure 8.4. Geoffrey's Team's Feedback

him over the years, and he questioned whether he wanted to continue to live in this way. On days 2 and 3, Geoffrey started a journey of self-discovery that had been long overdue.

Context. The Johari Window is used by training groups, teams, and individuals to sensitize themselves to issues of self-knowledge, impact on others, and personal and group effectiveness. This is a highly adaptive tool and can be applied lightly as a context for other processes, or as a framework around which to structure activities.

Method. The Johari Window provides a framework for looking at interactions and ourselves differently. Typically, the process begins with learning about the model itself. This is followed with generating data about ourselves and others. Finally, perceptions are exchanged as individuals give and receive feedback. Use of the window can quickly take you into sensitive areas of personal feelings, fears, and perceptions, so it is important that application is led by experienced practitioners in human development. The Johari Window has been applied in countless team-building sessions around the world and is frequently used in educational and therapeutic contexts:

- Step 1: Educate. To benefit from the Johari Window framework requires a basic understanding of the core ideas, the dimensions, and the quadrants. This education is usually accomplished through lecture and reading. There are many sources to choose from, and some of the best are available for free on the Web. Depending on the depth of understanding needed and the purpose, you can select a short overview piece from Augsburg College (http://www.augsburg.edu/education/edc210/JoHari.html) or a more in-depth treatment by David M. Boje (http://cbae.nmsu.edu/ ~ dboje/503/JoHari_window.htm).
- Step 2: Self-assess. As a prelude to receiving feedback from others, it is often helpful to conduct some reflective self-assessment. What would others say about me? How open am I? Would it be better if I were more open? The two approaches to achieving this are to complete a brief self-scoring survey, or to draw the window, adjusting the size of the four quadrants to reflect how you see yourself.
- Step 3: Give and receive feedback. The transformative impact of the Johari Window is the result of the exchange of meaningful feedback. Feedback is a surprisingly powerful force and needs to be treated with care and respect. Safe conditions for all are necessary. Even then, the process will contain risk for participants. At times, it is helpful to stop and discuss the feedback process itself as people grow more comfortable in the roles of both giver and receiver. Beware of a tendency to become defensive in receiving or protective in giving feedback. Both are natural responses, but neither is particularly helpful. Feedback received should be about areas the receiver is willing to pursue. It is often best for the

recipient not to speak at all while receiving feedback, so he or she neither deflects nor misses important information. Feedback given should be honest, descriptive, and nonjudgmental. Sharing the feeling level impact of others' actions is particularly powerful and helpful.

• Step 4: Plan and experiment. It is possible to improve one's window configuration through active exploration in a discussion or group experience. To lock in gains, however, it is important to change some of our behaviors in the world. The goal is to be both more open and to learn from others on an ongoing basis. This step consists of making some specific commitments to being different that will maintain and increase progress.

References

Boje, D. M. "Johari Window and the Psychodynamics of Leadership and Influence in Intergroup Life." Sept. 2003. [http://cbae.nmsu.edu/~dboje/503/johari_window.htm].

Johari Window. [http://www.chimaeraconsulting.com/johari.htm].

Luft, J. *Of Human Interaction*. Palo Alto, Calif.: National Press, 1969.

⊞

Myers-Briggs Type Indicator
Isabel Briggs Myers and Katherine Briggs

The MBTI [Myers-Briggs Type Indicator] is primarily concerned with the valuable differences in people that result from where they like to focus their attention, the way they like to take in information, the way they like to decide, and the kind of lifestyle they adopt.
    —Isabel Briggs Myers[6]

The Myers-Briggs Type Indicator (MBTI) is the most widely used personality test in the world, completed by approximately 2 million people each year. Developed by the mother-daughter team of Katherine Briggs and Isabel Myers, the work is based on Carl Jung's personality theory described in his 1921 book, *Psychological Types*. Two basic cognitive functions define differences between humans: how we take in information and how we make decisions. Jung also looked at differences in how we get and expend energy. The survey produces sixteen individual profiles based on four sets of preferences (Table 8.2).[7]

The four sets of preferences used by the MBTI are:

• Introversion-Extraversion (I, E): A focus on the inner world of ideas and reflection versus the outer, external world

Table 8.2. The Sixteen Myers-Briggs Types

		Introverts — Judging Types	Introverts — Perceptive Types	Extraverts — Perceptive Types	Extraverts — Judging Types
Sensing Types	With Thinking	**ISTJ** I Depth of concentration S Reliance on facts T Logic and analysis J Organization	**ISTP** I Depth of concentration S Reliance on facts T Logic and analysis P Adaptability	**ESTP** E Breadth of interests S Reliance on facts T Logic and analysis P Adaptability	**ESTJ** E Breadth of interests S Reliance on facts T Logic and analysis J Organization
Sensing Types	With Feeling	**ISFJ** I Depth of concentration S Reliance on facts F Warmth and sympathy J Organization	**ISFP** I Depth of concentration S Reliance on facts F Warmth and sympathy P Adaptability	**ESFP** E Breadth of interests S Reliance on facts F Warmth and sympathy P Adaptability	**ESFP** E Breadth of interests S Reliance on facts F Warmth and sympathy J Organization
Intuitive Types	With Thinking	**INFJ** I Depth of concentration N Grasp of possibilities F Warmth and sympathy J Organization	**INFP** I Depth of concentration N Grasp of possibilities F Warmth and sympathy P Adaptability	**ENFP** E Breadth of interests N Grasp of possibilities F Warmth and sympathy P Adaptability	**ENFJ** E Breadth of interests N Grasp of possibilities F Warmth and sympathy J Organization
Intuitive Types	With Feeling	**INTJ** I Depth of concentration N Grasp of possibilities T Logic and analysis J Organization	**INTP** I Depth of concentration N Grasp of possibilities T Logic and analysis P Adaptability	**ENTP** E Breadth of interests N Grasp of possibilities T Logic and analysis P Adaptability	**ENTJ** E Breadth of interests N Grasp of possibilities T Logic and analysis J Organization

Note: For more detailed information, see http://www.mtr-i.com/mb-types/mb-types.htm.

- Sensing-Intuiting (N, S): Perceiving and acquiring new information through intuition versus the five senses

- Thinking-Feeling (T, F): Making decisions based on reason versus values

- Judgment-Perception (J, P): A basic orientation toward either judging (thinking/feeling) or perceiving (sensing/intuiting)

The Myers-Briggs team developed their survey and related methods and materials over a twenty-year period, producing a rich and comparatively stable instrument. It is a model in which there are no good or bad personality types. There is a need and a place for all of us. Your psychological type indicates what you are naturally drawn to, but you still can choose to pursue other kinds of endeavors and succeed at them. The MBTI does not measure functional strengths and weaknesses or intelligence. Understanding type preferences gives us a language to appreciate the interests and benefits of unique individual orientations. Combining education with personal feedback, the framework helps both individuals and groups to make crucial decisions, improve effectiveness, and resolve conflicts.

The two inner scores—how we take in information and how we make decisions—provide a useful introduction to MBTI assessment (see Figure 8.5). We focus on these as a way to become more familiar with one of the most important diagnostic tools available for understanding ourselves and others. *This is not intended as a working tool.* The MBTI should be administered by a qualified and trained professional in the psychology or social work fields. For those

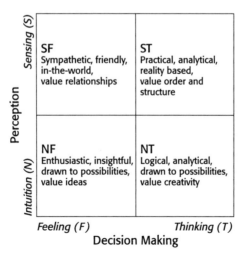

Figure 8.5. Perception and Judgment Matrix

interested in delving further into the MBTI, a good next step is to take the quick self-scoring survey created by Personality Pathways, available on-line at http://www.personalitypathways.com/.

The Two Dimensions and Their Extremes. It is reasonable to think of Perception and Judgment as cognitive functions and the remaining two (introversion-extraversion and judgment-perception) as orientations. It was Isabel Briggs Myers's insight that combinations of all four preferences painted a full picture of individual personality. We encourage interested readers to learn more by checking out some of the authoritative sources listed at the end of this section. However, let's examine what we learn by creating a basic 2 × 2 matrix with the two core functions.

Perception: Sensing versus Intuition. How do you acquire information? Sensing types experience the world through their five senses. They tend to be practical and able to quickly accept and work with constraints in a given situation. They are realistic and tend to be good at remembering lots of facts. Intuiting types go beyond the five senses to identify meaning and patterns. They look at the big picture and see new possibilities. They value imagination and inspiration.

Decision Making: Thinking versus Feeling. How do you make decisions? Thinking types make decisions based on analysis and logic. They explore logical consequences and try to be objective even if some of the facts are unpleasant. Feeling types make decisions based on what is important to themselves and others. They are interested in others and tend to be sympathetic and ready to get involved if they can help out.

The Four Quadrants. In *Introduction to Type,* Isabel Briggs Myers examines the combinations of cognitive types for direction in selecting a suitable career:

• Upper left: SF. People with an SF orientation are caring and practical, often making them ideally suited to service-oriented careers. They are efficient and drawn to applying their efforts to work that makes a difference to others. Typical careers for SF types are in health care and teaching.
• Lower left: NT. NTs are the theoretical modelers and problem solvers. They are interested in exploring possibilities by applying methods and logic. NTs are drawn to careers in computers, engineering, management, and law.
• Lower right: NF. NFs are passionate, caring dreamers. They are drawn to inventing rather than implementing and are particularly adept at seeing the possibilities in any situation. They thrive in careers like research, art and music, and teaching.

• Upper right: ST. ST types care about facts and tangible evidence and draw their conclusions from logical analysis. They can be counted on to investigate matters in a very reasoned and empirical fashion. With their real-world, practical orientation, they excel at careers like law enforcement, applied science, and banking.

Example: A Work Team Composition Case. The MBTI is often used extensively in team situations for diagnosing problems, resolving conflicts, and increasing understanding among members. Once people understand type differences, it becomes easier to accept a range of behaviors and work out accommodations. Teams need to address different issues as they progress through stages of maturation and project completion. The MBTI helps to tackle interpersonal issues in a dispassionate and constructive way. The example here looks at how conflicts are reframed and energy is rechanneled using MBTI modeling. We have constructed the analysis around the two dimensions of perception and decision making (Figure 8.6).

Conflicts in teams often arise around role definitions and decision making. Differences that appear to be about direction and content may well have more to do with style.

As conflicts intensify, people sometimes stop listening to each other or trying to understand what is motivating their behavior. Small misunderstandings grow into major problems as people increase their efforts to influence others and protect their own interests. This creates a downward spiral, leading to more conflict and dysfunction.

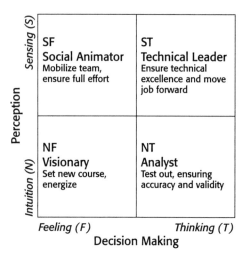

Figure 8.6. Harnessing Type Power Matrix

By understanding the type profiles of team members, motivations and actions come into better focus. What at first may appear as irreconcilable differences can be viewed as uniquely different styles. As indicated in Figure 8.6, each type has strengths that can be accessed for the benefit of the group. The NF member challenges norms and initiates new direction, the NT member qualifies and validates the proposed path, the SF member engages others on the team and rallies participation, and the ST member makes sure work proceeds in a professional and economical way.

Context. The MBTI is well suited to a range of individual and group situations, extending from career counseling and personal awareness to conflict resolution and staff planning. In all situations, a qualified, trained professional should be engaged to administer and help interpret and process test results.

Method. Methods may vary depending on the purpose and context. The following steps are offered as a general map relevant to most situations:

- Step 1: Establish purpose and context. The MBTI produces a set of results that can be applied in general or to assist with a specific need. It is advisable to establish the context in which results will be reviewed. Respondents should feel at ease completing the survey honestly and trust the method and administrator of the overall process.
- Step 2: Complete the survey. The survey is processed after completion.
- Step 3: Orient to the MBTI. Respondents must understand key MBTI concepts to derive the benefits of the survey process. Readings and presentations help to accomplish this.
- Step 4: Report and interpret results. Survey scores are delivered, interpreted, and applied to the specific goals of the intervention.

References

Jung, C. *Psychological Types.* Princeton, N.J.: Princeton University Press, 1976.

Myers, I. B. *Gifts Differing: Understanding Personality Type.* Palo Alto, Calif.: Davies-Black Publishers, 1995.

Myers, I. B. *Introduction to Type: A Guide to Understanding Your Results on the Myers-Briggs Type Indicator.* Gainesville, Fla.: Center for Applications of Psychological Type, 1998.

⊞

Learning Styles Inventory
David Kolb

Tell me, and I will forget. Show me, and I may remember. Involve me, and I will
understand.
  —Confucius

Adults learn differently from children. They are not empty vessels seeking to be
filled or clay in need of shaping. Adults have knowledge, values, relationships,
and intentions that influence how they behave and learn new things. Often
unlearning is half the battle.

David Kolb has recognized these factors in his development of the Experiential Learning Cycle. Most learning for adults occurs in natural settings as opposed
to formal situations and institutions. Learning and problem solving are closely
related. Typically, learning involves four phases: concrete experience (feeling),
reflective observation (reflection), abstract conceptualization (thinking), and
active experimentation (doing). The Learning Styles Inventory (LSI) identifies four
different orientations to learning, depending on the parts of the Experiential Learning Cycle one prefers (Figure 8.7). The LSI has been completed by millions of people and is used frequently in group, educational, and career counseling situations.

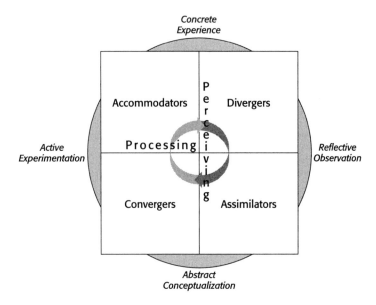

Figure 8.7. Learning Styles Inventory

The Two Dimensions and Their Extremes. The Learning Styles Inventory explores two key dimensions: Perceiving and Processing:

Perceiving. This describes our preferred means of acquiring new information, ranging from Concrete Experience to Abstract Conceptualization.

Processing. This refers to how we make sense of things, ranging from Active Experimentation to Reflective Observation.

The Four Quadrants. The four learning styles represent preferences, as opposed to strengths and weaknesses. Each of the styles is legitimate and well represented in the general population. It is common for people to draw on more than one style, indicating a degree of flexibility. Understanding one's learning style can be helpful in improving learning speed, depth, retention, and enjoyment:

• Upper left: Accommodators. Accommodators are activists who learn best when they become fully involved. They enjoy simulations and case studies and are adventurous types who will try anything. They are intuitive problem solvers who will often rely on others for information and analysis.
• Lower left: Convergers. Convergers are pragmatists interested in finding the practical application of ideas. They enjoy solving problems, and tend to prefer technical tasks over social and interpersonal issues. They learn well in laboratories and through fieldwork.
• Lower right: Assimilators. Assimilators are theorists who enjoy working with ideas and constructing models. They tend to be concise and logical and are more concerned with abstract concepts than their practical or human implications. They learn well with lectures and papers.
• Upper right: Divergers. Divergers are reflective learners who prefer to learn by observing and making sense of experiences. They enjoy lectures and benefit from recording their thoughts in a learning log. Divergers are imaginative and tend to be interested in people and their emotions.

Method. The Learning Styles Inventory can be employed with individuals or groups. Sample surveys can be found on the Web at http://www.ncsu.edu/felder-public/ILSpage.html. Presurvey orientation and postsurvey completion debriefing may need to be adjusted:

• Step 1: Complete the survey. This takes less than thirty minutes and should be done within a psychologically safe context to ensure candor.
• Step 2: Score the LSI. Results to the LSI are easy to calculate and can be done electronically or by respondents themselves.

• Step 3: Education: Prior to discussion of the results, it is helpful to teach the core set of ideas pertaining to the Experiential Learning Cycle and the LSI.

• Step 4: Interpret and apply. Scores are reviewed and implications examined. The approach taken for this will vary depending on the purpose and context.

References

Kolb, D. *Experiential Learning: Experience as the Source of Learning and Development.* Upper Saddle River, N.J.: Prentice Hall, 1984.

Smith, N. J., Kolb, D. M., and David, A. *The Users' Guide for the Learning-Style Inventory: A Manual for Teachers and Trainers.* Boston: McBer & Company, 1986.

⊞

I'm OK, You're OK: The Four Life Positions
Thomas Harris

We do not drift into a new [life] position. It is a decision we make. In this respect it is like a conversion experience.
    —Thomas Harris[8]

Thomas Harris's best-selling book, *I'm OK, You're OK,* helped jump-start the modern self-help phenomenon when it was released in 1967. It was based on the principles of Transactional Psychotherapy, first formulated by Eric Berne in an article, "Transactional Analysis: A New and Effective Method of Group Therapy." TA (as it came to be known) sought to shorten the time required for traditional therapy by dealing directly with the problems of adult behavior here and now. TA defined three dimensions of a person's ego: Adult, Child, and Parent. The Parent represented discipline and rules; the Child, spontaneous emotions; and the Adult, the rational perspective that made decisions based on data and experience.

The basic unit of analysis in TA is a transaction, an interaction between two people. Our propensity to transact in the Parent, Child, or Adult mode is set in early childhood by our nurturing, or lack of it. Berne's belief was that people play parent-child "games" throughout life, adopting roles that help us get the positive responses we need to survive. How successfully we learn to give and get positive responses—*strokes* in TA parlance—determines our ability to interact successfully with others. The goal of Transactional Analysis is to liberate the Adult from painful and often unconscious behavior patterns imposed on it by the Parent and the Child, enabling freedom of choice and rational decision making.[9]

The Two Dimensions and Their Extremes. The I'm OK, You're OK matrix explores two key dimensions: You and Me:

You. The You axis measures the extent to which one values and respects others.

Me. The Me axis describes how one values and feels about oneself.

The Four Quadrants. Healthy relationships between adults are based on respect that begins with acceptance of self and the other. The I'm OK, You're OK matrix (Figure 8.8) presents this relationship in the upper right quadrant, along with the three remaining suboptimal options. These are known as the Four Life Positions:

• Upper left: I'm Not OK, You're OK. The newborn begins life in a state of dependency with a sense of Not-OK-ness based on helplessness. Normally, the child cycles out of this quadrant as she matures. People who maintain this role live in anxious dependency, often feeling at the mercy of others. Two life roles or "scripts" often present themselves. One is the person who continuously seeks the approval and strokes of Parents—people who enjoy the power to give or withhold approval. The other is a perennial bad boy or girl who is always proving to him- or herself that "I'm Not OK."

• Lower left: I'm Not OK, You're Not OK. As a child matures, he needs positive stimulus or strokes. If those are not forthcoming as the infant becomes a young child, the person may get stuck in this quadrant. Unable to get strokes, the person eventually gives up on life. The I'm Not OK, You're Not OK person rejects positive reinforcement later in life and resists interacting with others as an Adult.

Figure 8.8. I'm OK, You're OK Matrix

• Lower right: I'm OK, You're Not OK. The child whose psychological needs are ignored turns inward, in effect, nurturing herself. Career criminals often characterize this life script—the fault in any situation lies with others. A more successful depiction of this quadrant is the powerful man who surrounds himself only with "yes" men. Since there are no OK others, they remind him that only he can provide authentic approval to himself.

• Upper right: I'm OK, You're OK. The goal in TA is for a person to make a conscious and concerted decision to assume the Adult role. Rather than operating on feelings programmed into us in childhood, one learns the skills of interacting as a responsible Adult.

Method. To benefit from TA, people need to become more competent and astute transactional analysts. By understanding interactions more accurately, we are able to step out of an unhealthy interaction or role and consciously assume the Adult perspective. TA is practiced in individual and group sessions:

• Step 1: Diagnose. Identify your role (Child or Parent) in unsatisfactory transactions and why you are in it.
• Step 2: Envision. Analyze how life interactions could be improved by adopting a more rational adult position in your interactions with others.
• Step 3: Commit. Make a decision to transact as an Adult. Experiment with approaching interactions from this perspective. Expect some challenges, and proceed with patience and an openness to feedback.

References

Berne, E. "Transactional Analysis: A New and Effective Method of Group Therapy," *American Journal of Psychotherapy*, 1958, *12*, 293–309.

Harris, T. *I'm OK, You're OK.* New York: HarperCollins, 1967.

⊞

Conflict Mode
Kenneth Thomas and Ralph Kilmann

The conflict behaviors which individuals use are therefore the result of both their personal predispositions and the requirements of the situations in which they find themselves.
—Kenneth Thomas and Ralph Kilmann[10]

Conflicts arise when people hold different views on a subject. Although conflict is a natural part of human experience, it can be problematic if it becomes entrenched or destructive. The Thomas-Kilmann Conflict Mode Instrument (Figure 8.9) is widely used to sensitize individuals to conflict styles and options for resolution. Response to conflict situations is a combination of one's dominant style and the attendant circumstances. No one is limited to one conflict style; however, our natural inclination and prior experiences cause us to favor one response style over the others. By understanding ourselves better and learning about a range of conflict approaches, we can consciously choose to respond in the most helpful and effective way.

The Two Dimensions and Their Extremes. The Conflict Mode matrix explores two key dimensions: Assertiveness and Cooperativeness:

Assertiveness. Assertiveness is the extent to which an individual acts to satisfy his or her own needs and interests.

Cooperativeness. Cooperativeness describes the extent to which one acts to satisfy the needs and concerns of the other party.

The Four Quadrants. Each conflict style has strengths and weaknesses and is more appropriate for some circumstances than for others:[11]

• Upper left: Competing. Might makes right. Assertive and uncooperative, this is a power-oriented approach. Competing is appropriate when quick, decisive action is needed or when an unpopular but necessary course must be followed.
• Lower left: Avoiding. Leave well enough alone. Unassertive and uncooperative, this is a delay-action approach characteristic of the ostrich with its head

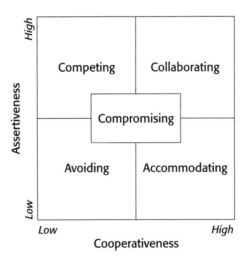

Figure 8.9. Conflict Mode Matrix

in the sand. Avoiding is useful when the issue is superficial, when more time would be helpful, or when others are better suited to resolving the matter.

• Lower right: Accommodating. Kill your enemy with kindness. Unassertive and cooperative, proponents of this style will sacrifice their own needs in the interest of satisfying the other party. Accommodating is beneficial when it is crucial to preserve harmony and when an issue is much more important to the other party.

• Upper right: Collaborating. Two heads are better than one. Assertive and cooperative, this involves working with the other party to find a mutually agreeable solution. Collaborating is ideal when seeking to integrate diverse approaches or to maintain commitment and goodwill.

• Center: Compromising. Split the difference. Intermediate in both assertiveness and cooperativeness, this approach leads to expedient and acceptable outcomes that fall short of ideal but which both parties are willing to accept. Compromise is suitable when goals are only moderately important, time is short, and equally powerful parties remain strongly committed to their points of view.

Method. The Thomas-Kilmann Conflict Mode Instrument is at the heart of this method. Follow these steps to conduct a high-level intervention to increase awareness and help resolve conflict:

• Step 1: Set the context. Establish a meaningful context. Is this to resolve a conflict or to promote personal insight?
• Step 2: Test. Complete the Thomas-Kilmann Conflict Mode Instrument.
• Step 3: Score. Calculate scores and examine for insights. What can we learn, and what changes in approach should be considered?

Reference

Thomas, K. W., and Kilmann, R. *Thomas-Kilmann Conflict Mode Instrument.* Santa Clara, Calif.: Xicom, 1974.

PROFESSIONAL EFFECTIVENESS FRAMEWORKS

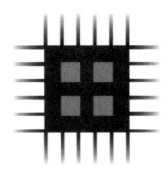

What are my unique professional strengths, interests, orientation, and values? How can I be more effective at work?

Each year, industry spends billions of dollars on professional development in the hope that employees will update their skills, knowledge, and outlook. Businesses don't tend to fail all at once. Deterioration is gradual, and the way to fight it is through ongoing investment, focus, and reinforcement.

2 × 2 frameworks are at the core of many of the most important professional development systems. Three key areas are addressed: career planning, leadership, and interpersonal effectiveness.

⊞

Social Styles
David Merrill and Roger Reid

> We should point out again here that we are talking mostly about the tensions created between people because they act differently. Behavioral differences are causing the problem, not differences in belief or values.
> —David Merrill and Roger Reid[12]

As unique as we each are, our social style, that is, the way we behave with others, is likely to fit one of four patterns. We may be a decisive Driver seeking action and results, a warm Amiable interested in relationships and others' welfare, a systematic Analyst concerned with order and facts, or an energetic Expressive looking for enthusiastic buy-in (Figure 8.10). These Social Styles are behavioral tendencies that form naturally in the give-and-take of life experiences. While we are capable of assuming alternate approaches, our style is the stance in the world that feels most comfortable and that others are likely to expect from us. There are no "bad" styles, although different styles have been found to predispose people to one or another kind of career.

Social Style is a function of two sets of behavioral preferences: Assertiveness, ranging from active, forceful initiating to quiet inquiring and waiting, and Responsiveness, ranging from openly displaying feelings to hiding our feelings from others. The four styles represent combinations of the polar extremes of these dimensions. Developing the model in the 1960s, Merrill and Reid found significant numbers of each of the types in the general population. Subsequent studies have confirmed the validity of the model and four styles in different countries and cultures around the world.

Interpersonal effectiveness is improved when we become aware of the interplay between different Social Styles and adjust our responses and behaviors accordingly. For example, you would present carefully chosen facts when trying to influence an Analyst, whereas to convince a Driver, you would be wise to point out urgency and describe concrete actions they should take. By understanding behavior as a function of Social Style, we are able to separate out issues of form from those of substance. This makes it easier to defuse unhelpful and unnecessary conflicts arising from misunderstanding rather than genuine disagreements.

Merrill and Reid describe a basic four-phase approach, beginning with knowing yourself (awareness), controlling yourself (self-utilizatization), knowing others (observing), and doing something for others (communicating with sensitivity).

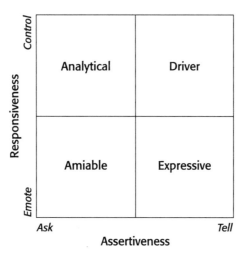

Figure 8.10. Social Styles Matrix

The Two Dimensions and Their Extremes. The Social Styles matrix explores two key dimensions: Responsiveness and Assertiveness:

Responsiveness. This dimension of behavior describes how much feeling a person tends to display, whether one tends to openly Emote or to Control feelings in social situations.

Assertiveness. This aspect of behavior describes whether a person tends to Tell versus Ask, and the extent to which others see one as trying to influence their decisions. People viewed as assertive are described as likely to take a stand and to make their position clear on matters.

The Four Quadrants. Each of us has a dominant Social Style. By understanding the behavioral preferences of ourselves and others, we can tailor communications in ways that increase comfort levels and improve interpersonal effectiveness. According to Robert and Dorothy Bolton, "Any style can conflict with another style, but our point is that if you can recognize and accept style differences, you can do much to minimize tensions which are unnecessary and clearly unproductive."[13] Understanding is the first step. Although our Social Styles are relatively set, we can improve our Versatility by being thoughtful and sensitive in communicating with others. Merrill and Reid found that although Social Styles do not in themselves diffferentiate those who are more or less successful in their undertakings, Versatility is consistently an ingredient of success, and it can be learned:

• Upper left: Analytical. Analyticals are organized, cautious individuals, interested in facts and reason. They tend to be thorough in whatever they do, gathering information and processing it thoughtfully and objectively. They are sometimes seen as overly structured, stubborn, or indecisive.

When communicating with an Analytical, be specific and concrete, following up with action, not promises. It matters to Analyticals that you agree with their carefully derived ideas and principles. Let them know your opinion. Although they cannot be hurried, it helps to be persistent and clear with this kind of person.

• Lower left: Amiable. Amiables place high value on personal relationships, cooperation, and affiliation with others. They are often warm individuals who bring positive energy and freshness to social situations. They prefer to achieve objectives with others, acting with respect and understanding rather than power or coercion. They can also be seen as emotional, sentimental, or easily influenced by others.

When communicating with an Amiable, it is important to recognize the human aspects of the issue. Who is involved, how do they feel about it, and how will this affect them? They care about relationship and trust. Remember to establish rapport and to work at defining mutually agreeable goals and methods.

- Lower right: Expressive. Expressives are assertive; however, they share their inner feelings and are experienced by others as enthusiastic and friendly. They tend to be influential people, engaging others with their energy and optimism. Expressives can overwhelm and be perceived as too talkative or domineering. They tend to be weak on details.

When communicating with an Expressive, it is important to recognize their dreams and intuitions. Remember that they are interested in the new and innovative aspects of the message and are less concerned with details. When reaching agreements, make sure to be specific about terms and next steps.

- Upper right: Driver. Drivers tend to be serious, assertive people, interested in action and results. Often viewed as decisive and pragmatic, they live in the here-and-now. They go to great lengths to tell others what they think and require, while revealing little about their feelings. They can appear severe, tend to be task focused, and are most comfortable when they are in charge. They can appear pushy or impulsive, ready to act without enough preparation.

When communicating with a Driver, focus on the what and how, not the why or who questions. Drivers don't necessarily require a personal relationship or deep philosophical alignment. Pay more attention to desired outcomes and the actions needed to realize them.

Example: Company Acquisition: The Negotiation. Social Styles training and skills have been used in thousands of corporate settings over the years. Application of the framework raises interpersonal awareness and provides a common language participants can draw on to communicate effectively and resolve conflicts. The hypothetical situation described here illustrates the impact of communication effectiveness on feelings and outcomes.

BigCo is interested in acquiring SmallCo. The fit appears ideal for both sides of the transaction, and four players, two from each firm, have gathered to iron out final issues and conclude the deal. The participants are the BigCo vice president of acquisitions (a Driver), the BigCo human resources director (an Amiable), the SmallCo founder (an Expressive), and the SmallCo chief scientist (an Analytical).

Each participant in the meeting has good intentions and will need to play a critical role in arriving at a successful outcome (Figure 8.11). The different Social Styles can become a barrier, however, if people feel pressured or wary. In intense negotiations, this happens too easily and often.

For example, the BigCo vice president might lead off by selling the financial virtues of the deal, looking for a speedy conclusion, while the Expressive and Analyst SmallCo representatives are looking for enthusiastic engagement and reliable facts. The BigCo vice president needs to begin by addressing the felt needs of the SmallCo representatives before forcefully pursuing her own agenda to close the deal. She might consider allowing her human resource director to engage the founder and provide concrete benefits information to the Analytical

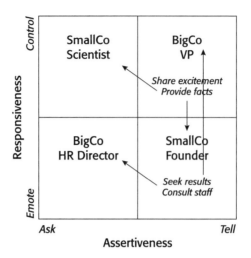

Figure 8.11. Improving Negotiations Matrix

scientist. In her offer, it will be important to recognize the pride and sense of accomplishment of the SmallCo reps. She needs to listen to the founder and demonstrate excitement.

The SmallCo founder might naturally be inclined to share his business vision in an animated manner, only to feel deflated at the lack of uptake by the BigCo representatives. The founder needs to consider the vice president's needs and offer her reassurances about his shared desire for speedy progress and a concrete outcome. In communicating with the human resources director, it would be useful to describe his company's staffing philosophy and commitment to full and fair consultation with employees.

By attending to each others' style needs, all parties feel more at ease and respected, and are less likely to be negatively distracted from the primary purpose of the transaction.

Context. The Social Styles approach is deployed to improve performance across a wide range of individual and team situations, and has been used by over 10 million people in more than twenty countries since it was introduced in the 1960s. The framework is particularly well suited to improving skills in leadership and sales.

Method. Follow the steps here to benefit from Social Styles insights:

- Step 1: Determine the context: individual, team, organizational, educational?
- Step 2: Complete the Social Styles Diagnostic Survey, available from the Tracom Group.

- Step 3: Score and debrief results in the context set for the process.
- Step 4: Improve communication with others based on personal insights and understanding of the model.

References

Bolton, R., and Bolton, D. P. *Social Style/Management Style.* New York: Amacom, 1984.

Merrill, D., and Reid, R. *Personal Styles and Effective Performance.* Philadelphia: Chilton, 1981.

TRACOM Group. [http://www.tracom.com].

⊞

Getting It Right
Peter Drucker

> There is surely nothing quite so useless as doing with great efficiency that which should not be done at all.
> —Peter Drucker[14]

This commonsense framework comes out of the study of highly effective leaders and their organizations. One view is that managers do the job right, while leaders ensure that the right job is being done (Figure 8.12). This leadership responsibility is especially pertinent in bureaucratic settings where work is too

Figure 8.12. Doing Things Right Matrix

easily abstracted from its larger purpose and context and the assigned task becomes an end in itself. The framework raises useful questions about the relevance and importance of the work being done by an individual, a team, or a larger unit within an organization. As organizations distribute more authority to knowledgeable workers, it becomes everyone's job to ensure the validity and design of their own work.

The Two Dimensions and Their Extremes. The Doing Things Right matrix explores two key dimensions: Right Job and Job Done Right:

> Right Job. This dimension describes the content of work activity. Not all task definitions are equally useful or aligned on purpose. Success begins with getting the Right Job defined.

> Job Done Right. This dimension describes the process of work activity. Work can be completed well or poorly.

The Four Quadrants. Of the four possible scenarios, only one, Yes-Yes, has any real chance of success. Improvement begins with diagnosis. Knowing the need helps you decide where to place your efforts:

• Upper left: Could Succeed. In this case, there is a chance of success because the work is properly defined, but there are problems getting in the way and undermining efforts. Diagnosis of the situation and course correction are required.

• Lower right: No Chance. Both the job definition and the methods being applied are wrong. Although this situation appears almost comically obvious, groups often find themselves here. This is because the two problems attract each other. In such an unhealthy atmosphere, it can become very difficult to challenge the status quo and launch corrective steps.

• Lower right: Waste of Time. This is perhaps the most tragic of the four states. Good work is being accomplished, but to no particularly useful end. Things could be turned around, but leadership is required.

• Upper right: Excellent Chance of Success. High performance requires both of the qualities measured by this framework. Great leaders provide focus to their teams and help members to work at their best.

Method. Follow these steps to improve organizational priority setting and to diagnose possible causes of performance ineffectiveness:

• Step 1: Focus. Pick an individual or business unit engaged in a defined work activity.

• Step 2: Assess. Assess current effectiveness by using the matrix and responding to the questions, "Are they doing the Right Job [validity]?" and "Are they doing the Job Right [quality]?"

- Step 3: Correct. Depending on the assessment, take appropriate action. For example, if the job is poorly defined, get clear about what is really needed. If the work is being done poorly, launch an effort to find out why, and then tackle the problem. If neither job nor work effectiveness is acceptable, rethink the legitimacy of the function or unit, and consider fundamental redesign or elimination.

Reference

Drucker, P. F. "Managing for Business Effectiveness." *Harvard Business Review,* May 1963, p. 56.

⊞

Leadership Coaching
Bryan Smith and Rick Ross

Nobody is more powerful than a passionate leader; particularly in terms of his or her impact on others. That is why the coaching that leaders receive is arguably one of the highest-impact leverage points available to a team.
—Bryan Smith and Rick Ross[15]

People in leadership positions face unique learning challenges when they want to improve their leadership effectiveness. Formal courses are often irrelevant and artificial, free time is scarce, and subordinates are often fearful of delivering honest feedback that may be received negatively. Bryan Smith and Rick Ross suggest coaching as a more practical and useful option.

Leadership Coaching opens the door to learning directly from what is or is not working well in the daily execution of leadership responsibilities (Figure 8.13). Acting as part mentor, part mirror, the coach encourages and supports honest reflection and improvement efforts.

The Two Dimensions and Their Extremes. The Leadership Coaching matrix explores two key dimensions: Message Content and Evaluation:

Message Content. The content of the coach's message ranges from Ambiguous to Specific. Specific performance feedback is most helpful.

Evaluation. Feedback ranges from Judgmental to Descriptive. Judgmental feedback risks provoking defensive, emotional responses, and damaging the connection between coach and leader. Descriptive feedback makes valuable information available to the leader.

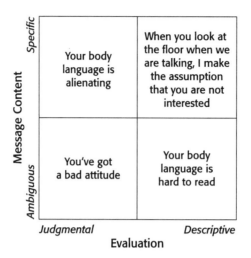

Figure 8.13. Leadership Coaching Matrix

The Four Quadrants. Effective feedback is Descriptive rather than Judgmental and Specific versus Ambiguous:

• Upper left: Judgmental and Specific. This is a dangerous and conterproductive approach. Even when the feedback is accurate, the leader is likely to feel judged and try to rationalize her behavior.

• Lower left: Judgmental and Ambiguous. It is difficult for the recipient to respond to nonspecific criticism or feel good when judgments are emotionally loaded. The goal is to move toward the Descriptive and Specific.

• Lower right: Descriptive and Ambiguous. Descriptive feedback is empty if it is not accompanied by relevant observations and examples. The leader needs this information to understand what exactly has occurred and what is worth changing.

• Upper right: Descriptive and Specific. As we move from the Judgmental to Descriptive, and Ambiguous to Specific, areas of improvement can be identified in a constructive and open manner.

Method. Coaching is a continuous process, as leadership skills are constantly tested and refined.

• Step 1: Set the scene. Coaches begin with establishing rapport and trust with the leader, and they take responsibility for successful coaching outcomes.

• Step 2: Observe behavior. It is ideal for the coach to attend meetings and other events to collect firsthand information. When this is not feasible, the coach is restricted to working with the leader's own account of events, helping the leader make sense of experiences.

- Step 3: Recreate the scene. It is helpful to review difficult and challenging situations, asking questions like, "How did you do in that encounter?"
- Step 4: Share observations. Using descriptive, specific language, provide feedback and help the leader to expand self-understanding and set meaningful leadership improvement objectives.

Reference

Senge, P., and others. *The Dance of Change: The Challenges of Sustaining Momentum in Learning Organizations.* New York: Doubleday/Currency, 1999.

⊞

Career Transitioning
Based on the work of Richard Nelson Bolles

There is a vast world of work out there in this country, where at least 111 million people are employed in this country alone—many of whom are bored out of their minds. All day long.
—Richard Nelson Bolles[16]

With over seven million copies sold in the past two decades, few books have been as influential as Richard Nelson Bolles's *What Color Is Your Parachute?* The book's premise is that most people choose a career path without properly evaluating their own skills, interests, and aspirations. As a result, millions of people are in jobs that are a poor fit for them. They miss their true calling and waste their working lives.

Bolles boils the issues involved in determining a career down to two main questions: What do you want to do? and Where do you want to do it? The book arms those who are seeking new careers with simple tools for finding out all of the information they need in order to make a meaningful career decision.

The Career Transitioning matrix (Figure 8.14) looks at two key variables involved in considering a new career.[17] Taken together, these determine the degree to which changing jobs will be simple or complex.

The Two Dimensions and Their Extremes. The Career Transitioning matrix explores two key dimensions: Job Title and Field:

Job Title. Job title refers to the nature of the work itself. One can remain in the same profession or switch.

Field. Field refers to industry context. One can stay in the same industry or move to a new one.

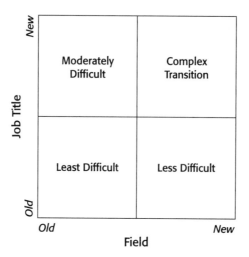

Figure 8.14. Career Transitioning Matrix

The Four Quadrants. The complexity and challenge of a career change increase with the addition of new elements. The Career Transitioning matrix illustrates how the two variables of Job Title and Field define a meaningful range of options with varying levels of difficulty:

• Upper left: Moderately Difficult. Changing Job Titles while remaining in a familiar industry context, as when an accountant moves into sales or a copyeditor moves into reporting, is moderately difficult. The challenge for the job seeker is to demonstrate aptitudes and abilities for the new position, which is often a move up.

• Lower left: Least Difficult. Staying in the current job and changing employers (while remaining in the same industry) is a common transition when one is happy in one's career but seeking a better opportunity or new geography.

• Lower right: Less Difficult. In professions such as sales, accounting, human resources, and graphic design, skills are standardized across industries. Moving from one industry to another constitutes a relatively easy transition.

• Upper right: Complex Transition. Finding lifelong fulfillment—the color of one's parachute—often means changing Job and Field. This is the toughest transition of the four. Many employers seek specific experience or technical skills. In addition, there is the risk that the job seeker will choose a career for which she is not prepared or temperamentally suited. The key to this transition is being realistic about what is possible and the amount of effort it will take to become fully competent.

Method. Follow these steps to create a high-level plan to effect the transition from one career to another:

- Step 1: Select a career direction. Identify the career or job you would like to attain, and locate it on the matrix. Consider the difficulty of attaining the desired job.
- Step 2: Interview. Prepare a list of informational interview questions for workers in that job. Include questions about skills, the daily nature of the work, education, coworkers, salary, lifestyle, personal fulfillment, success factors, work, and personal challenges. Conduct informational interviews with up to five people working in that field.
- Step 3: Acquire skills. Identify the skills that you will need in order to be happy and successful in the new career or position. Put a plan together to fill those skills gaps.
- Step 4: Switch jobs. Create the plan that will take you from your current position to the one you have identified.

Reference

Bolles, R. N. *What Color Is My Parachute?* Berkeley: Ten Speed Press, 1974.

DECISION-MAKING FRAMEWORKS

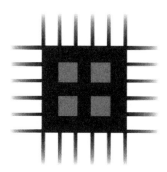

What is the best course of action?

We live in an era of overload and ambiguity. Information, alternatives, and advice bombard us daily. Ultimately, we must make decisions, often without completely understanding the terrain or being as prepared and clear as we would like to be. Decision-making frameworks help us to prioritize and on occasion reframe to gain a clearer perspective.

The frameworks in this section are highly scalable, as helpful at the personal level as they are for tackling organizational and national challenges.

⊞

Prisoner's Dilemma
Merrill Flood and Melvin Drescher

> This remarkable result—that individually rational action results in both persons being made worse off in terms of their own self-interested purposes—is what has made the wide impact in modern social science. For there are many interactions in the modern world that seem very much like that, from arms races through road congestion and pollution to the depletion of fisheries and the over-exploitation of some subsurface water resources.
> —Roger A. McCain[18]

Flood and Drescher created the Prisoner's Dilemma in 1950 as part of the Rand Corporation's investigation of the risks associated with nuclear arms development. Based on game theory, the Prisoner's Dilemma was popularized by Albert Tucker, who formalized the basic concepts and taught them to Stanford psychology students. A powerful modeling tool that scales from couples to business partnering to global conflict resolution, the framework cuts to the heart of risk situations where predictability and transparency are limited, and trust and self-interest are the key determinants (Figure 8.15).

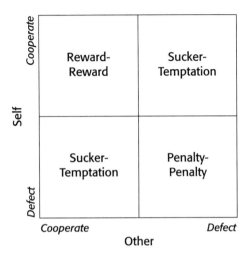

Figure 8.15. Prisoner's Dilemma Matrix

An example of this is the application of Prisoner's Dilemma logic to explain the competitive dynamics of NASCAR racing car drivers. To win, drivers are forced to alternately compete and collaborate with the other contestants. Positioning for "drag" is the main motivator, placing each driver in the position of giving and receiving help at different points in a race. Self-interest becomes complex, as drivers need the others to trust them in spite of the fact that they all want to win.

Since its introduction, over a thousand articles have been written on the Prisoner's Dilemma, as well as hundreds of doctoral dissertations.

The Two Dimensions and Their Extremes. Each axis represents the two prime options available to two parties to an interdependent risk situation. They can choose to Cooperate and hope for a win-win, or they can Defect by exclusively pursuing their self-interests. The classic situation is two guilty prisoners being asked to "rat" on their partner in exchange for personal freedom. The catch is that they are told the other prisoner is being offered the identical deal, and they must make their choice without consulting the other. Each combination of choices creates a unique set of outcomes for the two parties, ranging from win-win if both cooperate, to win-lose if one cooperates and the other defects. Assumptions about the other's position intermingle with personal values and goals to determine each side's decision. Students of the Prisoner's Dilemma point out the consistent irrationality of players, opting to defect in spite of the clear advantage of a mutually cooperative set of choices. The two dimensions are:

Self. One can Cooperate, hoping the Other will do likewise, or one can pursue self-interest and Defect.

Other. As above, the Other can Cooperate or Defect.

The Four Quadrants. Outcomes are composed of combinations of the following states:

R-reward: The reward payoff each party gains if both choose to cooperate (win-win).

T-temptation: The high personal gain one receives by defecting while the other cooperates (win-lose).

S-sucker: The loss one party suffers by cooperating when the other defects (lose-win).

P-punishment: The punishment each receives if both parties choose to defect (lose-lose).

The quadrants describe the four possible outcomes of choices made by the participating parties:

• Upper left: Reward-Reward. The greatest overall gain is achieved when both players cooperate. In the case of two criminals, this might result in a lighter sentence or possibly no sentence at all. If there is a stash of stolen money, each gets his or her half of that.

• Lower left/Upper right: Sucker-Temptation. Outcomes 2 and 3 are mirror images, where one player decides to cooperate while the other defects. This results in the worst possible outcome for one and the best for the other. In the case of the two criminals, one is set free and keeps all the money, while the other is sentenced to the maximum amount of prison time. An additional unfortunate consequence is that the loser is unlikely to cooperate if given the chance at some point in the future.

• Lower right: Penalty-Penalty. The worst possible outcome results when both parties defect. In the case of the two criminals, both go to jail, although for a slightly shorter time than if only one had defected.

Example: Pricing War. Price wars tend to be messy, painful exercises for the combatants, with both or all parties losing. In Prisoner's Dilemma terms, they represent the lower right quadrant, where both parties defect or act in their own best interest. The computer industry provides a colorful example of this as the industry itself enters a phase of maturity, and key players reposition and compete for continued relevance. Although the personal computer market continues to be sizable, two things have changed: it is no longer growing at a fast pace, and all the major manufacturers are capable of satisfying customer expectations. In other words, it has become a commodity market.

In this context, Dell Computer has emerged with the winning commodity strategy. With its direct sales channel, on-line configuration capability, and low-cost virtual value chain, it consistently wins the pricing battle. Key competitors like IBM, Gateway, HP, and Compaq have had to respond to the Dell fact. How do they win in this situation?

In February 2001, Dell announced it was embarking on a campaign to increase its share of the market by intentionally undercutting the price of its competitors. All had to respond. With less overhead, an efficient and reliable value chain, and scale economies due to high sales volume, Dell has proved formidable.

Michael Bean, president of Forio Business Solutions, models the HP/Compaq versus Dell situation as the Prisoner's Dilemma on his company's Web site (Figure 8.16). A game simulation is available where visitors can play out the logical dynamics of the competition to discover the outcome for each of the competitors.[19]

Context. The Prisoner's Dilemma is used primarily as a scenario-building and risk-assessment tool to guide decision making. Parties engaged in a conflict can model their situation and glimpse the consequences of various strategies. Real-world applications of the Prisoner's Dilemma tend to involve iterative opportunities to cooperate or defect, each with associated gains and losses. This may result in the development of learning and trust, increasing the possibility of a cooperative outcome. The Kyoto Agreement on Global Warming comes to mind as an instance of such a multiround process, replete with the complexity and inability to predict the follow-through of other parties that makes modeling a necessary aid.

Method. Follow these steps to model a multiparty decision-making or conflict process to gain useful insights:

• Step 1: Identify the parties and the issue. Identify the two (or more) parties and define the issue. What is at risk, and what can be gained?

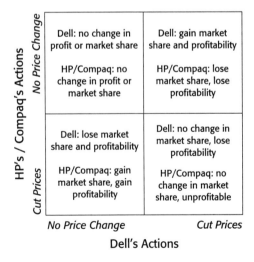

Figure 8.16. Payoff Matrix for PC Makers

- Step 2: Create the Prisoner's Dilemma matrix. Construct the Prisoner's Dilemma matrix, defining the positive and negative decision options for each of the parties. For example, in the case of the criminals, the decision is to confess or not confess. If we were applying the model to couples in a relationship, we might consider sacrifice versus cheat as the two options, representing the cooperate and defect choices. If the situation is a pricing war, we might look at lowering price or not.
- Step 3: Complete the matrix. Complete the Prisoner's Dilemma matrix, naming the outcome for each of the four combinations. These represent four different future scenarios. Scenarios can be developed independently by a third party or by each participant, or they can be co-created by the parties involved in the conflict.
- Step 4: Examine the implications. Consider the implications of the scenarios. This is a chance to step back from an intense situation and be more reflective about risk, self-interest, and options. As in step 3, this work can be completed in various groupings and forms, with the highest impact likely to result from dialogue between participating parties. Unfortunately, full openness and sharing is not always possible, especially in competitive market contexts where questions of collusion exist.

Tips on Prisoner's Dilemma. The Prisoner's Dilemma is not a zero-sum game: both parties can win or lose to some degree. Look to the advantages inherent in your own competitiveness, in the situation, or the needs of the other party or the customer.

The dilemma is broken when trust is increased and transparency into the other's motivations and actions is achieved. We don't have to proceed to lose-lose when we are able to define a mutually advantageous goal and trust each other to work toward it.

References

Brandenburger, A. M., Nalebuff, B. J., and Brandenberger, A. *Co-Opetition: 1. A Revolutionary Mindset That Redefines Competition and Cooperation; 2. The Game Theory Strategy That's Changing the Game of Business.* New York, Doubleday, 1997.

Poundstone, W. *Prisoner's Dilemma.* New York: Doubleday Anchor, 1993.

⊞

Urgency and Importance
Stephen Covey

Organize and execute around priorities.
—Stephen Covey[20]

For many of us, life is filled with tasks that are Urgent, leaving little time for more fundamental and long-term activities necessary for personal and professional development. Early versions of time management systems focused on efficiency and saving time, often at the expense of rich experiences, personal development, relationships, and spontaneity. Stephen Covey found that highly effective individuals take greater control of their lives and how they spend their time. Integrity and character grow when we act in accordance with intention rather than emotion or desire. This deceptively simple matrix (Figure 8.17) provides a clarifying mirror into how we are managing our life and where balance and investment into values clarification and goal setting are needed.

The Two Dimensions and Their Extremes. The Time Management matrix explores two key dimensions: Importance and Urgency:

Importance. Things that are important are reflective of one's values and contribute to achieving higher-priority goals and personal mission. Importance is about results that matter.

Urgency. Urgent things require immediate attention. They tend to be visible, popular with others, and to act on us.

The Four Quadrants. The Time Management matrix defines four sets of relationships between the variables Importance and Urgency. Finding time for High Importance–Low Urgency items is key to taking charge of one's life:

• Upper left: High Importance, High Urgency. These items are significant, and results are necessary. We all have some of these, but for many, this becomes the norm. The more you focus on this, the bigger it gets, and like the pounding surf, it knocks you down and wears you out.

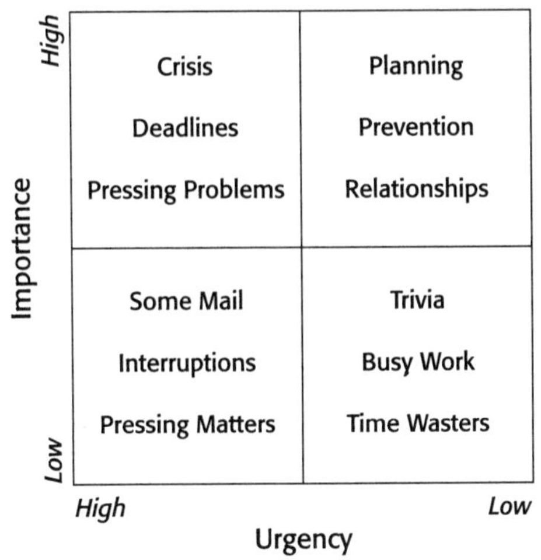

Figure 8.17. Time Management Matrix

- Lower left: Low Importance, High Urgency. Activities sometimes feel as if they are important, but the priorities tend to be those of other people, not our own. Driven by Urgency, this is a highly reactive and ultimately frustrating mode of existence.
- Lower right: Low Importance, Low Urgency. We all need to spend some time relaxing. This is the positive view of quadrant 4. However, even time off can be aligned with our values and interests, making it more important and ultimately satisfying. Too much time spent here is wasteful and destructive.
- Upper right: High Importance, Low Urgency. We take control of our lives by clarifying values and goals and working toward outcomes we truly care about. These kinds of activities tend be Important but not Urgent, and we need to set time aside for them or they won't happen. Saying yes to a quadrant 2 commitment means saying no to others in quadrants 3 and 4.

Method. Personal effectiveness requires integrating long-term and short-term priorities and plans. Here are two approaches:

Upgrading Your Current Agenda

- Step 1: Define. Make a list of how you use the majority of your time, and place each activity on the matrix.
- Step 2: Plan. Reflect on the balance. What can you stop doing to create time for some more important activities?

Becoming Principle Driven

- Step 1: Define. Identify the key roles you play in your life, such as spouse, friend, and manager.
- Step 2: Plan. Develop plans for each based on results you hope to accomplish; schedule, monitor, and adapt in line with core values.

References

Covey, S. *Seven Habits of Highly Effective People.* New York: Simon & Schuster, 1990.

Covey, S. *Principle-Centered Leadership.* New York: Simon & Schuster, 1992.

⊞

Influence and Concern
Stephen Covey

Lord, give me the courage to change the things which can and ought to be changed, the serenity to accept the things which cannot be changed, and the wisdom to know the difference.
—Alcoholics Anonymous prayer

We can choose to be proactive and take responsibility for our actions and feelings, or we can be reactive victims of circumstances and our own anxieties. We gain energy each time we get involved in improving things that matter, just as we lose energy by worrying about things outside our control. When we focus on areas that truly matter and where we can make a difference, we expand what Stephen Covey calls our circle of influence. "Proactive people focus their efforts in the Circle of Influence. They work on the things they can do something about. The nature of their energy is positive, enlarging and magnifying, causing their Circle of Influence to increase." This work typically begins with changing our own thoughts and actions, reclaiming time and energy tied up in anxiety about things we cannot change, which create feelings of powerlessness.[21]

The Two Dimensions and Their Extremes. The matrix explores two key dimensions: Influence and Concern:

Influence. This is the degree to which we are able to affect outcomes.

Concern. This is the degree to which we care about situations.

The Four Quadrants. Personal effectiveness and satisfaction increase when we work on tasks that are meaningful and where we can make a difference. The Influence and Concern matrix helps one to become clear about the things that matter and to be proactive in areas where one can reasonably influence outcomes:

• Upper left: Reactive Focus. When we focus here, we allow our anxieties to control and diminish us. We feel powerless and waste energy on resentment

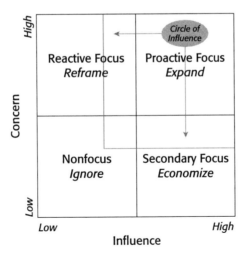

Figure 8.18. Influence and Concern Matrix

and regret. Some problems need to be accepted more gracefully; others need to be reframed and converted to actions available in the Circle of Influence.

• Lower left: Nonfocus. These are other people's problems or challenges and are best left to them to address.

• Lower right: Secondary Focus. On occasion, our knowledge, professional position, or relationships give us more influence than we care to use. If we are not careful, these demands can consume a disproportionate amount of our time. Economize to be helpful while limiting involvement.

• Upper right: Proactive Focus. Highly effective people and organizations spend their time working on things they value that they can do something about. The goal is to expand this zone by taking responsibility for our actions and reactions. We positively alter our circumstances by how we choose to view them.

Method. We expand our Circle of Influence by taking responsibility for our actions and reactions:

• Step 1: Identify concerns. Make a list of the major sources of your concern.

• Step 2: Assess the ability to influence. For each item, ask if this is something clearly beyond your ability to influence. If it is, set it aside, and focus on steps 3 and 4.

• Step 3: Address concerns you can influence. Take each concern you can affect, and build a vision of an ideal situation.

• Step 4: Construct action plans. Develop a set of actions you can take to realize this vision.

References

Covey, S. *Seven Habits of Highly Effective People.* New York: Simon & Schuster, 1990.

Covey, S. *Principle-Centered Leadership.* New York: Simon & Schuster, 1992.

NOTES

Foreword

1. We would be remiss not to point out this potential 2 × 2, on which all readers of this statement reside: Teeth: Clenched or Relaxed; Mind: Idling or Active!

2. George Will, *Men at Work: The Craft of Baseball* (New York: Macmillan, 1990), p. 324.

Chapter One

1. "Does the Human Brain Compute, or Does It Do More?" *Science Frontiers Online*, Jul.–Aug 1996.

2. R. J. Heuer, *Psychology of Intelligence Analysis* (Washington, D.C.: U.S. Government Printing Office, 1999).

3. A. N. Whitehead and B. Russell, *Principia Mathematica* (Cambridge: Cambridge University Press, 1927).

4. I. Ansoff. *Corporate Strategy* (New York: McGraw-Hill, 1965).

5. I. Nonaka and R. Toyama, "A Firm as a Dialectical Being: Towards a Dynamic Theory of a Firm," *Industrial and Corporate Change*, VII, no. 5, 2002, pp. 995–1009.

6. S. Covey, *The Seven Habits of Highly Effective People* (New York: Simon & Schuster, 1989).

7. S. Maier, M. Seligman, and C. Peterson, *Learned Helplessness: A Theory for the Age of Personal Control* (New York: Oxford University Press, 1996).

8. C. Peterson, S. Maier, and M.E.P. Seligman, *Learned Helplessness: A Theory for the Age of Personal Control* (New York: Oxford University Press, 1993).

9. R. Wiseman, *The Luck Factor: Changing Your Life, Changing Your Luck: The Four Essential Principles* (New York: Miramax, 2003).

Chapter Two

1. K. Hammonds, "No Risk, No Reward," *Fast Company,* Apr. 2002, p. 84.

2. G.W.F. Hegel, *Science of Logic* (Humanity Books, 1927).

3. K. Simmons, "How to Cure Delegation Deficiency," *Executive Update Online,* May 2000. [http://www.gwsae.org/executiveupdate/2000/May/Deficiency.htm].

4. I. Nonaka and H. Takeuchi, *The Knowledge Creating Company: How Japanese Companies Create the Dynamics of Innovation* (New York: Oxford University Press, 1995).

5. C. H. Fine, *Clockspeed* (Boston: Perseus Books, 1998), p. 49.

6. Growth calculated using GE financial statements throughout the 1990s. See http://ge.com/en/company/investor.

7. H. Saint-Onge, interview with the authors, Dec. 2002.

8. B. Johnson, *Polarity Management: Identifying and Managing Unsolvable Problems* (Human Resource Development Press, 1997).

Chapter Three

1. For a sampling of the diagnostic and modeling power of the archetypal dilemmas, try out Exhibit 3.1, a self-assessment guide.

2. The eight archetypal dilemmas were identified in a three-step bottom-up process. More than 160 unique 2×2 frameworks were collected in step 1. Step 2 consisted of classifying the frameworks into major themes by three researchers working separately. Step 3 involved careful synthesis of the themes into the smallest possible number of categories.

3. M. Macoby, *The Gamesman* (New York: Bantam Books, 1977).

4. Macoby, *The Gamesman,* p. 90.

5. "Nokia to Cut 1,000 Jobs as Slowdown Bites," *Financial Times,* June 28, 2001.

6. J. Duffy, T. Green, and P. Hochmuth, "Nortel Layoffs, Losses, Have Industry Asking: What's Next?" *Network World,* Oct. 8, 2001.

7. "Motorola Announces a Further 4,000 Job Cuts," *Financial Times,* Sept. 2, 2001.

8. "Where Layoffs Are a Last Resort," *Business Week Online,* Oct. 8, 2001.

9. P. Lawrence and J. Lorsch, *Organization and Environment* (Cambridge, Mass.: Harvard University Press, 1967).

10. M. Canellos and J. Spooner, "IBM's Outsider: A Look Back at Lou," *CNET,* Feb. 1, 2002.

11. P. Loftus, "Tales of the Tape, Consolidation Seen in Tech Services," *Dow Jones Newswire,* Jan. 6, 2003.

12. It is somewhat ironic that "risk-managed" projects have contributed significantly to placing the world at greater risk than ever before in history.

13. P. L. Bernstein, *Against the Gods: The Remarkable Story of Risk* (New York: Wiley, 1996).

14. M. Warren (ed.), *The Cunard Turbine-Driven Quadruple-Screw Atlantic Liner "Lusitania": Constructed and Engined* (Somerset, U.K.: Patrick Stephens Publishers).

15. Ansoff, *Corporate Strategy,* p. 128.

16. G. Moore, *Crossing the Chasm* (New York: HarperBusiness, 2002).

17. "Borland Software: Back in the Black," *Fast Company,* no. 60, p. 76.

18. R. Ackoff and F. Emery, *On Purposeful Systems* (New York: Aldine-Atherton, 1972).

Chapter Six

1. S. D. Alinsky, *Rules for Radicals: A Pragmatic Primer for Realistic Radicals* (New York: Vintage Books, 1971).

2. A. D. Chandler, *Strategy and Structure* (Cambridge, Mass.: MIT Press, 1962). I. Ansoff, *Corporate Strategy* (New York: McGraw-Hill, 1965).

3. H. Mintzberg, *Structure in Fives: Designing Effective Organizations* (Upper Saddle River, N.J.: Prentice Hall, 1983).

4. G. Hamel and C. K. Prahalad, *Competing for the Future* (Boston: Harvard Business School Press, 1994), p. 100.

5. Hamel and Prahalad, *Competing for the Future,* p. 105.

6. Hamel and Prahalad, *Competing for the Future,* p. 101.

7. Hamel and Prahalad, *Competing for the Future,* p. 101.

8. P. Wiefels, *The Chasm Companion: A Fieldbook to Crossing the Chasm and Inside the Tornado* (New York: HarperBusiness, 2002), p. 11.

9. G. Moore, *Inside the Tornado: Marketing Strategies from Silicon Valley's Cutting Edge* (New York: HarperCollins, 1995), p. 11.

10. From a private research report delivered as part of a research project: N. Klym, "The Customer as Product Manager" (Toronto: Digital 4Sight, 2000).

11. From a privately published set of workshop tools by A. Lowy and others, *Customer Fulfillment Networks Toolkit* (Toronto: Digital 4Sight, 2000).

12. B. T. Gale, *Managing Customer Value: Creating Quality and Service That Customers Can See* (New York: Free Press, 1994), p. 288.

13. P. Schwartz, *The Art of the Long View* (New York: Doubleday, 1992), p. 36.

14. This section was developed from conversations with Nicole Boyer of Global Business Network and internal documents supplied by GBN.

15. L. Wilkinson, "The Future of the Future," *Wired* (special edition), 1995, pp. 77–81. [http://www.wired.com/wired/scenarios/build.html].

16. T. Wilson, "The Role of the Librarian in the Twenty-First Century" (keynote address for the Library Association Northern Branch Conference, Longhirst, Northumberland, Nov. 17, 1995). [http://www.shef.ac.uk/ ~ is/wilson/publications/21stcent.html].

17. P. Schwartz, *The Art of the Long View* (New York: Doubleday, 1992).

18. W. Bennis, *On Becoming a Leader* (New York: HarperBusiness, 1997), p. 105.

19. N. Brown, private communication. Brown is the former director of marketing of government systems for EDS.

20. W. Wacker, J. Taylor, and H. Means, *The Visionary Handbook* (New York: Harper-Collins, 2000), p. 31.

21. R. Branson, chairman, Virgin Group, http://www/greatest-quotations.com.

22. C. Shapiro and H. R. Varian, *Information Rules: A Strategic Guide to the Networked Economy* (Boston: Harvard Business School Press, 1999), p. 17.

23. D. Hussey and I. Ansoff, "Continuing Contribution to Strategic Management," *Strategic Change,* 1999, *8,* 275–292.

24. I. Ansoff, *Corporate Strategy* (New York: McGraw-Hill, 1965).

25. http://www.greenmountaincoffee.com/investor_services/ annual_report_01_pdfs/front%20of%annual%203.pdf.

26. M. Porter, *Competitive Advantage* (New York: Free Press, 1985), p. xvi.

27. Porter, *Competitive Advantage,* p. 12.

28. The information from this section is drawn from *Automotive History: A Chronological History,* 4. [http://inventors.about.com/gi/dynamic/offsite.htm?site = http://www.aaca.org/history/].

29. A. Lowy and others, *Digital Economy Toolkit* (Toronto: Alliance for Converging Technologies, 1998).

30. Developed by Andy De and Alex Lowy for the *Digital Economy Toolkit,* Alliance for Converging Technologies, 1998.

31. W. Keegan, *Global Marketing Management* (Upper Saddle River, N.J.: Prentice Hall, 1999), pp. 346–351.

32. C. Shapiro and H. R. Varian, *Information Rules* (Boston: Harvard Business School Press, 1999), p. 224.

33. B. J. Pine II, *Mass Customization* (Boston: Harvard Business Press, 1993), p. 86.

34. T. H. Davenport and J. C. Beck, *The Attention Economy: Understanding the New Currency of Business* (Boston: Harvard Business School Press, 2001), p. 16.

35. W. Reinartz and V. Kumar, "The Mismanaging of Customer Loyalty," *Harvard Business Review,* July 2002, p. 88.

36. S. Majaro, *The Essence of Marketing* (Upper Saddle River, N.J.: Prentice Hall, 1993), p. 87.

37. A. Slywotzky and D. Morrison, *The Profit Zone* (New York: Times Business, 1997).

38. The 2 × 2 matrix presented here is a generic representation of core ideas pertaining to business decision making based on revenue and profitability modeling.

39. M. Porter, *Competitive Strategy: Techniques for Analyzing Industries and Competitors* (New York: Free Press, 1998).

40. S. Trussler, BCG head of knowledge management, interview with A. Lowy, Dec. 2002.

41. G. Stalk and T. M. Hout, *Competing Against Time: How Time-Based Competition Is Reshaping the Global Market* (New York: Free Press, 1990), p. 15.

42. E. Fromm, *Man for Himself: An Inquiry into the Psychology of Ethics* (New York: Holt, 1947).

43. The material on the future of energy for private clients at SRIC-BI was supplied by William Ralston.

44. William Shakespeare, *As You Like It,* Act II, Scene 7.

45. R. H. Hayes and S. C. Wheelwright, "The Dynamics of Process-Product Life-Cycles," *Harvard Business Review,* Mar.-Apr. 1979, pp. 127–136.

Chapter Seven

1. J. Collins, *Good to Great* (New York: HarperBusiness, 2001), p. 122.

2. Collins, *Good to Great.*

3. F. Herzberg, "One More Time: How Do You Motivate Employees?" *Harvard Business Review,* Sept.-Oct. 1987, p. 117.

4. The 2 × 2 presentation of this framework is our careful adaptation of Herzberg's original formulation. Although Herzberg clearly described the two dimensions and their interaction, he did not publish it in matrix form.

5. J. R. Harbison and P. Pekar Jr., *Smart Alliances* (San Francisco: Jossey-Bass, 1998), p. 6.

6. Presentation by T. Harris and C. Daniels, University of Connecticut, Storrs, Nov. 25, 1996. [http://www.ucc.uconn.edu/ ~ WWWIOPSY/teams.htm].

7. Interview with P. Hersey, Nov. 5, 2003.

8. R. M. Stogdill, "Personal Factors Associated with Leadership: A Survey of the Literature," *Journal of Psychology,* 1948, *25,* 64. In 1948, Stogdill investigated a wide range of traits in order to identify personality variables that might be positively correlated with leadership.

9. K.-E. Sveiby, *The New Organizational Wealth: Managing and Measuring Knowledge-Based Assets* (San Francisco: Berrett-Koehler, 1997), p. 54.

10. Sveiby, *The New Organizational Wealth.*

11. R. Nelson-Jones, *Group Leadership: A Training Approach* (Pacific Grove, Calif.: Brooks-Cole, 2003), p. 20.

12. Although this framework is drawn from the T-group context, its message is relevant to all leadership situations.

13. I. Nonaka and H. Takeuchi, *The Knowledge-Creating Company: How Japanese Companies Create the Dynamics of Innovation* (New York: Oxford University Press, 1995).

14. In a recent article, "A Firm as a dialectical being: Towards a dynamic theory of a firm," Nonaka and Toyama explore the dialectical process of knowledge creation as an exchange between a firm and its environment.

15. Interview with Larry Prusak conducted by Alliance for Converging Technologies, 1997.

16. J. S. Brown, "Learning, Working and Playing in the Digital Age" (paper presented at the Conference on Higher Education of the American Association for Higher Education, Washington, D.C., 1999). [http://serendip.brynmawr.edu/sci_edu/seelybrown/seelybrown4.html].

17. T. Stewart, *Intellectual Capital: The New Wealth of Organizations* (New York: Doubleday, 1997), p. 89.

18. Stewart, *Intellectual Capital*, p. 91.

19. GM corporate Web site, http://www.gm.com/company/investor_information/?section = Company&layer = CorporateInfo&action = open&page = head.

20. J. Gharajedaghi, *Systems Thinking: Managing Chaos and Complexity* (Boston: Butterworth-Heinemann, 1999), p. 92.

21. Gharajedaghi, *Systems Thinking*, p. 191.

22. The authors named the four quadrants, based on a case report by Jamshid Gharajedaghi.

23. Gharajedaghi, *Systems Thinking*, p. 192.

24. An architecture is a general description of a system, including its vital parts, relationships, and processes. It comprises a set of interrelated platforms reflecting key dimensions.

25. R. L. Ackoff and F. E. Emery, *On Purposeful Systems* (Chicago: Aldine Atherton Inc., 1972), p. 205.

26. C. Darwin, *The Origin of Species* (New York: Colliers, 1909).

27. The Change Grid is adapted from the work and writings of Elizabeth Kübler-Ross.

28. Conversation with Hubert Saint-Onge, CEO Konverge and Know, www.konverge-andknow.com.

29. J. Gharajedaghi, *Systems Thinking*, p. 116.

30. B. J. Pine II and J. H. Gilmore, *The Experience Economy* (Boston: Harvard Business School Press, 1999), p. 11.

31. Adapted from the suggested method presented in Pine and Gilmore, *The Experience Economy*.

32. The Book Beat, "Interview with Charles Fine." [http://www.clockspeed.com].

33. Douglas Engelbart invented the mouse and many key aspects of today's PCs while at Stanford Research Institute in the 1960s. He is a leading thinker on using computers to enhance collaboration and augment human intellect.

34. Beginning in 1973, Bob Johansen worked on the design, implementation, and evaluation of the first computer conferencing system on the Internet (then called the

ARPANET). He is the author of six books, including one on global cross-cultural teams, *GlobalWork* (with Mary O'Hara-Devereaux, San Francisco: Jossey-Bass, 1994), and *Groupware: Computer Support for Business Teams* (New York: Free Press, 1988).

35. C. H. Fine, *Clockspeed: Winning Industry Control in an Age of Temporary Advantage* (Boston: Perseus Books, 1998), p. 30.

36. W. Buxton, "Integrating the Periphery and Context: A New Model of Telematics," in *Proceedings of Graphics Interface* (San Francisco: Morgan Kaufmann, 1995), pp. 239–246.

37. Private interview with B. Buxton, 2003.

38. A. Lee, A. Girgensohn, and K. Schleuter, "NYNEX Portholes: Initial User Reactions and Redesign Implications," in *GROUP 97: Proceedings of the International ACM SIGGROUP Conference on Supporting Group Work* (New York: ACM Press, 1997), pp. 385–394. [http://www.wecbcollab.com/publications/lee97a.pdf].

39. R. Martin, "The Virtue Matrix: Calculating the Return on Social Responsibility," *Harvard Business Review*, Mar. 2002, p. 5.

40. Roger Martin, the dean of the Rotman School of Business at the University of Toronto, helped develop a Virtue matrix while leading a workshop at the Aspen Institute. We have adapted this matrix from their work.

Chapter Eight

1. P. Hawken, A. Lovins, and L. H. Lovins, *Creating the Next Industrial Revolution* (New York: Little, Brown and Company, 1996), p. 176.

2. A. Chandler, Jr. *The Visible Hand: The Managerial Revolution in American Business* (Cambridge, MA: Harvard University Press, 1977), pp. 245–246.

3. R. Burns, "To a Louse." From *The Canongate Burns*, edited by A. Noble (Canongate Books, 2003).

4. Development Dimensions International, "Labor Day Survey Reveals Many Top Leaders Landing in the Rough," press release, Sept.-Nov. 2001. [http://www.akronbusinessmagazine.com/press%20releases/090701laborday_ddi_survey.htm].

5. D. M. Boje, "Johari Window and the Psychodynamics of Leadership and Influence in Intergroup Life." [http://cbae.nmsu.edu/ ~ dboje/503/JoHari_window.htm].

6. I. B. Myers, *Introduction to Type* (Oxford: Oxford Psychologists Press, 2000), p. 4.

7. I. B. Myers, *Introduction to Type: A Description of the Theories and Applications of the Myers-Briggs Type Indicator* (Palo Alto: Consulting Psychologists Press, 1987).

8. T. Harris, *I'm OK, You're OK* (New York: HarperCollins, 1967), p. 51.

9. The I'm OK, You're OK matrix has been adapted from the information and models presented in Harris, *I'm OK, You're OK*.

10. K. Thomas and R. Kilmann, *Thomas-Kilmann Conflict Mode Instrument* (Palo Alto, Calif.: Davies-Black, 2002). [http://www.cpp.com/products/tki/index.asp].

11. This model incorporates a fifth cell in the model, Compromising.

12. D. Merrill and R. Reid, *Personal Styles and Effective Performance* (Philadelphia: Chilton, 1981), p. 79.

13. Bolton and Bolton, *Social Style/Management Style* (New York: Amacom, 1984), p. 79.

14. P. F. Drucker, "Managing for Business Effectiveness," *Harvard Business Review,* May 1963, p. 56.

15. P. Senge and others, *The Dance of Change: The Challenges of Sustaining Momentum in Learning Organizations* (New York: Doubleday, 1999), p. 108.

16. R. N. Bolles, *What Color Is Your Parachute?* (Berkeley, Calif.: Ten Speed Press, 1970).

17. We adapted the Career Transitioning matrix based on a reading of Richard Bolles's work, although he did not specifically present it as a 2 × 2 matrix.

18. R. A. McCain, *Game Theory: A Non-Technical Introduction to the Analysis of Strategy* (Cincinnati, Ohio: South-Western, 2003), pp. 9–11.

19. Forio Business Simulations, "The Price Strategy Simulator: Anatomy of a Price War, Hewlett-Packard/Compaq vs. Dell," 2001. [http://www.forio.com/pricing20010912.htm].

20. S. B. Covey, *The Seven Habits of Highly Effective People: Powerful Lessons in Personal Change* (New York: Simon & Schuster, 1989), p. 83.

21. Covey presents these ideas as the Circles of Influence and Concern in *The Seven Habits of Highly Effective People.* This 2 × 2 interpretation has been created with the permission and support of the author.

INDEX